Identity Anecdotes
Translation and Media Culture

Identity Anecdotes
Translation and Media Culture

Meaghan Morris

SAGE Publications

London ● Thousand Oaks ● New Delhi

First published 2006

SAGE Publications Ltd
1 Oliver's Yard
55 City Road
London EC1Y 1SP

SAGE Publications Inc.
2455 Teller Road
Thousand Oaks, California 91320

SAGE Publications India Pvt Ltd
B-42, Panchsheel Enclave
Post Box 4109
New Delhi 110 017

British Library Cataloguing in Publication data

A catalogue record for this book is available
from the British Library

ISBN-10 0 7619 6115 1   ISBN-13 978 0 7619 6115 4
ISBN-10 0 7619 6116 X (pbk)   ISBN-13 978 0 7619 6116 1

Library of Congress Control Number: 2005938341

Typeset by C&M Digitals (P) Ltd., Chennai, India
Printed on paper from sustainable resources
Printed and bound in Great Britain by Athenaeum Press, Gateshead

In memory of

DONALD HORNE

1921–2005

Contents

Acknowledgements

My first debt is to Chris Rojek, who talked me into planning this book and then waited very patiently for me to finish it. This is what people lightly call 'a book of essays', as though you put together some texts already published, and bingo – instant book. That is unfortunately not my way, and the work of revising the essays into chapters and then discovering what makes them cohere took much longer than I intended. During the worst phase of this task, Mila Steele, my editor at Sage, has been a pleasure to work with and a constant source of support.

This is perhaps the most sociable book I have written, in the sense that its materials mostly began as talks, lectures, articles or prefaces invited or, in a few cases, extracted from me by someone else. For their inspiration and the frameworks for thought they provided, I thank Phillip Adams, Ien Ang, Janet Bergstrom, Kuan-Hsing Chen, Denise Corrigan, the late Helen Daniel, Mike Featherstone, Paul Foss, John Hartley, Laleen Jayamanne, Jane Jacobs, Jenna Mead, Patricia Mellencamp, Tom O'Regan, Geraldine Pratt, Naoki Sakai, David Watson, Paul Willemen (who once told me to write a book about '"television culture" in the broadest sense of the term') and Kathleen Woodward. For help, advice and generous discussion at crucial times, I thank Tony Bennett, Margriet Bonnin, Fred Chiu, Helen Grace, Lawrence Grossberg, Trevor Johnston, Adrian Martin, Tracey Moffatt and Patrice Petro.

I owe a special intellectual debt to Kuan-Hsing Chen. Without his brilliance, drive and determination to see a new kind of cultural politics emerge across national borders in Asia, I would never have written this book. Kuan-Hsing also introduced me to Naoki Sakai, whose work on translation shapes my argument. There is no space to name all the other friends from the *Inter-Asia Cultural Studies* and *Traces* collectives whom I have met through these two people, in the process changing my life as well as my work. For conversations and shared experiences of labour decisive for a book about translation, however, I must thank Brett de Bary, Melani Budianta (who gave me the confidence to publish Chapter 11), Shun-hing Chan, Hae-joang Cho, Beng-huat Chua, Chris Connery, Naifei Ding, Jianping Gao, Yukiko Hanawa, Po-keung Hui, Myung-koo Kang, Nae-hui Kang, Soyoung Kim, Kiyoshi Kojima, Victor Koschmann, Tom Lamarre, Kin-chi Lau, Jeannie Martin, Tejaswini Niranjana, Tessa Morris-Suzuki, Ashish Rajadhyaksha, S.V. Srinivas, Shunya Yoshimi and Rob Wilson.

Over the years of the book's composition I had the privilege of fellowships providing precious writing time from the Humanities Research Centre, Australian National University, Canberra (1986 and 1998); the Literature Board of the Australia Council (1991–93); the Society for the Humanities, Cornell University (1993) and the Australian Research Council (1994–99). More recently, during the months of editing and writing the framework of the book, I have benefited immeasurably from the supportiveness of my colleagues in the Department of Cultural Studies at Lingnan University, who tolerated my lapses with kindness and grace – while teaching me a lot about translation and much else besides. I am deeply grateful, too, for the technical assistance of Joseph Man-kit Cho, Selina Tak-man Lo and Josephine Wai-shuen Tsui.

My earliest introduction to the critique of 'identity' and to political ways of thinking about the social force of aesthetics came from friends involved in the Gay Liberation Movement in Sydney in the 1970s, some of whom are thanked above. However, many other creative activists have died in the HIV-AIDS epidemic and I want to acknowledge their intellectual legacy; it should not be forgotten that their ideas and their flair for translating them changed the world. In one way or another, I am indebted here to Terence Bell, Barry Prothero, Dave Sargent and Paul Taylor.

As I was finalizing the manuscript, I learned of the death of my mentor, guide and friend of almost twenty-five years' standing: Donald Horne. A brilliant thinker, an accomplished author and a scholar-journalist who became an academic relatively late in a long, productive life, Donald had no problem combining sociology, political science and aesthetics in his version of 'cultural studies'; he believed you could translate any idea to anybody, if you really wanted to do it. Donald did not enjoy the theoretical essays in the middle section of this book, but he understood very well what they meant. This book is dedicated in gratitude to his memory.

* * * * *

An earlier version of Chapter 1 appeared as 'Afterthoughts on Australianism' in *Cultural Studies* 6:3 (1992): 468–475; reproduced with permission of Taylor and Francis (http://www.tandf.co.uk).

Chapter 2, 'Panorama: the Live, the Dead and the Living' appeared in Paul Foss, ed., *Island in the Stream: Myths of Place in Australian Culture* (Sydney: Pluto, 1988), pp. 160–187, and is reprinted in Graeme Turner, ed., *Nation, Culture, Text: Australian Cultural and Media Studies* (London and New York: Routledge, 1993), pp. 19–58.

Part of Chapter 3 featured in my 1991 Mari Kuttna Lecture on Film, Power Institute of Fine Arts, Sydney University. This version of the text first appeared as 'White Panic, or Mad Max and the Sublime', in Kuan-Hsing Chen, ed., *Trajectories: Inter-Asia Cultural Studies* (London and New York: Routledge, 1998), pp. 239–262; reproduced with permission of Taylor and Francis (http://www.tandf.co.uk).

Chapter 4, 'Beyond Assimilation: Aboriginality, Media History and Public Memory' was delivered as a BHP Petroleum Americas Distinguished Lecture for the Australian & New Zealand Studies Project of the School of Hawai'ian, Asian & Pacific Studies, University of Hawai'i at Manoa, October 1993. An earlier version of the text appeared in *Aedon* 4:1 (1996): 12–26.

An earlier version of Chapter 5, 'The Man in the Mirror: David Harvey's "Condition" of Postmodernity', appeared in *Theory, Culture & Society* 9:1 (February 1992): 253–279. Reprinted by permission of Sage Publications Ltd (© Theory, Culture and Society Ltd, 1992)

Chapter 6 appeared as the Introduction to Paul Willemen, *Looks and Frictions* (London and Bloomington: British Film Institute and Indiana University Press, 1994), pp. 1–23. Reproduced by kind courtesy of Paul Willemen and BFI Publishing.

Chapter 7 appeared as the Foreword to Naoki Sakai, *Translation and Subjectivity* (Minneapolis: University of Minnesota Press, September 1997), pp. ix–xxii.

An earlier version of Chapter 8 was published as 'Crazy Talk is not Enough' in *Environment and Planning D: Society and Space* 14:4 (1996): 384–394. Reproduced with permission of Pion Limited, London.

Chapter 9 first appeared in Phillip Adams, ed., *The Retreat from Tolerance: A Snapshot of Australian Society* (Sydney: ABC Books, 1997), pp. 145–161.

Earlier versions of Chapter 10 appeared as '"The truth is out there ... "' in *Australian Book Review* 181 (June 1996), 17–20; and *Cultural Studies* 11:3 (1997), 367–375.

An earlier version of Chapter 11 was published as '"Please Explain?": Ignorance, Poverty and the Past' in *Inter-Asia Cultural Studies* 1:2 (2000): 219–232; reproduced with permission of Taylor and Francis (http://www.tandf.co.uk).

Chapter 12 first appeared in the *TV Times* exhibition catalogue published by the Museum of Contemporary Art, Sydney (1992) and is reprinted in Heather Kerr and Amanda Nettelbeck, eds, *The Space Between: Australian Women Writing Fictocriticism* (Perth: University of Western Australia Press, 1998), pp. 115–119.

Introduction

Inside and outside and identity is a great bother. And how once you know that the buyer is there can you go on knowing that the buyer is not there. Of course when he is not there there is no bother.

Gertrude Stein, *Everybody's Autobiography*[1]

More than twenty years ago, the editor of a US feminist film theory journal, *Camera Obscura*, asked me for an essay discussing my 'national identity' in relation to feminism in Australia. A working film critic at the time, with a Master's degree in Paris well behind me, I was startled: I had not met many Americans, had never visited the United States or thought of doing so, and while I wrote for a variety of Australian publications, some distributed internationally through social movement circuits, I had written just twice for the vast elsewhere that we called 'overseas' (and then for people in places I knew). No doubt because of the fear that addressing a void induced in me, I was also earnestly shocked that this question of national identity should arise in raw form to position me as an informant to feminists who had spent years deconstructing the question of 'woman' and identity in cinema. Why should 'Australian' identity seem easy?

Taking the tough way out, I began an essay called 'Identity Anecdotes' (1984) with a sentence from Gertrude Stein ('Inside and outside and identity is a great bother'); with two diverging definitions of anecdote, one British ('narrative of *detached* incident'), the other Australian ('short narrative of a *particular* incident'); an obscure story about a British feminist (whom I later learned was Canadian) asking me, 'why does Australia matter?'; and a parodically clipped declaration that:

National identity occurs in an encounter with cultural difference when and only when that difference cannot be represented to the satisfaction of all concerned: or alternatively, the 'Australian' is that which irrupts as anecdotal in a theoretically rigorous exchange.[2]

Looking back, embarrassed as I am by the fuss I made over Janet Bergstrom's kind invitation, this hyper-precise formulation still strikes me as a true rendering of the *situation* of a scholar who writes internationally from, and ultimately for or to a place (it needn't be a nation) deemed unimportant or eccentric within a given economy of intellectual exchange. 'Marginal' is too plaintive a term for this situation, which offers full involvement in that economy at the simple cost of setting aside certain knowledges and concerns, which are localized *by* this transaction – only to emerge, in hapless moments of communicative failure, as floundering non-sequiturs, obscure phrasings, flares of irritation, or quaint stories and jokes. In these conditions (unlike those of trying to cross a border, seeking asylum or being conscripted for war), nationality becomes occasional; sometimes, it just happens.

For most of the English-using academic world today, this is part of what it means to acquire a discipline. In the early 1980s, I did not think about such things and my immediate inspiration for trying out an enunciative model of identity as 'occurring' in a dialogue was an essay on 'Antipodality' by Paul Taylor, then a brilliant young art critic, editor and entrepreneur whose impatience with the nationalist cowering and feminist piety of Australian critical culture in the 1970s was, while disturbing, the most liberating force on my horizon.[3] With the uneasy pomposity of someone being needled by pressures they do not understand while striving to seem to control them (the neo-liberal revolution was, in Deleuze and Guattari's scary phrase, 'knocking on the door' at this time), I went on from my reading of Taylor to offer, on the one hand, a caustic feminist critique of 'the meditation on national identity [as] one of the great genres of Australian speculative fiction', and, on the other, a prickly Australia-centred account of second-wave feminism and the depoliticizing impact within it of an emerging 'multinational spectacle' of academic feminist theory.

Having contributed a little to the latter myself by co-editing *Michel Foucault: Power, Truth, Strategy* (1979), a volume of translations and essays which *Camera Obscura* suggested I foreground for non-Australian readers,[4] I could only refuse to describe the theory phenomenon as, in the parlance of the day, an 'import' ('a trope', I claimed, which worked to reaffirm 'the enigmatic otherness of Australia itself'). Arguing rather that we should turn away from this simple imaginary of nation-based trade, I directed attention instead to 'matters of institutional politics and money', or what would now be called cultural policy:

> If cultural imperialism remains an issue in Australia, it is not because some Australian writers produce Gallicized prose or resort to un-Australian epistemologies, but because particular institutions – galleries, the music industry, universities, cinema distribution and exhibition chains, publishing companies – have a long history of confining Australian activities to a mimetic mode, and continue to monitor the limits – and the identity – of acceptably 'Australian' production.[5]

Today, with a multinational archive on the internet and American inflections of European thought installed in university courses world-wide, it is hard to convey the ferocity with which 'foreign' and 'imported' ideas were fought over in the 1970s and even the 1980s, although the word 'French' can still carry – in journalistic contexts, especially – a rancorous whiff of the past. Ambivalent myself about the academically American, rather than philosophically French, ambience of the new world then forming in bookshops, I declined the transnationally civil gesture of starting from Foucault (an American thing to do), and tucked away near the end of my essay the story of how the Australian export success of *Power, Truth, Strategy* over-stretched the unpaid labour distributing the book, inducing the collapse of the Gay Liberation-inspired collective that produced it. This deadpan economic response to the question of my interest in Foucault allowed me to end by returning to Gertrude Stein for the expanded quotation cited above, reframing the question of identity as a bother created by the pressure of a 'buyer', in Stein's words – or, in mine, of an emerging international *market* for talk about identity.

I should have been more grateful. Written between 1988 and 1999, the essays on nationality, translation and 'speech institutions' collected in this volume all proceed from that sketch for a *pragmatics* of identity and a *rhetoric* of critical practice written for Janet Bergstrom. Indeed, with one exception all of the chapters were initiated by other people or responded to an invitation; the exception is Chapter 10, 'The Scully Protocol', which I offered to a literary magazine in a rare burst of motivation after reading a Sydney newspaper editorial about the structuralist menace of 1996. It is also fair to say that I regarded each one of these essays as a *bother* – distractions into sidelines of professional theory and public controversy, dragging me away from the book about history in popular culture that I was struggling with in those years. In fact, this writing 'on the side' – for a general public in some cases and an expanding transnational academy of friends in others – helped me in practice to understand why so many appeals to history at this time (whether in tourism, action cinema or televised national politics) were trying to *manage* a profound transformation of the relations between professional, public and popular cultural spheres of national life.[6] For this was the period in which 'globalization' not only became a key issue in public debate but also began to reshape the institutional contexts – journalistic, cinematic and televisual as well as academic – in which this issue could be formulated and discussed.

Let me draw a contrast starkly. In 1983, when 'Identity Anecdotes' was written by a freelance journalist and part-time lecturer on an Olivetti manual typewriter, my work had to assume a primarily Australian readership, and there were plenty of places to publish; some even paid a hundred dollars for a thousand words. Life was vivid but relatively insular: Australia could still seem a remote sort of place, and its 'gadfly' critics flitting between media and teaching jobs looked eccentric to visitors who saw the research university as a scholar's natural home.[7] Today, the paying small magazines and journals are mostly gone, along with the plentiful part-time teaching, replaced for a new generation by the gruelling labour of serial casualization. While bloggers can write as they please for those with the means to read them, an export-driven federal research funding policy – together with what Lindsay Waters aptly calls the 'outsourcing' by universities of their assessment procedures to international corporations bulk-producing refereed journals and books[8] – inexorably pressures Australian critics who seek an academic base to sell their work in the first instance to trans-Atlantic readers *as a condition* of its publication and thus, in the fullness of time, its distribution to Australians. As the corporatization of universities spreads to countries where English is a language of education but not of most people's everyday lives (as in Hong Kong, where I now work as an academic), that eccentric gadfly condition is rephrased as 'multi-tasking' and looks more like a global norm.

Reductive as it certainly is, this contrast helps me to foreground some of the institutional changes that transformed the vocation of criticism as I was writing this book. One rapidly visible outcome of the disciplining of Australian research publication in the funding-starved 1990s, for example, was a growing number of scholars with no time and few incentives to experience live exposure to non-academic publics. I learned rhetoric in a world where you had to get up in front of an audience, look people in the eye and engage them or they would heckle; my first 'talk' on sexual politics was given in the early 1970s to a crowd of trade unionists and communists, in the company of a brave comrade (Barry Prothero) sporting a beard, high heels and a Chanel suit.[9] Two decades later, as US-style graduate schools appeared across the country, the riotous 'public forum' culture that once infused even academic conferences gave way to one in which speech becomes intransitive, an inefficient delivery system for draft publications – as tense heads hunch down over densely written papers and mutter them aloud at high speed for an exactly apportioned time.

This professionalization (though I prefer 'Taylorization') of the humanities prompted rising indignation in media columns, mostly content to blame 'jargon' and 'theory' rather than examine the redistribution of resources and the labour force replacement policies that were actually transforming higher education. However, new technologies and regulatory frameworks were also transforming the media as well. Even before use of the internet became widespread, satellite broadcasting from 1986 began to 'nationalize' as well as globalize a once-varied Australian media ecology, in which provincial or state-based TV and largely local newspaper and radio zones had thrived.[10] At the same time, the near-instantaneity of the new media intensified a long-entrenched cultural habit (traceable in the racial exclusion debates of the Australian colonies in the late nineteenth century[11]) whereby journalists convert hot news stories from the United States into hysterically pre-emptive frames for interpreting events that have not happened or could not happen elsewhere but which are thereby cast as imminent; the political correctness furore of the late twentieth century was a classic of its kind. In between these developments, Australian cultural institutions arguably became more powerful in their capacity to produce a national life, and yet also less visible in their structural particularity and material operations.

These mundane developments alter everything. Translation, in Naoki Sakai's sense of a 'heterolingual' effort to address an essentially mixed audience (whether within one language or between two or more) becomes an inescapable condition of practice, whether one is sweating to get an article about Rugby League past American referees; doing a broadcast about race relations in a country town, which can be heard by people who live there as well as by your colleagues; or just trying to persuade your mother that universities do not sack 'politically incorrect' staff for saying *ladies* rather than *women*. In turn, the pervasiveness of this effort reshapes our research agendas. Thus, in 1984 I could dismiss 'identity politics' in the American sense as I understood it then; today, the archive created by those politics is not only canonical for any cultural critic anywhere who wants to publish in English ('has the author made use of the relevant literature on the topic?', the refereeing question goes) but is also, as more journalists graduate from media and cultural studies courses, common currency in public debates *about* identity-related issues.

A unifying concern of this book, then, is how to sustain a critical relation to what is often (in my view) locally a phantom identity politics, industrially generated, from a position that cannot exist outside the sphere of influence of such politics and the global academic networks (and markets) in which they circulate, thereby helping to instil new elements of identity in us all. As I argue in Chapter 2, this situation requires embracing a critical *proximity* to our objects of study rather than seeking a distance from them. Each chapter at some point uses a more or less (often much less) personal anecdote as an allegory of this 'proximity', a term I use not only in the sense of establishing a position of nearness to a problem or an object but also in the sense of translatively trying to *touch* (address) a mixed audience; as any journalist knows, anecdotes *work* to make contact and catch people's attention, although they can fail in their nudging, insinuating mission.

Accordingly, the broad themes of the volume are, first, a critique of 'identity' understood as an institutionally productive circuit of demand and, second, an argument for a translative (rather than narrowly trans-national) practice of cultural work that can attend to institutional differences, moving, when need be, from one institution and/or speech situation to another. Such a practice involves thinking identity itself a matter of address; that is, as produced by desire and, undoubtedly, history, in an encounter with others which always involves a third party – not the discursive third person that so much analysis of 'othering' has closely attended to, but rather a medium or, more exactly here, a speech institution (such as the school, the media, or the family) which encourages particular ways of talking or writing, plays a role in deciding what 'resists' translation, and constrains what people can say. Any translator knows inadequacy or failure, but if translation is always impossible and indispensable my interest leans toward the latter as the more unpredictable, mysterious and pressing condition of practice.

Since these themes are afterthoughts or outcomes of the work of compiling this book, I can best clarify my interest in translation as a cross-institutional practice by first explaining my logic of organization. While this is a book which is very much marked by change, the chapters are not arranged in their order of composition. Chronology would be misleading in ways that matter to me. The oldest text is Chapter 2, 'Panorama: the Live, the Dead and the Living', a 'discontinuous' reading of *Australia Live* (a desperately continuous, four-hour, satellite-dependent media event held to mark the Bicentennial of January 1, 1988),[12] and the most recent is Chapter 11, '"Please Explain?": Ignorance, Poverty and the Past', a close reading of a few moments from a 1997 *60 Minutes* special report on Pauline Hanson, then a rising star of right wing populist and racist politics. Since the former ends with a tribute to the successful critical campaign waged in proximity to the Bicentennial by Aboriginal and other protest groups, while the latter analyses a failure by media professionals to address the backlash led by Hanson, chronology may suggest a pessimistic story of a golden age of experimental cultural politics falling to the wave of 'paranoid nationalism' that swept through many countries in the past decade or so.[13] In that before/after narrative, the awful moment of transition in Australia (others will come to mind elsewhere) is the election of Prime Minister John Howard in 1996.

If that story has descriptive and emotional force for me as a citizen of a certain age, it is not the one I am telling here. This is a book about some ordinary effects of neo-liberal globalization in concrete contexts of institutional practice, and about new problems and *possibilities* that emerge with those effects. The significant transition at issue here occurred in 1986–1988, as economic liberalization began working in tandem with new communications technology to transform Australian society in ways that had locally distinctive implications while none the less installing transnationally disciplined regularities – a process sketched for the un-heroic context of academic publishing by the first chapter, 'Afterthoughts on Australianism'. It follows that 'Panorama' is not about the end of an era but marks the beginning of a long aftermath by investigating something new and strange: a national cultural event, even (for some currents of feeling) a culturally nationalist event, designed for global media coverage and pitched to international investors and tourists.

Here, the national is neither opposed to nor displaced by the local and the transnational. While any nation has material foundations and frames of practice (economic, legal, institutional) that keep it going, these are not formed in isolation and all nations are shaped relationally by other forces and processes at work on varying scales; as Lauren Berlant points out, 'it is precisely under transnational conditions that the nation becomes a more intense object of concern and struggle'.[14] In this perspective, the politics of opposition to colonialism, racism and patriarchal narratives of nation arise in the same historical conditions as the reactionary lines of flight mobilized by the likes of Hanson, and then captured and normalized by the third force of government. Divergent as they are, all these politics (each incorporating elements of protest and mainstreaming) work to create continuity with organizations and principles inherited from the past; all are confronting the social consequences of the same 'new' economy (as we call the regrouping and expansion of capitalism); and all make use of new technologies to reach out to strangers and *move* them to their side. In other words, all these politics are potentials of the present and, as I see it, the balance of power and popularity between them is no less open to contestation than it was twenty years ago.

Rather than composing a narrative, then, the chapters are grouped into three parts respectively developing rhetorical, theoretical and institutional aspects of the argument I want to make. The first part, 'Rhetoric and Nationality', focuses on the *work* of translation involved in the bother of producing identity for discourse markets. Here, Australia matters as a minor field of globalizing experiment – created by the world-girdling British imperialism of the late eighteenth century, made national during phobia-ridden battles about free trade in the late nineteenth and early twentieth centuries – in which cultural industries have been dealing with an export imperative from a weak position for more than thirty years. Looking at some of the changes that the pressure of imagining an outside buyer has wrought on media projections of history and nationality, I see much of this change as a good thing and examine ways in which Aboriginal groups, in particular, have at times been able to utilize that pressure to further their political struggles and transform historiographical practices. Next, the readings in the second part, 'Translation in Cultural Theory', render explicit the *models* of translation I find useful for understanding the conditions of social and linguistic heterogeneity in which cultural politics must work. Taking up in practice the argument that such heterogeneity operates within as well as between so-called national languages, the third part, 'Institutionally Speaking', follows some of the issues discussed in the first two parts through to their scandalizing uptake in media polemics, their translation as 'culture wars'; taking part in those polemics,

I also try to draw out the *constraints* on translation that operate in and between diverse institutional speech situations, and the benefits as well as the costs of working with those constraints.

If these broad divisions between rhetoric, theory and institution tell the reader something about the emphases (and critical genres) to expect in each section, they do not operate neatly within or between chapters and all three aspects are worked on throughout the book as a whole. For example, the first four chapters trace ways in which the historical 'depth' of nationally formative experiences of colonialism and racism is marked in popular culture, whether in formulaic turns of phrase, in the knowing or humorous use of a stereotype, in the editing of a scene of terror in one film or the colours saturating the *mise en scène* of another; perhaps unreadable or invisible to 'buyers' indifferent to the history invoked, these markings are no less powerfully capable of moving (in social as well as affective directions) those who see them and sense their involvement. This capacity of phrases, clichés and images to mobilize historical knowledges and act with temporal force is a theme of my critique in Chapter 2 of Fredric Jameson's theory of postmodernism, and a key issue for my reading in Chapter 5 of David Harvey's influential uptake of that theory; then, in Chapter 11, I discuss the price of ignoring this capacity paid by a journalist trying, in the context of a nationally televised debate, to use a display of cosmopolitan cultural 'attitude' against the popular historical *affect* mobilized by a phrase-savvy politician.

Several threads of this kind run though the book. However, the point of an anecdote for me is not only the wider conversations in which it plays a part but also the import of the incident it narrates. For a quick definition of anecdote, I still prefer 'short narrative of particular incident' (*Macquarie Dictionary*) to 'narrative of a detached incident' (*Concise Oxford Dictionary*) because the latter suggests that an incident has been separated, like a stray button or a lost tooth, from a prior and larger whole. An ideal of epic or the nineteenth century novel probably moulds this definition, making it unhelpful for thinking about varieties of narrative and their powers in media-saturated conditions. In contrast to this pathos of the fragment is the pointed, energetic brevity of the *singular*: one particular incident may well be detached from a larger narrative, but another will initiate a longer narration, link two or more stories and arguments together, or enable (as is most often the case in this book) the elaboration of another, non-narrative discourse. The point of an anecdote depends on its content as well as its telling and the contexts in which it is told and taken up; a pointless anecdote is one in which nothing works to give the incident itself a meaning or a resonance for us. For this reason the idea of detachability better applies to the 'case study' than to the incident at the heart of an anecdote, at least as the former is used in a literary analysis which subjects all its materials (whether ethnographic data, film texts, personal experience or a media event) to the primary task of illuminating the works of Freud, Marx, Heidegger, Lacan, Derrida or Foucault.

Before talking particulars, I should stress that while much of my material is Australian in an obvious but, I hope, meticulously situated way, this is not a book about 'being Australian'. I can imagine writing something like that, although I might not find a buyer unless my book were a lyrical memoir or a 'my hard life in the back-blocks' expatriate autobiography; a British publisher once told me that the words 'Australia' and 'Canada' can kill an academic book in any market, even Australia and Canada (and, true or not, the prediction is self-fulfilling). Nevertheless, *this* book is about transnationally circulating problems of identity production. Chief amongst these for culturally engaged academics in many places around the world is how to balance or negotiate between the diverse claims of community, locality and nation on our time, imagination and energy for commitment – when a globalizing university increasingly disciplines our 'work time' with productivity demands and professional performance norms that are indifferent or inimical to any 'outside' claims of belonging.[15]

I emphasize 'culturally' engaged academics not because I think that cultural work displaces or is synonymous with social or political engagement (this is not a view I hold) but because the *kind* of disciplinarity imposed by what Simon Marginson and Mark Considine call 'the enterprise university' is particularly difficult to handle for activist scholars who do work in cultural domains.[16] The demand that scholars must publish primarily in English-language international refereed journals to secure research funding (Australia) or renew their contracts (Hong Kong) is a clear example. Basically, if you live and breathe as well as 'work on' non-Anglophone cultural issues, being an academic these days means writing in a language (English) that few people around you will read for a journal nobody sees except for readers who won't care – unless you put time into reconstructing or transfiguring the significance of those issues, which means acquiring the cultural capital to do this effectively.

I caricature a little to underline the *industrial* nature of the difficulty as it arises from a globally uneven distribution of academic labour (involving linguistic and cultural effort as well as highly variable time, pay, job security and working conditions) and thus is not entirely helped by an Anglo-American representational politics of making 'space' for 'others' – who must then do extra work to take advantage of that space. On the other hand, in good conditions this work of linguistic and cultural translation is immensely rewarding for those who do it, and, it is also politically fruitful when the labour is shared in a spirit of willingness to confront the inequalities involved. Such work builds transnational communities of effort which, while striving towards a mutual understanding that may never finally arrive, have the capacity to create those conditions of confidence and trust which shape solidarity (if they do not alone sustain it) and make possible new conversations that genuinely do cross borders.

The two communities of effort which have shaped this book are the *Inter-Asia Cultural Studies (IACS)* network, and the collective of *Traces: A Multilingual Journal of Cultural Theory and Translation*. Both work across linguistic as well as national and disciplinary boundaries. Emerging from an earlier initiative by Kuan-Hsing Chen, *IACS* is an English-language refereed journal edited from Taiwan and Singapore; it sustains a regional Society, holds a conference that has travelled from Taipei to Fukuoka, Bangalore and Seoul, and often translates articles from Asian languages.[17] Both Chapter 3, 'White Panic or Mad Max and the Sublime', and Chapter 11, 'Please Explain?', were delivered as papers to international symposia in Taipei (in 1992 and 1998 respectively) and written for an inter-Asian rather than an exclusively Australian or 'Western' readership. *Traces* publishes each issue separately in Chinese, English, Japanese and Korean, and each article appears in all four language editions. This means that while writers can choose not to use English, every writer must keep readers of all four languages in mind. Few people are familiar with the diverse intellectual cultures, institutional contexts and generic expectations active in all four languages, and so each writer must take the risk of addressing 'the multitude of foreigners' in every language of the journal.[18] *Traces* was founded by Naoki Sakai, whose work is the subject of Chapter 7, 'An Ethics of Uncertainty'. However, it also motivates the inclusion in the last section of essays written for general publics and exploring heterolingual tensions and pleasures inhabiting everyday English.

The particulars that I want to stress raise issues of translation in the sense I have just outlined. Beginning with a story about a translation mistake (my own) within English, the first chapter explains why it can be hard labour to convert a local talk about the Australian socio-cultural institution of 'mateship' into a global English article. In writing, Australian English is very close to standard American or British varieties; compared to the effort of translating a Cantonese talk into an English text, my problems of proximity certainly partake of what Marjorie Garber, drawing on Freud for a discussion of discipline envy, calls 'the narcissism of minor differences'.[19] My argument, however, is that such problems arise not with words marked as specific ('Australianisms') but in usage and with memories or allusions inhabiting unmarked phrases. My *effort*, then, is to draw out the difficulty of saying when a minor difference marks and, if it is suppressed or remains untranslated as 'too local', *masks* a major divide, in this case not between Australians ('mates') and Americans ('buddies') but within the former category, as when an egalitarian majority is seized by minority envy and complains of its marginalization. This leads me to query the tendency in cultural studies on the one hand to *nationalize* work not British or American in provenance, and on the other to *over-extend* notions of 'expatriation' and 'migrancy' as models for a transnational practice.

Writing about disciplines, Garber argues that differentiation is a strategy which they use 'to protect themselves against incursion and self-doubt', thereby creating an evil twin or 'closest other' which returns to haunt the discipline so secured.[20] This strategy is, of course, far more widely employed (or, to put it another way, this model of narcissistic self-composition is allegorical in force) and in 'Panorama', 'White Panic' and 'Beyond Assimilation: Aboriginality, Media History and Public Memory' I variously examine the white woman settler as a haunting as well as haunted 'closest other' within media zones of narrative dealing with violent historical matter while striving for cross-cultural appeal. I was not aware of whiteness studies when I wrote these texts but, at the risk of creating another minor difference, I think I would prefer to see them as *majority* studies, in Deleuze and Guattari's sense of majority as 'the determination of a state or standard in relation to which larger quantities, as well as the smallest, can be said to be minoritarian'.[21]

By this I mean that while these chapters unequivocally deal with the historical production of whiteness, they also analyse historical moments in which a majority is caught up (for concrete, often socio-economic reasons) in a wave of fear, resentment or panic about becoming minor, a becoming that would, adapting Deleuze and Guattari once again, 'rend us from our major identity'.[22] Pauline Hanson's 1996 warning that Australians were at risk of 'being swamped by Asians' is a vulgar but classical expression of this fear, which, as I suggest in accounts of the gendered erasure of Aboriginal and Asian figures in twentieth century landscape writing ('Panorama') and in the film *Mad Max* ('White Panic'), mixes not only with desire but also with that strange energy that Marjorie Garber calls *envy*.

For Garber, envy, understood as the 'opposite' strategy to differentiation, involves 'a kind of energy, an exhilarating intellectual curiosity, as well as what Veblen called emulation'.[23] While I certainly do not conflate the harmful, socially aggressive crises of white majoritarian identity with the process of discipline formation, Garber's account is useful for understanding what can happen when these interact. The work of Fanon long ago drew attention (from the perspective of a man of colour burdened and battered by a white colonial gaze) to the envy, curiosity and emulation at work in racist masquerades of becoming minor;[24] Charles Chauvel's film *Uncivilised* (1936) is exemplary of the more complex but no less violent formations of stereotype which I examine in this book. More recently, the conscription of otherwise sober scholars to the anti-political correctness campaign against so-called 'other studies' and 'victim studies' in universities showed once again that if discipline envy is not in itself socially noxious, it can become so when it mixes with other, more dangerous movements.

In the media events and texts discussed in 'Panorama' and 'White Panic', this volatile amalgam of fear and envy is rendered anecdotally by translator figures who articulate boundary problems for an audience as well as marking them in representation. One such figure in 'Panorama' is the travel writer Ernestine Hill (1899–1972), with her explicit reflections on translating outback life into stories for urban consumption; within Hill's work is the figure of 'Mrs Witchetty', a white woman who married an Aboriginal man, lived with his people and dreamed of writing an autobiography. In counterpoint to this story of the 1930s is the 1988 tale of Mrs Smith of Kingoonya, a white woman living without television in an outback town and a 'formerly iconic' national remnant whom the globally pitched *Australia Live* purports to celebrate but does not and cannot address.[25]

'White Panic' gives a detailed account of the inside/outside boundary thinking and ambivalence about alterity which animated late nineteenth century racial exclusion policy, and its pathological hostility to the too permeable, reproductive bodies of women. Examining the relay of that policy's logics a century later, in popular cultural translations of 'the plot of the sublime' and in policy rhetoric about dynamic Asian economies threatening a lazy, complacent Australia, I turn to action cinema's role as a field of experiment projecting other possible ways of narrating the nation. The major translator figure here is Mad Max, the go-between or *carrier* between inner and outer worlds, past and future. Another is the figure of Aunty Entity played by Tina Turner in *Mad Max Beyond Thunderdome*, as she translates for a global marketplace the possibility of black jurisdiction over the deserts of an Australia in which Aboriginal people and Asian women can only be glimpsed in peripheral vision.

For thinking about translation as a cultural politics, the most important chapter for me is 'Beyond Assimilation', on Tracey Moffatt's *Night Cries* (1989), a short film about a situation arising from the assimilation policy pursued by govern-ments in the twentieth century of rending Aboriginal people from their kin and cultural identities most deeply through the institution of the family: a black daughter is trapped in the desert, caring for her dying white mother. Picking up the theme of temporal depth in images, this chapter explores the homage paid in *Night Cries* to the painting of Albert Namatjira, an immensely popular Aboriginal artist of the 1940s and 1950s who made landscapes in a Western mode. Drawing on recent scholarship about his life, this chapter spells out the difference between seeing his painting as an expression of 'split identity' and conceiving of it rather as a translative *act* by which Namatjira spoke to non-Aboriginal Australians about his country in a visual language which he judged, correctly, that we could under-stand. It seeks to describe the rhetorical effectiveness of a short film which played a significant role in widening public debate about the stolen children of Aboriginal

Australia by entwining a universal mother–daughter story with a historically specific white–black story – creating a 'doubled' field of address in which anybody may struggle to secure a single place from which to perform identification.

The next four chapters deepen the basis for understanding Moffatt's film and Namatjira's painting as works of translation. In my reading of Harvey's *The Condition of Postmodernity* I follow Rosalyn Deutsche's analysis of its logic of 'mistaken identity' (a misrecognition of the burden of feminist and post-structuralist texts) in order to ask why this logic comes into play and what happens when it does so.[26] The feminist debate about this book is an old one now, and I revisit it here to identify the obstacles to thinking about translation which arise from the 'tradition and modernity', 'general and particular' dyads which organize Harvey's text but also, much more widely, script recurring problems of translation between social and cultural theorists. Super-imposed on an opposition between 'narrative' and 'the image', these dyads also make it impossible to conceptualize aesthetic and media *practice*.

This discussion of Harvey's account of the 'fragmentations' of postmodernity recalls my earlier distinction between an anecdote conceived of as detached from a wider narrative, and an anecdote understood as a singular force with the capacity to initiate contact in conditions of heterogeneity. The chapters on Paul Willemen and Naoki Sakai explore the practical implications of thus distinguishing heterogeneity from fragmentation and singularity from particularism. Willemen's *Looks and Frictions* proposes a theory of cinematic experience *as* translation, taking as its premise the constitutive heterogeneity of all psychic and cultural activity, while Sakai's study of cultural nationalism and the subject of 'Japan' in *Translation and Subjectivity* proposes a theory *of* translation based on the premise that any audience is 'mixed'.

In a move inconceivable for Harvey's version of the general–particular dyad, Willemen asks how to take location seriously in the *formulation* of critical work, while at the same time offering a critique of 'specificity as fetish' in film theory. Outlining the major concepts with which he develops an account of translation as constitutive of subjectivity and communication in cinema ('inner speech', 'the fourth look', 'double-outsidedness' and 'the in-between'), I relate Willemen's interest in an institutionally located and *directed* politics to his argument that the national in cinema is a question of address, and also to his vision for a transnational avant-garde. The critical anecdote in this chapter is that of Willemen's migration from Belgium to Britain and his encounter with the culture of literary English. Putting the frictions of translation at the core of British film theory in the 1970s and 1980s, his story affirms the value of sustaining a sense of non-belonging and non-identity with the culture one 'inhabits'.

The chapter on Sakai extends this critique to the historical arena in which geo-politics and discipline formation interact. Sakai's account of the complicity between universalism and particularism in social theory adopts what Willemen might call a 'doubly-outsided' location as it implicates both 'Asian Studies' in the West, and the discipline called 'Japanese Thought' in Japan, in the history of Japanese imperialism. In earlier work, Sakai argued that a rivalrous 'logic of co-figuration' (opposing and comparing 'tradition' with 'modernity', 'particularism' with 'universalism', and 'East' with 'West') took hold in Japan as an *outcome* of a theory of translation and thence a concept of national language that emerged in the eighteenth century. *Translation and Subjectivity* refines this argument with a critique of 'homolingual' theories of communication and translation based on the model of a unified national language. Focusing on the enunciative effort (the work of address) which precedes the possibility of a communication which may always fail to occur, Sakai insists that translation is a *social* relation, and that the art and politics of creating transnational critical space involves accepting to speak in a state of uncertainty about whether one will be understood or what the outcome might be.

Following these discussions of disciplinarity (Harvey, Sakai) and institutional practice (Willemen), 'Crazy Talk Is not Enough: Deleuze and Guattari at Muriel's Wedding' turns to the question of the 'outside' that boundary-marking operations always instate. I do a little translation myself to draw out from the dense prose of *A Thousand Plateaus* a model of *home-making* capable of bringing *in* to the home the outside term of the identity problem that bothered Gertrude Stein, while conceiving of the home as a workplace as well as a dwelling. A theory of translation consistent with those of Willemen and Sakai could be based on Deleuze and Guattari's pragmatics of 'several regimes of signs', which assumes the inadequacy of linguistic presuppositions for semiotic analysis and shifts the emphasis away from the circularity of signs referring to other signs and towards 'the *multiplicity* of the circles or chains' and the things that can happen or 'jump' between them.[27] My purpose is very much more modest: I take from *A Thousand Plateaus* a way of thinking about inside and outside which escapes not only the circularity of 'white panic' thinking but also the blockage of a simplistic (non)-deconstruction of the inside/outside *binary* that reveals its impossibility without accounting for its practical uses, and I do this to enable a discussion of the academy as an institutional home which is open to outside forces. P.J. Hogan's film *Muriel's Wedding* (a tragi-comedy of small town globalization) helps me to read Deleuze and Guattari in this way and to situate feminist pragmatics in a mundane social landscape.

In a little-read passage of *A Thousand Plateaus*, Deleuze and Guattari stress that 'crazy talk is not enough' to secure translation from one semiotic to another, and that translation is very difficult when we confront a 'dominant atmospheric' semiotic.[28] Academics who have defended the humanities, theory, feminism or cultural studies in the bellicose ambience of the media in recent years may wonder if any sort of talk could get their point across. Of course, some scholars are also media practitioners and education policies fostering 'industry links' are bringing the two professions perhaps more closely together than ever before in their modern history as distinct. At the same time, the academy–media interface has become a fraught and merciless, even a perilous place for academics suddenly caught up in a whirlwind of scandal or controversy which takes them by surprise.[29]

I have always disliked the term 'culture wars', not because the martial image is melodramatic but because the phrase so successfully lent a fuzzy, pluralistic alibi to a hard-edged *ideology* war, waged over two decades or more, to attach credibility (our beliefs about other people's beliefs) to neo-liberal ideas of the common social and economic good, thereby securing recognition value (effective 'interpellation') for ruthlessly limited ways of imagining the actual and the possible. Now that the dust of culture wars has packed down into the iron-hard ground of military globalization, on which the violence of terrorism and 'war against terror' supports a spreading militarization of civic everyday life, it is obvious that the former rhetorically prepared for the latter; ten years before the destruction of the World Trade Center, President George Bush Snr warned Americans that 'political extremists roam the land ... setting citizens against one another on the basis of their class or race', urging them to 'join in common cause without having to surrender their identities'.[30] As the word spread, in the blink of a cursor it became commonplace in Australia, too, to hear talk of feminist and 'multiculturalist' terrorists not only on campus but in government as well, and to meet passionately angry citizens, colleagues and family members for whom the term *terrorist* worked as an objective correlative of their feelings about seemingly endless criticism of their values and ways of life ('of course, I don't mean you, dear').

Like many others I took a small part in some of the brawls of the 1990s, in particular those over sexual harassment in universities, precipitated for Australians by *The First Stone: Some Questions about Sex and Power* (1995), an attack by the novelist Helen Garner on two young women who 'went to the cops' about the Master of their college;[31] the hoaxing of *Social Text* by Alan Sokal, who persuaded the journal to publish pastiche as science studies;[32] and the savage impact of educational reform on the working conditions and prospects of academics, especially the young.[33] The bile and brutality stirred up by the first two scandals was, to put it mildly, thought-provoking beside the indifference inspired by the third in media professionals who would also aspire (one must imagine) to a good education for their children.

Yet all three situations manifestly involve shop-floor issues of, as it were, occupational health and safety. Arising in academic workplaces undergoing rapid change, they concern the codes of conduct (and industrial safeguards) we should expect to operate there, as well as the terms on which highly diverse bodies of people working very long hours can feel at home as they work; a hoax, no less than an assault or a redundancy campaign, acts to undermine other people's sense of security. These links were rarely picked up in the media. The first two scandals merged in a moral panic over PC 'feminazis' who were bad scholars as well,[34] but the third, with its unsettling news for families about stress-related illness and insecure employment – in a country where universities are major employers ensuring the survival of some quite large towns – was isolated to education features or mocked in op-ed pieces about the whiners in the ivory tower. The common source of conflicts over sexual harassment, refereeing ('quality assurance') and an erosion of job security, pay and quality of *life* in a productivity-driven process of institutional restructuring – an experience shared by academics with other workers, including journalists – failed to attract attention away from excitingly perennial topics such as 'eros' in the classroom or infelicitous prose.

This deep, empathetic disconnection between academics and journalists has a rich professional history which merits complex explanation. The two sallies from the culture wars included here for their emphasis on translation focus merely on one element, the cultivated habit of professional people who are not academics themselves to think of the university not as a workplace, conflicted and changing like any other, but as a site of personal *memory* that evokes strong emotions and remains frozen in time. It is not uncommon for media folk and creative writers like Garner to frame a shocked revelation of bizarre goings-on in universities today with a contrasting story of 'the way we were' when they themselves were students (a tactic I use without shame myself in Chapters 9 and 12). It usually goes unmentioned in such baby-boomer *bildung*-anecdotes that their authors, who may elsewhere heartily endorse dismantling 'welfare' and opening the economy to 'global competition', enjoyed the option in their youth of an excellent, cheap education courtesy of the taxpayers within a highly protected national economy structured by racial and gender exclusion.

The seventies-style subtitle used by Garner ('some questions about sex and power') *places* sexual harassment in this faded world of her youth and mine where a white student pestered by an authority figure could indeed 'knee him in the balls', as Garner puts it, while gazing past him to a social horizon of plentiful employment, jobs for life, free medical care and a decent old age pension.[35] Even then, far less freedom of movement was afforded Aboriginal people who had no such horizon, and migrants who were battling to attain it.[36] Today, the vista has changed for all and harassment is a life-shaping question of *work*, power and sex. In a moment of empathy with the humiliation of women who do not fight back, Garner recalls how she once responded with infantile denial to a masseur's advances, paying his bill as she left.[37] However, this private transaction is beside the point, a bad translation of workplace harassment. Kerryn Goldsworthy pinpoints the difference when she recalls with her colleagues an academic serial pest: 'why didn't we deal with him? ... "We needed his signature", we said. On postgraduate progress reports; on references; on applications for leave, for funding, for promotion. *Not once, but over and over and over.*'[38]

It is hard to convey to outsiders the grinding yet touchy quality of daily life in academies, which have now become corporate bureaucracies. Chapters 9 and 10 highlight broad changes which have affected universities and some of the practical reasons for today's institutional obsession with managing socio-cultural identity and difference. 'Sticks and Stones and Stereotypes' tells an inside story of why speech codes have emerged, and what they mean to achieve in conditions that do not easily translate to those presumed by pundits. 'The Scully Protocol' follows the PC panic outwards to the anti-government conspiracy narratives with which TV drama in the 1990s heralded the triumph of neo-liberalism, and thence to the muddled stories of post-structuralism and identity politics promoted by David Williamson, a popular playwright who shared Harvey's impulse to conflate the two. Contesting these tales as a *bad* popular translation of academic work – a judgement I believe we must be willing to make within a public culture which is more a non-stop tournament of values than a forum for reason – I direct attention outwards, once again, to the identity skirmishes widely occurring over a resurgent Darwinism on the one hand, and the uses of new technologies on the other. Like the battles of belonging everywhere waged around large-scale movements of migration, urban renewal, rural crisis, genetic engineering and environmental change, these struggles over *human* identity are on-going.

Even as academics gain media opportunities (welcome and unwelcome) to share our specialized views of culture with unpredictably mixed publics, powerful new modes of politics arise from the outside to demand our involvement. The institution framing the final two chapters is the family, taken as a site where contending politics are not only evaluated as worth the trouble or not, but also relayed and socially *ignited* as casual media consumption translatively interacts with the hearsay, orthodoxy and affect circulating through domestic and neighbourly life. These chapters address intermingled but divergent politics *of* family and belonging in Australia, exclusionary and expansive respectively. 'Please Explain?' analyses a televisual moment of mass convergence in which a single working mother voiced a resurgent ethnic nationalism of class-based white identity by demanding explanation of a word, *xenophobia* – in the process, shredding the homolingual media mode of address which presumed a multicultural, middle class nation. 'Uncle Billy, Tina Turner and Me', a family romance of sorts, ends the book with a short, utopian reflection on the sense of community sparked between strangers forming an 'active audience' for sport, and on the strangeness always abiding within an extended family.[39] Dealing with different instances of community mobilization, both chapters consider identity as a product of how we attend to what other people are saying, as well as of what we say to them or about them, while also exploring intimately public *responses* to the accounts of popular life which circulate between the academy and media.

Over the past twenty years, 'identity and difference' has phased in and out of fashion as a concern of the Anglophone cultural academy. At my time of writing in the Hong Kong Special Administrative Region (HKSAR) of the People's Republic of China, I often hear that identity is 'over' in Western elite research environments, as these settle back down to tending a cosmopolitan canon now including 'theory' classics, while in new and/or teaching-oriented institutional settings (like my own at Lingnan University) complex affirmations and *questions* of identity pour in every day from the community, the greater urban or rural environment, an unsettled, locally emergent national formation, a fluctuating region and an unpredictably intrusive wider world.[40] Whether they come through the gates or over the airwaves, pop up on our personal computer and TV screens or simply materialize with the mainland Chinese or foreign exchange student present for class discussion of a historically sensitive topic, these questions cannot be avoided or rendered parenthetical, and they stimulate theorization – in the midst of what feels like a growing relevance gap with that canonical body of theory.[41]

However, 'identity' (or 'difference', for that matter) is not necessarily the most useful discursive framework for thinking about those questions; as Lawrence Grossberg succinctly puts it, if political intellectuals must 'begin with identity' in some contexts, 'it does not follow that they should end up there as well'.[42] My theme is *translation* rather than 'identity' taken as the object of a vast literature which I do not review in this book.[43] Here, identity is broadly the name of a 'dominant atmospheric' semiotic which enveloped us during the period (for my purposes, roughly 1985–1997) in which globalization gained rhetorical force for neo-liberalism as a sticky, all-purpose slogan while unfolding across institutions as a *project* composed of concrete policy initiatives.[44] While the slogan glowingly affirmed that 'pervasive logic of market exchange' in which Adorno (as Christopher Connery reminds us) saw 'the totalizing identity of all things', the policies worked in a necessarily much more hit-and-miss manner towards creating the imagined optimal environment for realizing that logic.[45] In education as in media-spheres and the economy of family life, the effects of neo-liberal policies have been real and consequential but by no means always scripted by the logic of the slogan – which by its very form calls up counter-utopian spaces in which alternative visions of the global and other ways of 'worlding' can emerge.[46]

Identity in the relative sense, however, is now a dominant, in that during this period identitarian interpretation was installed as *customary* in a bewildering variety of situations. As academics and other citizens learned a new, self-cataloguing protocol to authorize acts of public speech (and 'speaking as a W, X, Y, Z' became a socially safe rather than a personally revealing statement), a semiotic fluidity of identity as *consumable* and *disposable* became the mark of middle class cosmopolitanism;[47] meanwhile, legal and administrative codings multiplied occasions of need for persons to *prove* identity as a condition of their entitlement to participate openly in economy and society. Identity is also 'atmospheric' in that it is everywhere, life-giving and inescapable. As thinkers, artists and activists struggling to breathe another air are diagnosed as 'in denial' of identities which others insist must matter, a globally circulating aesthetic pedagogy of 'queer eye', 'nip/tuck' and 'extreme make-over' sells dreams of an infinitely plastic personal identity to those with the economic reach to acquire the props, teaching anyone within reach of a TV set that identity is an *asset* in which we must invest.[48] Meanwhile, as Tom Nairn observes, 'for growing masses of people issues of identity are not metaphorical but treasured, if deplorable, bits of cheap plastic: matters of everyday life and death'.[49]

I find it hard to disagree with American critics such as Berlant and Grossberg, who variously suggest that the most effective identity *politics* of recent decades has been pursued from the right.[50] Following Berlant, Melissa Deem argues that in the United States the category of identity was, more specifically, 'deployed by the right through a rhetoric and affect of intimacy within the public sphere', reinvesting legitimacy in the 'hetero-normative', privatized family.[51] In identity-card-resistant Australia, where truly patriotic sporting heroes must (I still firmly believe) mumble rather than sing the few bars of the national anthem they are willing to be seen to know, this operation unfolded slowly, deviating as it did so; it took twenty years of public sector unravelling for an affective politics of 'family first' to push through the deep reserves of egalitarian homosociality and carnivalesque low culture which render the hetero-*normative* model of family a shaky proposition and a fertile subject for humour.[52] It was rather a rhetoric and affect of *security* (no doubt, intimacy's partner in a privatizing world) which in 2004 allowed a Christian-based, homophobic 'Family First Party' to displace 'One Nation' at the semiotic centre of national politics.[53] However, in a climate of alarm about transnational threats ranging from terrorism and an 'influx' of asylum seekers to internet-based child pornography rings and interest rate rises menacing the family home, the shift from nation to family is a smooth one of emphasis, and visa categories and tax file numbers no less starkly decide the identity politics which counts.

The frictional work of what I have, loosely and a little eccentrically, called *speech* institutions is then all the more vital in producing both spaces of 'worlding' and opportunities in *time* for projects contesting fascism and militarization to take shape, to gain social traction in people's everyday lives and to disseminate models other than a violent defensiveness for living in proximity with strangeness and uncertainty. By 'speech institutions', I simply mean those in which bodily speech acts of all kinds (face-to-face or technically relayed and enhanced) are central to the conduct of daily affairs and fundamental to realizing their *purposes*.[54] Of course, all institutions mix speech with other material practices, writing included, but some institutions are more talkative than others. Churches, the military, prisons, libraries and some arts institutions tend to *ration* speech in the interests of achieving transcendence, abolition, or redemption of human mundanity; a monastic order or a taciturn militant group may even seek perfection in an erasure of speech. The school or academy, the media and the family share an emphasis on *producing* speech, to the extent that, while its use is disciplined in the interests of good pedagogy and socialization, an unexpected absence, withdrawal or failure of speech creates a sense of crisis, whether acute (the radio and TV static that signals disaster, the break-down of a teacher whose sentences fail in front of a staring class) or chronic, as for the child who finds it hard to handle the demands of a noisy outside world. My interest, however, lies not in distinguishing institutional types but in situating academic work on a broad though definitely not smooth social continuum, and thus in a wider community of effort.

Theoretically speaking, anecdotal tactics are of interest to me for their practical value in translating effort across that necessarily heterolingual, socially rubble-strewn continuum. There are other ways to think about anecdote, many of them making it the minor/feminized term which is held to disrupt a major mode of discourse: anecdote is to grand narrative, say, as small talk is to theory.[55] In an interesting critique of this set of assumptions, David Simpson marks the importance of anecdote for 'the culture of conversation', where it works to distinguish competence from incompetence; noting the fondness for it avowed by Samuel Johnson, Simpson suggests that anecdote became a 'compulsive mode of representation' in the eighteenth century.[56] His discussion, however, is itself more narrowly lodged in a corner of US literary theory established by Joel Fineman's 1989 essay on 'The History of the Anecdote', with its much-quoted remark that the anecdote, 'as the narration of a singular event, is the literary form or genre that uniquely refers to the real'.[57]

In a spiral required neither by a culture of conversation nor by Fineman's erudite reading of Thucydides and the medical case history in Hippocrates, but possibly irresistible in a culture of identity, this corner is given over less to debates about 'the literary' and 'the real' than to reflecting on 'the theoretical' and 'the personal' in academic speech. Indeed, both for Simpson, who invokes Derrida against the yearning for a 'pre'-professional literary freedom and for the 'presence' of a lost public sphere which he senses in anecdotal criticism,[58] and for Jane Gallop who, writing *as* a Derridean, embraces in *Anecdotal Theory* the anecdote's occasional and eventful force,[59] a slide from 'telling anecdotes' to 'speaking personally' seems almost to go without saying. Insofar as support for this slide is provided, it comes from associating feminism with the quotidian and with the idea of personal experience.

My sympathies lie with Gallop's version of deconstruction, which is more finely in tune with Fineman's insistence on grasping the *impact* of the anecdote's production of 'the occurrence of contingency'; for Fineman, the anecdote does not merely produce that 'effect of the real' which leads Simpson to talk of nostalgia, but also *'lets history happen'* by introducing 'an opening into the teleological, and therefore timeless, narration of beginning, middle and end'.[60] At another level, while Gallop 'thinks' institutionally from a variety of situations and roles, whether as a teacher investigated for sexual harassment or as a sister addressing a fiftieth birthday party, Simpson implicitly affirms a socially sedentary, one-career model of university-based critical professionalism. However, there is professional and other life outside but not prior to ('pre-') the American tenured academic mode; most students graduate to other modes of institutional life, some critics move from one to another, and certain professions can be all about articulating presence for multiple networked publics in lieu of a single sphere – sometimes, as live reporters do, making history in the process.[61]

However, journalistic and other more or less banal practices of anecdote are not necessarily *personal* in the narcissistic and literary but truth-seeking mode affirmed by Gallop but unsettling to Simpson, and also to me. Oddly enough, it was as a way of extricating myself from the grip of the academic personal on my first trip to the United States that I first tried out this model of anecdote to frame an argument that the admission of a personal *truth* from an Australian TV newsreader signified catastrophe:

> I take anecdotes, or yarns, to be primarily referential. They are oriented futuristically towards the construction of a precise, local, and *social* discursive context, of which the anecdote then functions as a *mise en abyme*. That is to say, anecdotes are not expressions of personal experience but allegorical expositions of a model of the way the world can be said to be working. So anecdotes need not be true stories, but they must be functional in a given exchange.[62]

While I would no longer want to claim an Australian sanction for this view (not least because the personal is transnationally more pervasive a public mode than it used to be), this *futurism* of the anecdote, along with its expository, sociable force, still seems to me its most salient feature for ventures in translation. If the impact of an anecdote is microscopic as well as context-specific, this small quantity of force does not mean that it disrupts, subverts, transgresses or dramatically feminizes a 'grand' discursive other. For an ethics of uncertainty, to 'introduce an opening' into teleological narration may simply mean taking advantage of proximity to hazard an initiative ('what do you make of this story?'), to accept the bother of not having a clue what might come next, and to make room in time for history to happen.

The stakes of attempting this in historically fraught contexts of cross-cultural and transnational discussion are clear, and they have been formulated eloquently over the years by Homi Bhabha, whose writings have, like those of Judith Butler, done a great deal to work a more complex rhetorical notion of identity as enunciative, rather than expressive, into a literary-critical tradition that persistently reduces the rhetorical to the figural;[63] in doing so, it recurrently generates intensely moralized but formal problems of representation rather than a politics of cultural redistribution and participation that may begin but cannot end with 'culture' alone.[64] However, I want also to highlight the stakes of cross-institutional practice, and therefore of allowing institutional limitation and diversity to register in what Willemen calls 'the actual formulation of our work'.[65]

To univerzalise the *habitus* of the elite university as the emblematic ground of an ambitiously theorized 'cultural politics' of interpretation with paradoxically little desire and power to engage in translation is of limited value even for criticism as a 'vocation' (in Bruce Robbins' sense of that term), especially in contexts where this *habitus*, insofar as it has ever existed, is rapidly being dismantled under the impact of globalization on education systems, along with other sites of cultural production.[66] Much as I love my opening quotation from Gertrude Stein, its wonderful cadence carries us into a time-rich world where the bohemian artist or genteel scholar can close the door and *create* in the absence of market pressure; when 'the buyer is not there … there is no bother'. This is not our world, and an academic writer without a market these days is in deep trouble. In part, it follows from this that a 'buyer' – or, in Deleuzian terms, an outside-oriented critical practice which translates between academic, media and other institutions, needs to operate with an un-inflated sense of its own political potential; translation is a technical business and a highly constrained mode of interpretation. However, translation can do more than interpret; always modifying, as Sakai shows, the social context in which it occurs, it can also initiate cross-institutional 'openings' that can be imagined but less effectively produced without it.[67]

It is with some reluctance that I use the empty, even vapid term 'media culture' to invoke spaces and times in which some such openings form, especially since my concern here is mainly with the 'old' media of print journalism, cinema and television. My subtitle designates many topics which this book does not address, ranging from the roles played *by* forms of translation (dubbing, subtitling, remaking, glocalizing) in the circulation of media narratives, to large debates about the politics of consumption, audience activity and cultural policy frameworks.[68] It serves, though, to bring together three sets or clusters of issues: the production of national culture *by* the media, and the uses of participating in this process for groups with other affinities and different stories to tell; the status of translation *in* theories of media and culture; and the value of translation as a model of cultural action *for* media practitioners and critics.

The third cluster defines for me the distinctive emphasis of this book. I find almost wholly unproductive the recurring, envious face-offs between sociological and so-called 'textualist' approaches to media cultural studies. My practice is not sociological but this does not mean that it is textual in the narrow, pre-structuralist sense reiterated by those for whom 'text' is a shibboleth or a boo-word. Something more than a precious nuance is lost in this reiteration. The sociologically driven shift away from the fine art of individuating texts and towards an interest (which I share) in researching what Nick Couldry nicely calls 'textual environments' is often accompanied, unnecessarily in my view, by a curious neglect of one of the primary *social* aims of textual pedagogy – making text production accessible as something which *we do*, all of us (researchers included), using techniques that can be taught, learned, modified and shared with others. Even in Couldry's careful, sympathetic account of the debates around text, his expression of hope for a 'wider synthesis of the sociological and aesthetic concerns to which texts give rise' ultimately locates its 'questions of aesthetics and pleasure' on the receiving end of someone else's textual power – that is, in consumption rather than in the pleasure and power of text-making ourselves.[69] In this perspective, we feel pleasure but do not give it, and aesthetics is a problem to be explained but not a guide to everyday practice.

I am interested in problems of rhetoric, textuality and institutional location as these arise for media *practitioners*, and by this I mean people who act 'anecdotally' (occasionally, momentarily, eventfully) as active participants in media fields, as well as those who want to work professionally as journalists, programme-makers and pundits. For this, competence is important; to be effective, such action requires aesthetic skills as well as social knowledges that neither conflict nor wholly overlap with those needed to study audiences, media ownership or the impact of new technologies, just as these, in turn are not wholly interchangeable with the skills and knowledges required to formulate and effect cultural policies. To defend the value of cultivating and transmitting aesthetic skills for students of media is the personal purpose of this book.

NOTES

1 Gertrude Stein, *Everybody's Autobiography* (London: Virago, 1985), p. 50.

2 Meaghan Morris, 'Identity Anecdotes', *Camera Obscura* 12 (1984): 41–65 (p. 41).

3 Paul Taylor, 'Antipodality', *Art & Text* 6 (1982): 49. An extraordinary person who made a lasting impact in art criticism over ten hectic years of activity, Paul Taylor died of an AIDS-related illness in 1992. A brief biography and a wonderful photograph of Taylor by Robert Mapplethorpe is at http://home.vicnet.net.au/~bookman/paultay.htm.

4 Meaghan Morris and Paul Patton, eds, *Michel Foucault: Power, Truth, Strategy* (Sydney: Feral Publications, 1979).

5 Morris, 'Identity Anecdotes', p. 59.

6 See Meaghan Morris, *Too Soon Too Late: History in Popular Culture* (Bloomington and Indianapolis: Indiana University Press, 1998).

7 Meaghan Morris, 'A Gadfly Bites Back', *Meanjin* 51:3 (1992): 545–551.

8 Lindsay Waters, *Enemies of Promise: Publishing, Perishing, and the Eclipse of Scholarship* (Chicago: Prickly Paradigm Press, 2004).

9 I do not remember the date but I can never forget the courage with which Barry elegantly walked through the Newcastle (NSW) Workers' Club in this then utterly outrageous outfit, nor the warmth with which his bravery was saluted by the men drinking there. Later a respected art gallery director and curator in the UK, Barry Prothero died of an AIDS-related illness in 1996. He and his partner Tim Lunn are commemorated by a patients' garden in the Ian Charleson Day Centre at the Royal Free Hospital in London:http://www.positivenation.co.uk/issue92_3/regulars/news/news92_3.htm.

10 See Tom O'Regan, *Australian Television Culture* (Sydney: Allen & Unwin, 1993).

11 See Andrew Markus, *Fear and Hatred: Purifying Australia and California, 1850–1901* (Sydney: Hale & Iremonger, 1979).

12 The book that inspired me and many others to think about discontinuity as a mode of narration was Frank Moorhouse, *The Americans, Baby – a Discontinuous Narrative of Stories and Fragments* (Sydney: Angus & Robertson, 1972).

13 I take the phrase 'paranoid nationalism' from an eloquent, hopeful book by Ghassan Hage, *Against Paranoid Nationalism: Searching for Hope in a Shrinking Society* (Annandale and London: Pluto Press Australia and The Merlin Press, 2003).

14 Lauren Berlant, *The Queen of America Goes to Washington City: Essays on Sex and Citizenship* (Durham, NC and London: Duke University Press, 1997), p. 13.

15 See Evan Watkins, *Work Time: English Departments and the Circulation of Cultural Value* (Stanford, CA: Stanford University Press, 1989); and Elspeth Probyn, *Outside Belongings* (New York and London: Routledge, 1996).

16 Simon Marginson and Mark Considine, *The Enterprise University: Power, Governance and Reinvention in Australia* (Cambridge: Cambridge University Press, 2000).

17 The earlier initiative was a series of international symposia called 'Trajectories'. See *Trajectories: Inter-Asia Cultural Studies,* ed. Kuan-Hsing Chen with Hsui-Ling Kuo, Hans Hang and Hsu Ming-Chu (London and New York: Routledge, 1998).

18 See Naoki Sakai and Jon Solomon, 'Addressing the Multitude of Foreigners, Echoing Foucault' in *Traces 4: Translation, Biopolitics, Colonial Difference,* eds Naoki Sakai and Jon Solomon (Hong Kong: Hong Kong University Press, 2006). I must admit to an interest as Senior Editor of the *Traces* series.

19 Marjorie Garber, *Academic Instincts* (Princeton, NJ: Princeton University Press, 2001), pp. 54–55.

20 Garber, *Academic Instincts,* p. 57.

21 Gilles Deleuze and Félix Guattari, *A Thousand Plateaus*, vol. 2 of *Capitalism and Schizophrenia,* trans. Brian Massumi (Minneapolis: University of Minnesota Press, 1987 [1980]), p. 291.

22 The sentence I am adapting is: 'In a way, the subject in a becoming is always "man", but only when he enters a becoming-minoritarian that rends him from his major identity' (Deleuze and Guattari, *A Thousand Plateaus,* p. 291).

23 Garber, *Academic Instincts,* p. 60.

24 Frantz Fanon, *Black Skin, White Masks* (New York: Grove Press, 1991 [1952]).

25 I borrow 'formerly iconic' from Berlant: 'today many formerly iconic citizens who used to feel undefensive and unfettered feel truly exposed and vulnerable … They sense that they now have *identities*, when it used to be just other people who had them': *The Queen of America Goes to Washington City,* p. 2. However, I argue in Chapter 2 that the pre-televisual Mrs Smith fascinates *Australia Live* because she has no way of knowing and does not care whether she is or is not 'iconic'.

26 Rosalyn Deutsche, 'Boys town', *Environment and Planning D: Society and Space* 9 (1991): 5–30.

27 Deleuze and Guattari, *A Thousand Plateaus,* pp. 111–113; emphasis mine.

28 Ibid., p. 138.

29 A visionary text on the politics of scandal within an emerging 'new world order' is Patricia Mellencamp, *High Anxiety: Catastrophe, Scandal, Age, and Comedy* (Bloomington and Indianapolis: Indiana University Press, 1992).

30 George Bush, excerpt from a speech at the University of Michigan, May 4, 1991, in *Beyond PC: Towards a Politics of Understanding,* ed. Patricia Aufderheide (Saint Paul, MN: Graywolf Press, 1992), p. 227.

31 Helen Garner, *The First Stone: Some Questions about Sex and Power* (Sydney: Pan Macmillan, 1995). Ostensibly non-fiction, this book multiplied and dispersed across several distinct characters the identity of a female academic whose job it was to counsel the young women, thus inventing a feminist conspiracy. See Jenna Mead, 'Introduction: Tell It Like It Is' in *Bodyjamming: Sexual Harassment, Feminism and Public Life,* ed. Jenna Mead (Sydney: Random House, 1997), pp. 1–41. See also the dossier of pieces by Jenna Mead, Meaghan Morris and Wendy McCarthy, 'Bodyjamming, Feminism and Public Life', *The Sydney Papers* 10:1 (1998): 69–85.

32 'Toll of a Hoax', *The Australian's Review of Books* November 1998, pp. 16–19.

33 'Losing Our Minds', *Weekend Australian* July 22–23, 2000, pp. 19, 22.

34 Melissa Deem notes that 'the mainstream is never so fascinated with feminism as during a sexual harassment case'; 'Scandal, Heteronormative Culture, and the Disciplining

of Feminism', *Critical Studies in Mass Communication* 16 (1999): 88. For a perspective on scandal from a feminist 'accused', see Jane Gallop, *Feminist Accused of Sexual Harassment* (Durham, NC and London: Duke University Press, 1997).

35 Garner, *The First Stone,* p. 201.

36 See Rosi Braidotti, 'Remembering Fitzroy High', in Mead, ed., *Bodyjamming*, pp. 121–147.

37 Garner, *The First Stone*, pp. 172–175.

38 Kerryn Goldsworthy, 'Needing His Signature', *Australian Humanities Review*, May 1998, http://www.lib.latrobe.edu.au/AHR/archive/Issue-May-1998/goldsworthy2.html.

39 A fascinating discussion of 'familial identity' is José Medina, 'Identity Trouble: Disidentification and the Problem of Difference', *Philosophy & Social Criticism* 29:6 (2003): 655–680, esp. p. 663.

40 On these issues see the articles in *Soundings* 29 (2005), 'After Identity'.

41 I discuss this in 'On the Future of Parochialism: Globalization, *Young and Dangerous IV*, and Cinema Studies in Tuen Mun' in *Film History and National Cinema: Studies in Irish Film II*, eds John Hill and Kevin Rockett (Dublin: Four Courts Press, 2005), pp. 17–36.

42 Handel Kashope Wright, '"What's Going On?" Larry Grossberg on the Status Quo of Cultural Studies: An Interview', *Cultural Values* 5:2 (2001): 133–162 (p. 150). See also Rita Felski, 'The Doxa of Difference', *Signs* 23:1 (1997): 1–22.

43 From this literature the three texts I would take to a desert island are Ien Ang, *On Not Speaking Chinese: Living Between Asia and the West* (London and New York: Routledge, 2001); Homi K. Bhabha, 'Interrogating Identity: The Postcolonial Prerogative' in *Anatomy of Racism*, ed. David Theo Goldberg (Minneapolis: University of Minnesota Press, 1990), pp. 183–209; and Stephen Ching-kiu Chan, 'Figures of Hope and the Filmic Imaginary of Jianghu in Contemporary Hong Kong Cinema', *Cultural Studies* 15:3 – 4 (2001): 486–514.

44 On globalization as a 'weasel word', see Doreen Massey, 'Problems with globalisation', *Soundings* 7 (1997): 7–12.

45 Christopher L. Connery, 'Actually Existing Left Conservatism', *boundary 2* 26:3 (1999): 9. On the utopianism of market talk in this period, see my 'Ecstasy and Economics' in *Too Soon Too Late*, pp. 158–194.

46 Rob Wilson and Christopher Connery, eds, *Worldings: World Literature, Field Imaginaries, Future Practices – Doing Cultural Studies in the Era of Globalization* (Santa Cruz: New Pacific Press, 2006). See also Fredric Jameson and Masao Miyoshi, eds, *The Cultures of Globalization* (Durham, NC and London: Duke University Press, 1998).

47 The best account of this is John Clarke, *New Times and Old Enemies: Essays on Cultural Studies and America* (London: Harper Collins Academic, 1991).

48 The TV series referred to here are *Queer Eye for the Straight Guy*, *Nip/Tuck* and *Extreme Makeover*. Also interesting as aesthetic pedagogy are the TV series *Alias* (with Jennifer Gardner) and Andy Tennant's film *Hitch* (with Will Smith), both of which affirm an anchoring social normality – that of the dysfunctional family and the romantic couple respectively – which allows wholesome people to engage in identity morphing while psychologically remaining the same.

49 Tom Nairn, 'A Myriad Byzantiums', *New Left Review* 23 (Sept.-Oct., 2003): 115–133 (p. 115).

50 Berlant, *The Queen of America Goes to Washington City*; Lawrence Grossberg, *We Gotta Get Out of This Place: Popular Conservatism and Postmodern Culture* (New York and London: Routledge, 1992).

51 Melissa Deem, 'The Scandalous Fall of Feminism and the "First Black President"', in *A Companion to Cultural Studies,* ed. Toby Miller (New York: Blackwell, 2001), pp. 407– 429 (p. 409). More recently, Grossberg has pointed to the violent division of this normativity by what he calls 'America's war on its children': Lawrence Grossberg, *Caught in the Crossfire: Kids, Politics and America's Future* (Boulder and London: Paradigm Publishers, 2005).

52 On this point see John Fiske, Bob Hodge and Graeme Turner, *Myths of Oz: Reading Australian Popular Culture* (Sydney, London, Boston: Allen & Unwin, 1987); and Meaghan Morris, 'Fate and the Family Sedan', *East–West Film Journal* 4:1 (1989): 113–134. Also at http://www.sensesofcinema.com/contents/01/19/sedan.html.

53 The 'semiotic' centre of Australian politics is accorded by the media to anyone who might end up holding the balance of power in Federal Parliament, no matter how small their electoral base. Led briefly by Andrea Mason, an Aboriginal woman (who stepped down when she failed to win a seat in the 2004 election), Family First differs from One Nation in disavowing racism: see http://www.familyfirst.org.au/.

54 I include signed languages used by deaf people as speech in this sense; thanks to Trevor Johnston for discussing this point with me. On the bodily in speech acts, see Judith Butler, *Excitable Speech: A Politics of the Performative* (New York and London: Routledge, 1997), pp. 152–153.

55 The *locus classicus* of this sort of argument is Jane Tompkins, 'Me and My Shadow', in *Gender and Theory: Dialogues on Feminist Criticism,* ed. Linda Kauffman (New York and Oxford: Blackwell, 1989), pp. 121–139.

56 David Simpson, *The Academic Postmodern and the Rule of Literature: A Report on Half-Knowledge* (Chicago and London: University of Chicago Press, 1995), pp. 54–55.

57 Joel Fineman, 'The History of the Anecdote: Fiction and Fiction' in *The Subjectivity Effect in Western Literary Tradition: Essays Toward the Release of Shakespeare's Will* (Cambridge, MA and London: The MIT Press, 1991), pp. 59–87 (p. 67).

58 Simpson, *The Academic Postmodern and the Rule of Literature,* pp. 41–91. See in particular pp. 62–64.

59 Jane Gallop, *Anecdotal Theory* (Durham, NC and London: Duke University Press, 2002), p. 5.

60 Fineman, 'The History of the Anecdote', p. 72, emphasis original. Ross Chambers persuasively argues that the 'getting personal' movement exemplified by Tompkins shares with Simpson's critique a misreading of post-structuralism shaped in US English Departments: 'Literature Against Disciplinarity?', *The UTS Review: Cultural Studies and New Writing* 4/1 (1998): 188–193.

61 See Meaghan Morris and Iain McCalman, '"Public Culture" and Humanities Research in Australia: A Report', *Public Culture* 11:2 (Spring 1999): 319–345.

62 'Banality in Cultural Studies', paper delivered to the Center for Twentieth Century Studies, University of Wisconsin–Milwaukee, September 1987. Published in *Logics of Television* ed. Patricia Mellencamp (Bloomington: Indiana University Press, 1990), pp. 14–43 (p. 15).

63 Homi Bhabha, *The Location of Culture* (London and New York: Routledge, 1984).

64 On the link between literary 'representation' campaigns and liberal interest-group politics in the United States see John Guillory, *Cultural Capital: The Problem of Literary Canon Formation* (Chicago and London: University of Chicago Press, 1993).

65 Paul Willemen, *Looks and Frictions: Essays in Cultural Studies and Film Theory* (London, Bloomington and Indianapolis: British Film Institute and Indiana University Press, 1994), p. 162.

66 Bruce Robbins, *Secular Vocations: Intellectuals, Professionalism, Culture* (London: Verso, 1993). I discuss this dismantling in 'Humanities for Taxpayers: Some Problems', *New Literary History* 36/1 (2005): 111–129.

67 An innovative example is the work of the Centre for Cultural Research at the University of Western Sydney in doing cultural research for museums, galleries, health centres, national parks, local councils and community organizations. The rationale for such work is developed by Ien Ang, *Who Needs Cultural Research?*, CHCI Working Paper, Walter Chapin Center for the Humanities, University of Washington, Seattle WA 98195.

68 These are brilliantly explored in Diana Crane, Nobuko Kawashima and Ken'ichi Kawasaki, eds, *Global Culture: Media, Arts Policy and Globalization* (New York and London: Routledge, 2002) and in Mette Hjort, *Small Nation, Global Cinema: The New Danish Cinema* (Minneapolis and London: University of Minnesota Press, 2005).

69 Nick Couldry, *Inside Culture: Re-imagining the Method of Cultural Studies* (London, Thousand Oaks and New Delhi: Sage Publications, 2000), pp. 86–87. An important counter to this tendency to neglect aesthetic skills formation is the work of John Hartley on media literacy: see John Hartley, '"Text" and "Audience": One and the Same? Methodological Tensions in Media Research', *Textual Practice*, 13:3 (1999): 487–508; and John Hartley, ed., *Creative Industries* (Oxford: Blackwell, 2005).

PART ONE

Rhetoric and Nationality

1

Afterthoughts on 'Australianism'

At a conference held in Fremantle, Western Australia, in 1991, I found myself placed oddly, I thought, on a panel called 'Australianism'.[1] Never having heard this word before, I was not sure what it meant. When speakers of English in Australia use an 'Americanism' or a 'Gallicism', we borrow from a foreign idiom and mix it with local speech. Presumably, speakers of any of the varieties of English in Fiji or Hong Kong or England can use an Australianism in that sense. But what could it mean for me – a white Australian with no familial or ethnic memories of a history in any other place – to talk metaphorically, in this alienating way, about 'Australianism' in Australia? Was I being asked to reproduce the ethnographic style of social critics in the 1950s and 1960s, who had to prove that Australians 'had' culture? Or was I being asked to reflect on the radical nationalist tradition deriving from the 1890s, with its passion for what John Docker calls 'impossible stories of uniqueness'?[2]

Any 'nationality-ism' is a travelling form that may acculturate in some destinations (becoming lexicalized, thus losing its mark of origin), keep on circulating in a homely way as 'foreign', or else lose currency in others once its value is used up. So, thinking of an international flow of trade in national and regional meanings, I decided that 'Australianism' must refer to the commodifying process of identity promotion whereby the old folklores of white Australia, like the contemporary arts of black Australia, can gain new social and economic currency in the export industries of tourism and culture – in film, television, music, advertising, the visual and performing arts. In other words, I interpreted 'Australianism' as a synonym for 'Australiana' – a term historically rich with that vague embarrassment about location with which high culture responds to 'kitsch'.

The conference theme was *Dismantle Fremantle*. However, I did not see why a cultural studies gathering in Fremantle – admittedly, a city in Australia's most secessionary state, and to me an exotic and in some ways foreign place – should reify its wider context in this way. So I chose as my dismantling topic one of the most solemn, classic, grand, comic, politically fraught and emotionally complex themes in the repertoire of *Australian* Studies, 'mateship'. Now usually construed historically as the major legitimizing myth of white male homosociality, mateship (loyalty, solidarity) is also an ethic without reference to which it can be hard to grasp – from any perspective of class, race, ethnic or sexual analysis – the nexus of culture and politics in contemporary Australia.[3]

Mateship is practised from Fremantle to Sydney, by no means only by white males. In Australian society, the practically oriented 'cultural technicians' whom Tony Bennett hoped to see emerging from cultural studies could not operate effectively without at least some awareness of the protocols and passions of mateship.[4] Since mateship is an everyday medium of micropolitical pressure – facilitating, for example, the kind of 'industrial relationship' between police and news media that Steve Mickler has analysed in the Western Australian context[5] – it also thrives in those oppositional milieux (feminist, anti-racist, multiculturalist, gay and lesbian activist) which most often affect to despise it for its historic exclusionary determinants and its current complicities with power. Mateship entails forms of conduct which may figure in other ethical codes as unjust or even corrupt. Mateship shapes social personalities (rather than 'selves') which are as ruthless as they are sentimental. My father hated mateship. My cultural access to it as an emotionally positive value comes entirely from my mother.

In putting mateship on a cultural studies agenda, then, and in 'dismantling' its connection to an exclusionary masculine national rhetoric, I thought to contest the reifying category 'Australianism'. Only later, when I read a paper on 'Expatriation' by one of the organizers, John Hartley, did I learn that 'Australianism' is not a variant of 'Australiana' but an ordinary lexical item meaning 'a word or phrase originating in or peculiar to Australia' (the Australian *Macquarie Dictionary* says), and that there is actually an Oxford *Australian National Dictionary* of such items.[6] I must see what it says about 'mateship', a word which is exactly an Australianism in that sense. For now, I am more interested in the afterthoughts of discovering that I had unknowingly performed, at the conference, my allotted Australianist task.

Hartley's model of cultural studies as expatriation immediately becomes productively troubling for me. Does not my incapacity to see my own Australianism from even so proximate an outside as that provided by 'English' English suggest that there is, after all, an important sense in which we are *not* all expatriates or migrants? There are historical depths and geopolitical twists to what Hartley aptly calls 'the power of deixis' in Australia:[7] I doubt that the Cambodian refugee and the English academic really do ever share the same boat, as his expatriation model suggests, although in the longer perspective which his text adopts it is true that their children or grandchildren may. Yet my main problem with expatriation as a norm for non-Aboriginal Australians finds its source in this same longer perspective. If the original class distinctions transported from Britain to New South Wales were tenuous ones between officers, soldiers and convicts (prisoners of distance, all), the primal colonial class distinction was drawn between free expatriates from Britain and Ireland (colloquially known as *sterling*), and the native-born children of the soldiers and convicts – semantically devalued as *currency*.

This history of distinction still lingers, shaping complex tensions between those born and not-born *here* that can snap between generations and stretch to touch the many cultures of Australia that have never referred to Britain or Ireland as *there*. We cannot seriously explore these tensions once we posit that we are all migrants. I would feel bogus saying that, or in claiming expatriate status. I have no experience of real emigration, and my links to my expatriated Welsh and Irish ancestors are little more than genetic. My most significant and motivating 'there' destinations are internal to Australia, and thus exert, in an everyday way, an other than 'national' attraction. Nothing here seems 'upside down' to me, and if the landmarks are sometimes perplexing it is not because they are new or strange, but because of an all too familiar difference between what I know of those landmarks and what my training prompts me to say. So even as I accept John Hartley's metaphor of cultural studies as a displacement from existing homelands of knowledge, I think that this metaphor, if over-extended, can act as a barrier or a trap.

For example, it has become important in recent decades for non-Aboriginal Australians to stress the recency of our arrival, the shallowness of our stake in the land; what is the difference between 10 and 200 years in Australia, we can say, when set against 40,000 years, 60,000 years, or forever? There are many reasons to suspend, with this question, the differences and conflicts dividing the non-Aboriginal mass of the population: the damaging impact of the long-entrenched doctrine of *terra nullius* and an ongoing failure to negotiate a treaty, the radical exclusion of Aboriginal people from the most basic rights and opportunities enjoyed by other Australians, and continuing vicious racism despite the reshaping of Australian culture by Aboriginal pedagogy over the past twenty years.

Yet even here, where the model of expatriation is so obviously helpful, it can be an obstacle once we ask 'why', 'where' and 'how' questions about that continuing racism. Peter Sutton has suggested that one source of indifference to Aboriginal people among Eastern white suburban Australians – that large majority, still, who may say that they have 'never met an Aborigine' – can be traced to our own history of assimilation and amnesia, of growing up post-war without a sense of ancestry or tradition, and above all without any cultural means with which to *miss* such things.[8] Faced with immemoriality, we are sceptical. We have learned to be polite about it and to exploit the contribution that Aborigines make to the national image economy, but deep down – we suspect it's a scam. We may be outraged by sporadic exposés of grossly racist behaviour (those wretched country towns, those brutal Redfern police) but, when faced with stories of tragic dispossession, we are puzzled and easily bored. We don't like 'clinging to the past', and so we don't always distinguish the rhetoric of Aboriginal 'militants' (who are, we like to imagine, more in touch with 'white radicals' than with 'ordinary Aborigines') from the claims of 'ethnic lobby groups' who extract 'special privileges', 'at our expense', from 'the rest of the community'. In short, we have forgotten our own ancestral expatriation and – egalitarian as we are – we expect that everyone else should too.

There is a distinctness to the complacency of this position, which needs to be marked as incommensurable not only with a mythology of origins and authenticity, but with a romance of travel and displacement as well. It is a position from which Australia is quite stolidly experienced as home. But it is also a position which comfortably depends on a sense of history which is not experienced as fractured or fragmented, but, in a positive and affirmative way, as patchy, partial, vague. I would not want to call this an 'Australianist' position, still less to claim it (though I know it well) as 'mine'. On the contrary, it structures experience and behaviour in ways that I would like to see changed. Yet for this very reason, I am resistant to the erasure of what I will call 'dominion' or 'white settler' subjectivity from accounts of Australian culture.

Settler subjectivity, primarily but not exclusively articulated in Australia by Anglo-Celtic people, is oddly placed by contemporary cultural studies. The old dominions (like Australia, Canada, New Zealand) mess up the maps, drawn in Britain and the United States, that determine what counts as 'sterling' in global intellectual exchange. To use an Australianism, dominion subjects are the 'whingeing whites' of international cultural studies.[9] Dubiously postcolonial, prematurely postmodern, constitutively multicultural but still predominantly white, we oscillate historically between identities as colonizer and colonized. Economically, we are perhaps more aware of being (re)colon*ized* now in the era of global 'free trade' than at any time in the past, and yet this awareness – with its intimations of a hostile future context for current forms of cultural activism – is becoming more difficult to communicate internationally as the old political empires disintegrate. So we are sometimes caustic Cassandras in Anglophone cultural studies: accustomed to being objects as well as subjects of experiment for global 'restructuring' programmes, always thinking in terms of identity *in* exchange, we are practised and prescient readers of prevailing trends in international (intellectual) trade. We rarely expect to affect them.

Moreover, as a function of our ambiguous role as 'human hinges' in past encounters between imperial and indigenous peoples, we have a history of representing the abject for histories narrated from both sides – in Australia, 'the scum of the earth', 'convicts and Irish' (Winston Churchill), 'the poor white trash of Asia'. Americans and Europeans often also assume that we are abstracted, like a footnote, from *their* history, and devoid of any complicating specificity in intellectual and cultural history: 'after all, what have you had here', a travelling reader of Foucault once told me, 'but 200 years of enclosure'? This exemption suits the amnesiac style of many dominion subjects, who accept and confirm it happily: if most white Australians are learning to recognize their role as invaders in Aboriginal history, and many are dreaming of a redefined part in an 'Asian-Pacific' history, few will register any awareness of our colonizing roles in Papua New Guinea, Nauru or Fiji. For in such awareness, dominion subjectivity would find itself installed, unequivocally, in a discomforting, perhaps unwanted position of fully responsible historical agency – and in a history of marginal concern to 'international' cultural studies.

More familiar to critical bearers of white Australianism is the homely splitting of awareness that occurs in any encounter with intellectual voyagers in search of that ultimate blank space – their last frontier (such voyagers are usually American), their mystic destination (German), their pre-Oedipal idyll (French) – on which to inscribe what European History always already knows.[10] It is easy to wince at this. Yet as I wince, I also wonder – watching another round of visitors setting off for the desert primed by their Foucault, their Kristeva, or their Chatwin – if our own expatriate ancestors went forth into the wilderness, just like that, brandishing their Burke and their Darwin. From one place in my experience, I know there is a difference between these modes of reading and travel, and at the same time, from another, I know that there is not. Somewhere in between, I always feel that sense of astonishment – one which I do share, after all, with John Hartley – which motivates my own pursuit of various 'mixed-up' (rather than mystic) destinations in the written spaces of Australian cultural history.

In a Romantic mood myself, I would then like to make this word 'Australianism' refer to a multilingual habit of reading and a polyphonic way of hearing, rather than to a singular type of speech or an impossible story of uniqueness. Interpreted in this way, Australianism would be an active practice of reception (emphasizing destination), not a code of production (origin). But a material problem for intellectuals is, unfortunately, elided here. Such reading and hearing is not always practised internationally, or reciprocally, and this in turn affects what writers and speakers of varieties of English in which *others* locate '[nationality]-isms' are likely to be able to (be heard to) say. It is my experience that, say, Americans of any provenance who speak internationally about problems, and in terms, specific to the United States (Americanisms), are heard as responsibly engaging with their society, in ways that are expected to resonate elsewhere. A white Australian or Anglo-Canadian who does exactly the same thing is much more likely to be heard as excessively concerned with *nation*, rather than society (thus, in this excess, as national*ist*), and, if using Australianisms or Canadianisms, will be expected to work to explain them.

So the problem I have in mind is not simply the dilemma of translation, but, even more materially, the burden of negotiating *in* translation an uneven distribution of labour. This problem arose, it always does for non-Anglophones and 'variant' speakers of English alike, when the time came to submit my mateship paper for publication in an international refereed journal, *Cultural Studies*. Live at *Dismantle Fremantle*, it was possible to discuss mateship and expatriation at much the same level of intellectual investment and effort. Neither topic required special justification, or demanded the adoption of a significantly national rhetoric. I spoke about mateship as a feminist; as a seventh generation Irish-Australian; as a 'Sydney' petty-bourgeois (i.e., as one expected to err towards cosmopolitanism rather than regionalism) visiting Western Australia; and, wryly, as a 'New South Wales Labor Party (right wing faction) sympathizer'. People unfamiliar with the cultural distinctions and historical debates subtending these highly specific positions could ask questions in the usual way. But in the shift from an Australian speech situation to an Anglo-American publication, this equivalence turns into hierarchy. It is not simply that there is a reversal in which 'I' find myself off 'home ground' – discursively ex-patriated, as it were – when writing in an international journal, but rather that the topics no longer have a comparable significance. An imbalance is introduced: mateship is over-coded there as an Australian issue, expatriation is not; mateship requires an extensive introduction, expatriation does not.

This is why something more than a difference between speech and writing can intervene between an international cultural studies conference and an international cultural studies journal. I cannot simply 'dismantle' mateship in such a journal, because I would first have to construct it as a cross-culturally intelligible object, and I would then have to maintain it as an internationally useful and interesting object. To put it baldly, it would be much more difficult, much more *work*, to write about mateship for *Cultural Studies* than it is to criticize, as if from the sidelines, an 'English' expatriate discourse. Contemplating the former, I quail merely at the thought of the footnotes I would have to write, and, more poignantly, of all the internationally unread and unavailable Australian texts with which I would like to presume an acquaintance. Doing the latter (criticizing Hartley), I can talk *about* displacement, without seriously displacing myself or my reader into the 'wilds' of Australian history, and I can talk *about* difference without confronting it in my text.

Through this comparison, I can say what 'Australianism' means to me in an international publishing context. What is peculiar (as the *Macquarie Dictionary* puts it) to an Australian practice is not having to assume the labour of glossing visibly local words and phrases, such as 'Australiana', 'whingeing', 'little Aussie battler', 'mateship' – a relatively simple task. It is more a matter of drawing out the cultural assumptions, the affects and the histories of usage investing all those unmarked travelling expressions (such as 'special privileges', 'currency', 'clinging to the past') in which a local experience may, if I do not do this work, *inaudibly* be speaking. Why bother? (I might think in a lazy or insular mood): this is one-sided labour; far easier and more intelligible to write yet another essay about Bakhtin on heteroglossia.

At this point of my argument, it is tempting to translate the difference that develops in transit between 'expatriation' and 'mateship' into the *sterling* vs. *currency* opposition (in twentieth century terms, 'cultural imperialism' vs. 'the little Aussie battler') with which I began. However, I would then be using John Hartley's essay as a means to claim for my discourse an edge of difference which it had, in practice, already declined to construct. I think it is more useful (and more honest) to work back from this moment of polemical reduction to the problem it pretends to solve. In this case, my problem is not with 'Australianism', nor with the co-existence in one country of many different modes and models of historical subjectivity, but with two different institutional forms of *internationalism*.

Dismantle Fremantle was a conference at which people working on what Dipesh Chakrabarty called 'non-metropolitan histories' could discuss differences, compare questions and share sources in the formal expectation that others should follow them up.[11] In this context, John Hartley's pursuit of Englishness made helpful and stimulating Australian sense to me. At the same time, I could also 'hear' new questions *about* Australia in papers on topics seemingly more distant from my concerns. For example, Chakrabarty's reflections on the 'everyday symptoms' of the asymmetric ignorance rendering subaltern any 'third-world, non-western histories' prompted me to wonder if I could even name the speaking subject of my own historical reflections; 'dominion or white settler subjectivity' is no solution, but an improvised index of the problem[12].

After hearing a talk by Luke Gibbons on the ascription of nationalism to agrarian insurgents in nineteenth century Ireland, I could ask more lucidly why a subject speaking about Australia in any name other than that of Aboriginality or that of a real or fictive expatriation is, in fact, so likely to be categorized now ('patriated', perhaps) as 'nationalist'.[13] When this happens, perhaps we encounter not so much an imperialism as a massively empowered, but largely unconscious, parochialism. The irony of this experience is that those of us who find it productive to enjoy such estrangement are often charged, by conscious parochialists in

Australia, with a glib or self-seeking 'internationalism'. My heart is impure on both scores. I am an internationalist, working 'locally' in a country where nationalism is (as a resurgence of republicanism in the 1990s suggests) a still unfinished business; a 'paradox', as Sylvia Lawson once put it:

> Metropolis, the centre of language, of the dominant culture and its judgements, lies away in the great Elsewhere; but the tasks of living, communicating, teaching, acting-out and changing the culture must be carried on not Elsewhere but Here. To know enough of the metropolitan world, colonials must, in limited ways at least, move and think internationally; to resist it strongly enough for the colony to cease to be colonial and become its own place, they must become nationalists.[14]

Lawson wrote this in the context of her study of journalistic culture in late nineteenth century Australia – a place which was colonial in the strictest sense. However, in the ambiguous, mixed-up and turbulent conditions that Australians negotiate today, the form of the paradox persists in our relations with a multiplicity of metropolitan centres: a cartoon I once saw about Australian identity had the republican talking in dollars-and-yen (that is, in terms of 'Pacific Rim' exchange) while the monarchist talked in sterling ('Europe'); both are economic internationalists, but only the former is a cultural nationalist. Consequently, the importance of working in an international space of 'non-metropolitan' exchange is that only from such a space is it possible to imagine a history which will not find its destination in, once again, this paradox – and the nationalist subjectivity it imposes.

In Lawson's terms, the internationalism of the refereed journal is rather of a metropolitan order. I support and I appreciate (to use an Americanism) the project of one such as *Cultural Studies*. It is not a journal that practises (as most British and American publishers regularly do) that subtle censorship of Australian language which makes it so arduous or even impossible to write serious cultural analysis, and so tempting to rest content with the conventions and repetitions of theoretical commentary. So if I was and remained reluctant to undertake that extra labour of writing on mateship for *Cultural Studies*, it is not that I feel that such efforts are wasted; on the contrary, I have always learned most about Australia by writing from here to an elsewhere and from somewhere else to here. The problem is, as usual, economic – a matter of imbalance and of one-way circulation. Because of its cost (subscriptions in sterling) and its method of distribution (university libraries rather than bookshops), *Cultural Studies* is a journal that relatively few Australians are ever likely to read. So in practice, my remarks published there were not really *destined* for Australians, and nor were the written proceedings of the *Dismantle Fremantle* conference. Dismantling expatriation therefore seemed to be the only logical choice.

NOTES

1 *Dismantle Fremantle*, June 1991, organized by Ien Ang and John Hartley. See the proceedings in their guest-edited issue of *Cultural Studies* 6:3 (1992).

2 John Docker, *The Nervous Nineties: Australian Cultural Life in the 1890s* (Melbourne: Oxford University Press, 1991), p. xi.

3 A classic feminist critique of mateship is Marilyn Lake's 'The Politics of Respectability: Identifying the Masculinist Context', *Historical Studies* 22:86 (1986): 116–131. Reprinted in *Images of Australia,* eds Gillian Whitlock and David Carter (Brisbane: University of Queensland Press, 1992), pp. 156–165.

4 Tony Bennett, 'Useful Culture', *Cultural Studies* 6:3 (1992): 406.

5 Steve Mickler, 'Visions of Disorder: Aboriginal People and Youth Crime Reporting', *Cultural Studies* 6:3 (1992): 334.

6 John Hartley, 'Expatriation: Useful Astonishment in Cultural Studies', *Cultural Studies* 6:3 (1992): 449–467.

7 Hartley, 'Expatriation', p. 450.

8 Peter Sutton, Artists Week Panel on 'Nation and Representation', Adelaide Festival of Arts, March 1992.

9 To 'whinge' (a word of Scottish origin) means 'to whine'.

10 Examples of these national genres are, respectively, John Greenway's travel memoir *The Last Frontier* (Melbourne: Lothian, 1972); Werner Herzog's film *Where the Green Ants Dream* (1984); and Jean Baudrillard's *Cool Memories* (London: Verso, 1990). Bruce Chatwin's *The Songlines* (London: Jonathan Cape, 1987) is a synthesis of all three.

11 Dipesh Chakrabarty, 'Provincializing Europe: Postcoloniality and the Critique of History', *Cultural Studies* 6:3 (1992): 337–357.

12 Chakrabarty, 'Provincializing Europe', p. 337. On 'locating' Australia, see Ross Gibson, *South of the West: Postcolonialism and the Narrative Construction of Australia* (Bloomington: Indiana University Press, 1992).

13 Luke Gibbons, 'Identity without a Centre: Allegory, History and Irish Nationalism', *Cultural Studies* 6:3 (1992): 358–375.

14 Sylvia Lawson, *The Archibald Paradox: A Strange Case of Authorship* (Ringwood, Vic.: Penguin Books, 1987 [first published 1983]), p. ix.

2

Panorama: the Live, the Dead and the Living

In memory of Cecil B. De Mille

I: MEDIA LANDSCAPE

'Live' was the operative word, and I couldn't help wondering why.

Peter Robinson, *Sun–Herald*, January 3, 1988

The first major media event of the Australian Bicentennial in 1988 was the multi-network satellite television broadcast, on January 1, of a four-hour landscape-special called *Australia Live: Celebration of a Nation*. There had been many other inaugural events that day: Prime Minister Bob Hawke led the countdown to New Year fireworks at a rain-soaked Melbourne concert; Aboriginal people cast wreaths into the waters of Botany Bay to launch their Year of Mourning; Prime Minister Hawke quoted Abraham Lincoln (while Aboriginal protesters were 'restrained' from approaching the dais) at a pavilion commemorating postmodernism in Sydney's rain-soaked Centennial Park. The reports of these events casually jostled each other, in the usual way, across the newspaper page. They prompted little explicit commentary. It was left to the interested reader to trace ironies running between them.

Australia Live, in contrast, was made an object of serious criticism. As a state-of-the-art communications panorama of Australia past and present, it was a media gift to the Bicentennial, not mere reportage of events. So it acquired the professional status of a self-reflexive text. Almost every 'personality' not seen on the show had something to say about its high-tech aesthetics, its conceptual insufficiencies and its investment of authority in media-celebrity speech. It was described as boring, glib, superficial, embarrassing, myopic and (by Peter Robinson) as a 'shallow, ockerish, noisome bouquet of snippet journalism'. Those critics who praised it seemed unctuous and sycophantic towards their fellow professionals.

It was left to a few letter-writers simply to admire the stream of sceneries as 'beautiful' and 'lovely'.

Most writers agreed, in a vexed sort of way, that the programme's content was deliriously formalistic. *Australia Live* had not celebrated a 'nation', in any substantive sense of that term, but rather its own technical demonstration that four hours of live television could simultaneously be produced and consumed around the globe without too many disasters. The technology itself, some added, wasn't even Australian. We just pushed the buttons, twiddled the knobs and put celebrities on planes to remote locations so we could see, when they were there, that they were there.

Australia Live was not riveting television. Nor, perhaps, was it meant to be in a dramatically *pointed* sense. Orchestrated by Peter Faiman (director of *Crocodile Dundee*), it placed three talk-show stars in a studio, and tested their skills at burbling into coherence a stream of: (1) spectacular landscapes: desert, mine, snow, jungle, sea, ice, mountain, bush, woolshed, beach, town; (2) histori-cized landscapes: old footage of fire and flood, live presentations of places (Gallipoli, Portsmouth) significant in white Australia's past; (3) celebrity discourse-locations: snatches of speech and song appropriately framed in space – Phillip Adams at Uluru, Olivia Newton-John in her living room, Ernie Dingo at Botany Bay. In this way was protest and dissent also made panoramic, not pointed: set-piece speeches about the heritage of Aboriginal Australia were smoothed into easy continuity with the spectacle of black English media-import Trisha Goddard gushing, from a hot air balloon, that 'everything in this country has been made by immigrants'.

The panorama is a tolerant form, infinitely indulgent of lapses of attention, momentary or lengthy distraction, shifts of mood, and variations of intensity in involvement. A classical panorama (whether produced by painting, cinema, literary description or formal look-out construction) may project this indulgence into the object constructed. So much space to see, so much time for seeing; duration as well as extension becomes an ennobling mythic property of a ('timeless') spatial *scene*, and together they signify a there-ness impervious, because supposedly indifferent, to the frailties of the viewer. The long-lasting but high-speed televisual montage of scenes developed in *Australia Live* is 'panoramic' in another way. It is the per-formance of keeping it going that matters, the *show* of co-ordinating disparate spaces in time, through time, while moving constantly from scene to scene with minimal jerks and bumps. So much space to see, so little time in any one place; duration and extension as properties of objects are displaced by the staying-power of monitoring subjects, and the reach of the technical system.

With this kind of panorama, there is no need for the viewer to try to watch closely or become absorbed in her vision. To participate, she only needs to check from time to time that it's all still going-on-happening. No single place or scene matters very much. Objects are unimportant. Segments count individually only as pre-texts for conversation later, or as hooks for vagrant story-telling ('I missed that bit, I was doing X or Y, and ...'). Where the libidinal economy of classical panorama is imperial, or proprietorial, in structure (seeing as possessing), the self-celebratory, high-tech panorama is primarily touristic (seeing as just passing by). The two structures share, however, a passion for *continuity*: the unbroken vista in the first case, the smooth connection in the second. A certain dullness was thus a generic feature, and not an aesthetic flaw, of *Australia Live*. Relentlessly repetitive aerial shots and domestic close-ups produced a look-alike effect, an echoing sameness linking places and personalities in a consistent indistinction, which was perfectly appropriate to the project of the show. Airline in-flight magazines and travel advertisements are 'dull' in precisely this way.

Australia Live was not a failed portrait of a national identity, nor a poor dramatization of an Australian social text. It was a four-hour tourist brochure for international, including Australian, consumption. It celebrated Australia as a vast reservoir of exotic yet familiar (cross-culturally accessible) resorts and photographic locations. One of the unifying formal motifs of the presentation was a circle flashing at a dot on a tiny bit of map so otherwise uninformative that it could only proclaim 'We are now somewhere else'. Another was a temporal conceit: allusions to racing the twilight across the face of Australia combined with references to time-pressure (the satellite agenda) to create a theme of the *schedule*. With map and schedule to fix our itinerary, a climate-controlled team of studio guides confirmed the touristic mode of address: Jana Wendt (cool and hard) and Ray Martin (warm and mushy) marked the national media context, while Clive James (tepid and oozy) was the international message.

Few other formats could more effectively have declared a gap between, on the one hand, a historical, critical conception of the Bicentennial as an opportunity (however artificial the occasion in a nation then eighty-seven years old) for analysis, appraisal and reform, and on the other, an entrepreneurial philosophy of its spectacular festive function. *Australia Live* had no commemorative or even nostalgic aspirations at all. It produced Australia as a space for visiting, investing, cruising, developing, and its basic theme was (capital) mobility. Comprehensive notes on the risks – drought, grasshopper plagues, restless natives – were included.

In that sense, critical disappointment with the programme's lack of historical 'depth' and 'vision' was, while understandable, inattentive to what it did achieve. One writer made fun of its uniformly 'joyous' image of a country without 'blemishes', 'pimples and blotches'.[1] But in a regime of representation where a Cromwellian 'warts and all' approach implies just another style of make-up and not a political shift in aesthetics, it might be more precise to say that *Australia*

Live produced a landscape without *shadows*: a surveillance-space where nothing secret, mysterious, troubling or malcontent could find a place to lurk or hide. This controlling fantasy of total visibility and access was, in turn, no secret. Commercial breaks were smoothed into the programme by cartoon images of satellite communication beams ping-ponging from dish to dish, and zapping in unerringly at dot after dot on the map. The immediate historical referent of the show was not two centuries (or even eighty-seven years) of 'Australian' experience, but a classic international video game – *Space Invaders*.

At least, that was its model referent in the history of technique (that is, of the media, the technology and the know-how defining the 'game' of space invasion). Another historical referent in the broader sense of history was a person brought on live to be enjoyed with relish by hosts and critics alike – as a model not just of the show, but of an old national myth that the show worked hard to displace. Mrs Smith of Kingoonya – the 'mover and shaker', Clive James drooled in anticipation, of a dusty little town with six inhabitants – was the figure who at once epitomized the regime of *Australia Live*, and marked its difference from the historic, pre-satellite, bush-based, white-pioneer, isolationist national mystique of days gone by. She did both by persistently misunderstanding questions, missing her joke cues, over-riding her husband and mixing up James with Martin. In this way, she guaranteed that the live was really *live*. However her propensity for error (like her cultural difference) had already been explained. The Smiths of Kingoonya do not have television.

Just as James announced that Mrs Smith was actually capable of changing her mind and refusing to participate, the camera tracked like a brave pioneer through the house to catch Mr and Mrs Smith in their lair (the kitchen). It was a rare First Contact experience: media modernity met two of the last surviving pre-televisuals, and the result, all agreed, was spectacular. In this moment, Mrs Smith of Kingoonya became both a temporary national relic, and a living stereotype.

Scenes of the Death of History

> I almost think we're all of us Ghosts, Pastor Manders. It's not only what we have inherited from our father and mother that 'walks' in us. It's all sorts of dead ideas, and lifeless old beliefs, and so forth. They have no vitality, but they cling to us all the same, and we can't get rid of them. Whenever I take up a newspaper, I seem to see Ghosts gliding between the lines. There must be Ghosts all the country over, as thick as the sand of the sea.
>
> Henrik Ibsen, *Ghosts*, 1881

In the gloomy theory of media developed by Jean Baudrillard, a programme like *Australia Live* could be considered a symptom-text of 'our' terminal living-condition.

It wouldn't be enough to claim that certain media practices now package a commodified set of differences (national in this case, sexual, ethnic, or cultural in others) for an increasingly undifferentiated, international, consuming class. For Baudrillard, the media actually do generate as (hyper)*reality* the spectacles they present. Not only is all television like *Australia Live* – shadowless, depthless, invasive – but reality, or rather what's left of it, is really like *Australia Live* (even, though not especially, in Australia).

According to this scenario, there is no point in calling for historical analysis or for critical perspective. After television, imagining the past in any other relation to the present than that of a period-piece becomes ontologically impossible for mediatized human beings. Costume dramas like the mini-series *Captain James Cook*, or the associated theatrics of historical re-enactments, function so strongly as simulacra – creating a past which never before existed – that we become incapable of thinking either past or future except as genres in the present. Baudrillard's argument is not that these practices distort the truth of history, or naturalize it as myth, nor even that they displace alternative and dissident versions of the histories to be narrated. His claim is much more drastic: television destroys the imagination. In its regime of the all-seeing eye, the fully visible space, the inescapable network, there are no obscure places left to shelter enigma, and so to prompt speculation.[2]

It follows that criticism has become a futile business, at least in its traditional projects of highlighting 'hidden' principles of organization, revealing faults and clarifying virtues, or looking between the lines and behind the scenes of a text. When everything is all out in the open, there's nothing much to say. That Paul Hogan could introduce *Australia Live* with a joke about giving the place 'back to the abos [*sic*]' may (and did) give rise to indignant commentary about offensiveness and racism. But the problem is that such a response is programmed by the joke. Because the joke openly exists to provoke the criticism (shock-horror publicity value), it is not vulnerable to 'exposure'. As the representative national viewer, Hogan also supplied *Australia Live* with its own critical backchat. Asked what it had said about Australians today, he admitted for us, 'not much'.

A more sober version of the idea that historical sense is weakening and critical distance diminishing in contemporary culture is given by Fredric Jameson in his analysis of postmodernism as a 'cultural dominant' of late capitalism. Jameson attempts to be argumentatively plausible in a way that Baudrillard (who takes the post-critical logic of his own theory seriously) does not. In Jameson's scenario, an electronics-based and globally integrated capitalist system is increasingly invading the enclaves of resistant or merely, in Ernst Bloch's phrase, 'non-synchronic' life forms tolerated by previous modes of capitalist organization. These enclaves are not only localized cultures and residual non-capitalist social systems – once economically exploited, perhaps, but symbolically left alone, in semi-autonomy, to get by – but also what Jameson calls the two 'big targets' of contemporary expansion: Nature and the Unconscious.[3]

This expansive, invasive, integrationist world-capitalist cultural system bears little relation to the culture once said by Marxists to 'reflect', in various intricate ways, the determinant structures of economic organization. Since the base–superstructure distinction has collapsed, so, therefore, has the possibility of reflection, and of 'representation', which always assumes a gap of some sort between at least two orders of reality. In electro-capitalism, culture becomes a determinant. The tourist industry provides an excellent example of the systemic integration of economic activity and exploitation, political struggles for power, a technical streamlining of nature, the production of dreams and desires, and popular cultural practices of having (and making) fun. Tourism, in turn, is laterally connected to a vast range of other enterprises and activities.

To stress integration in this context does not imply that no differences or inequalities remain. On the contrary: as the 'purest form' of capitalism to date, the order that Jameson sees emerging would imply an even greater extension of inequity and exploitation. What 'systemic integration' does entail is a decreasing tolerance of the very possibility of critical exteriority to the system. The sheer invasiveness of the latter precludes the establishment of positions 'outside' its field of operations; it follows that the 'critical distance' that once separated criticism from its political, social and aesthetic objects has also been abolished. Once again, this does not mean that there are no differences left, although as difference itself becomes commodified it may mean that the differences at stake in particular conflicts will need to be re-conceptualized. What Jameson does claim is that the spatial relation between criticism and its objects has changed: they can no longer effectively be considered as external or foreign to each other, for 'distance in general (including "critical distance" in particular) has very precisely been abolished in the new space of postmodernism'.[4]

Within this scenario, one sign of the collapse of critical distance is an increasing inability to distinguish past from present in a way that would allow us to analyse their 'real' relationship. At this point, Jameson's version of the death of history rejoins that of Baudrillard. Our access to the past's reality is choked off by a proliferation of historical simulacra (period 'styles', pastiche): 'the historical novel', for example, 'can no longer set out to represent the historical past; it can only "represent" our ideas and stereotypes about that past (which thereby at once becomes "pop history")'.[5] Although Jameson's unease with these developments is manifest, his point is not to denounce or decry pop history, but to argue that an 'oppositional' cultural politics becomes increasingly inappropriate to this new regime of space. With the erosion of distance, the collapse of distinction and the disappearance of any possibility of positioning 'outside' this new capitalist hyperspace, the old techniques of 'moral denunciation of the Other' have become, for Jameson, 'completely ineffective'. He proposes instead that new forms of political action must develop in response to our *spatial*, as well as social, confusion. Pop history, logically, and despite Jameson's own distaste, should provide one such space for action.

Baudrillard provides no comparable remedial scenario for articulating discontent. In his post-critical fables, the death of history is absolute. However, Jameson, rather than the more overtly experimental Baudrillard, is the one to point out the limits of his own scenario. Writing about 'contemporary entertainment literature', Jameson comments on the depressing determinism at work in the genre of *high-tech paranoia* – stories featuring 'labyrinthine conspiracies of autonomous but deadly interlocking and competing agencies in a complexity often beyond the capacity of the normal reading mind'.[6] However, he adds that conspiracy theory is at least an attempt to think the 'impossible totality' of the 'contemporary world system' – and so, of course, and in a similar way, is his theory of postmodernism.

Ephemera

> Ephemera: Pl. ephemerae, -as. ... Zool. An insect that (in its imago) lives only for a day.
>
> *Oxford English Dictionary.*

A conspiracy theorist might see *Australia Live* as evidence for these theories. History was certainly treated as an archival display (old footage) or as a tourist commemorative experience (recitation of 'For the Fallen' at Gallipoli). Moreover, one of its themes was indeed a cliché of Australian pop historiography – the end of the 'tyranny of distance'. Thanks to satellites, aeroplanes and computers (three enabling conditions of the show), at least one version of history was repeatedly declared dead: the one about Australia as a space of isolation, slow development and eccentricity. Ray Martin called distance 'freedom' (the wide open spaces), and in order to demonstrate the overthrow of the old tyranny two residual 'distanced' types were tracked down in the outback and flown in to Sydney to be filmed discovering big city life and total contemporaneity. With a thesis so clear to present, it's perhaps hardly fair to say that *Australia Live* had no historical implications.

However, there is no need to accept either the exorbitant literalness with which Baudrillard presents particular spectacles as co-extensive with all reality, or the literary nostalgia that animates Jameson's paranoia. An event like *Australia Live* is no more representative of 'television-in-general' than it was reflective of life in

Australia. So its uncanny resonance with the *terms* of these theories makes its fiction of Australia as a totally accessible televisual space a useful pre-text for questioning 'paranoia' as a critique of high-tech culture. As Alice Jardine has pointed out, paranoia involves both a 'fear of the loss of *borders*' and an experience of such a loss.[7] For many critics and historians of culture, to dispute and redraw borders is the same as creating knowledge: despite their differences, both Baudrillard's and Jameson's theories are based on a pained discovery that in the presumed new 'world space' of media, the practice of discrimination (dividing mountains from mole-hills, the wood from the trees) seems to have become more difficult. This is a temporal, as well as a spatial, problem. Because they are ephemeral, though not necessarily inconsequential, events in people's lives as well as 'texts' that can be recorded, stored in archives and analysed, media products are not easily assimilated to the problematic of the 'durable' which has animated so much classical Marxist criticism as well as the liberalism it opposes. The ephemeral, by definition, lives for one day only: it is transitory, short-lived, poorly differentiated (the *ephemeromorph* is the lowest form of life, 'not definitely either animal or vegetable'). Modern institutionalized criticism, however, has for over a century relaunched and revised its project not only by 'bordering', or differentiating, its objects, but by progressively taking a 'distance' from previous readings of texts that somehow survive through *time*.

Much of the hostility provoked by media criticism in recent decades derives, implicitly or explicitly, from assumptions about ephemera. It seems indecent for critics to perpetuate objects that should naturally die in silence after their single day of glory. One response to this assumption is to write histories of durability, and how it has been invested in canonical texts by literary critics. Another response is to say that mass-media history, far from being 'dead', has barely begun to be written; that the ephemerality of any television show is in part a product of ignoring the problem of how to think about its relationship to a *media*, and mass cultural, 'past' and present; and that we can write a critical history of this ignoring, as well as of ephemeral objects, their circulation and their modes of enduring through culture. It is possible, after all, that the disappearing sensation experienced by Jameson is as much a product of the rush of his analysis from early nineteenth century novels to late twentieth century media events, without pause to consider the history of mediating structures.

However, it is not simply a matter of looking at how media technology develops, and how it changes our experience of culture and our relationships to the past. A history of mediation also involves questioning the conceptual and rhetorical frameworks that have been used in the past to analyse the media and popular culture. The terms of discussion, and how the debates of the past may relate to those of today, are as much a part of the 'history' of media as the technologies on which they depend. As Andreas Huyssen points out in *After the Great Divide*, early twentieth century debates about 'high art' and 'mass culture' were already cast in paranoia-producing, borderline terms, which we haven't quite stopped using. Huyssen argues that modernism constituted itself *as* high art by relegating mass culture to the deathly realm of the Other: modernism's aesthetic and political programme depended on maintaining an 'anxiety of contamination' by an impure force invading from mass culture.[8] The 'great divide' is thus for Huyssen not merely a historical moment, but a discourse that can be analysed, and criticized, historically.

Nevertheless, in an Australian context the rhetoric of 'death', 'divide' and 'distance' – on which so many accounts of media culture still depend – poses a difficult problem for the writing of cultural history. On the one hand, these are terms historically fundamental to the European invasion of Australia, and the dispossession of Aboriginal people; they have immediate and concrete referents, both geographic, in European namings of the land ('The Great Dividing Range'), and historical, in the naming of our own experience (*The Tyranny of Distance*). On the other hand, they circulate back around as puns in Eurocentric media theory: Jameson's scenario in particular would be unimaginable without its conflation of intellectual and political activity (criticism) with spatial representation (landscape) in the metaphor of 'cognitive mapping'. It is easy to explain this convergence as a casual effect of imperialism, but rather than accepting this sort of generalization as an all-purpose conclusion, it is more useful to take it as a point of departure for asking questions. If contemporary critics represent media culture in general as a funereal landscape, how have media critics and practitioners in Australia in the past represented the space – political, geographic, conceptual – of their own activities? To consider this is a way of beginning to historicize the imaginary spacings of media, rather than simply to take them as given. So it is also a way to see shadows on the landscape of *Australia Live*.

II: SHADOWS

Wending her way for 1,500 miles north, white sails threading through seas and islands lovely as a dream, with her ghastly human cargo unable to stand upright in the hold where they carry the pearl-shell, the leper ship was a nightmare – and a streamer special for the southern Press. Such is a journalist's philosophy. The worse it is, the better it is, transcribing life in printer's ink. For your true journalist ... prefers a murder to a suicide, and both to a wedding. He skims the cream of science, and the practical experience of years in a few comprehensive phrases, and gives it a snappy title. He is all things to all men, and to him all men, living and dying, are copy.

Ernestine Hill, *The Great Australian Loneliness*, 1937.

One of the most interesting commentators on early media 'effects' in Australia was Ernestine Hill (1899–1972). Her description of the leper ship transporting Aborigines from an island near Roebourne to another near Darwin combines three of the recurring themes of her writing: a descriptive 'dream' of an idyllic land, the 'nightmare' history it contained and concealed, and the disturbing new relations created between classically opposed terms (dream/nightmare, description/ narrative, landscape/history) by the 'streamer special' of media sensationalism and a reductive 'snippet journalism'.

A journalist herself, Hill specialized in a kind of writing that was once easily recognizable and very popular in English-speaking countries but which is now quite hard to classify. In the major study of the social and aesthetic context in which Hill was working, *A Study of Australian Descriptive and Travel Writing 1929–1945*, Margriet Bonnin calls it 'the genre which has been described at various times as landscape writing, travel writing, descriptive writing, frontier writing, and several combinations of these labels'.[9] Each of Hill's books was as mixed as their general status was uncertain. Today, we might call most of them 'factions'. *The Great Australian Loneliness* (1937) was a volume of highlights from the 'location' journalism she published during several years of travel through Western, Northern and Central Australia in the 1930s. *My Love Must Wait* (1941) was a novel which combined historical romance with a researched biography of the explorer Matthew Flinders. *Water Into Gold* (1937) and *Flying Doctor Calling* (1947) were what Hill liked to call 'living history' – idealizing portraits of personalities (respectively the Chaffey brothers, pioneers in irrigation, and Dr John Flynn, founder of an airborne medical service) projected across an actively 'landscaped' historical account of their nation-building exploits. *The Territory* (1951) was a remarkable experiment mixing epic, romantic, Western and descriptive conventions to write regional and local history. *Kabbarli* (published posthumously in 1973), was a 'personal memoir' of Daisy Bates – a character sketch, a biography and, in part, an autobiography. In this book, Hill insisted that she had ghost-written Bates' own memoir serialized as *My Natives and I* by the Adelaide *Advertiser* in 1936, and subsequently edited by other hands for publication in book form as *The Passing of the Aborigines* (1938).[10]

During much of her lifetime, Hill was one of Australia's best-known and most widely read authors.[11] Her popular reputation was not confined to the considerable circulation achieved by her books. Beginning with *Smith's Weekly* after working as J.F. Archibald's last secretary, she published for over thirty years in almost every newspaper and magazine in Australia. She contributed for decades to *Walkabout*; she was a special correspondent and then editor of the women's pages for the influential war-time *ABC Weekly*, published by the Australian Broadcasting Commission; she was an ABC Commissioner from 1942 to 1944;

she wrote radio plays, a short centennial history of South Australia ('Story of the State: From Wilderness to Wealth in a Hundred Years'), and a Ure Smith proto-coffee-table book called *Australia: Land of Contrasts* (1943).[12] Yet today Ernestine Hill is a barely discernible figure in the field of Australian literature. She no longer really counts as an 'author', but as one of the innumerable, poorly differentiated ephemera whose writings form the context from which literary authors emerge. Her work had already died for most of the broad interpretive histories of Australian literature appearing after the 1960s, ranging from the conservative, tradition-constructing project of Leonie Kramer's *Oxford History of Australian Literature* (1981), to the feminist rewriting of tradition in Drusilla Modjeska's *Exiles At Home: Australian Women Writers, 1925–45* (1981).

There are many ways of explaining Hill's non-existence for today's literary past. She does not seem to have counted unambiguously as a literary figure even during the height of her popularity. This is partly a matter of landscape – the political geography of fame. Although she was in contact with many other writers,[13] Hill did not frequent literary circles nor spend substantial periods of time in Sydney and Melbourne when such circles were defining a national literature in the 1930s. While her books were read in Sydney and Melbourne, she favoured Adelaide, Perth and Darwin, and her privileged location was the outback. Those critics who praised her work (like the West Australian J.K. Ewers) were often precisely those who were about to be marginalized in the Eastern historical tradition not only as old-fashioned, but as 'regionalist'.

During her lifetime, Hill's work was most admired as Australian literature in precisely those media where much of the material of her books first appeared in 'story' form – popular newspapers and magazines. The most serious criticism of her books, trenchant to the point of being scathing, also came from a popular magazine, *The Bulletin*, where her writing was pilloried for the sentimentality, purple rhetoric and rosy optimism that made it appeal to a mass, not literary, and feminine, not robust, sensibility.[14] Her work began to go out of fashion generally towards the end of the 1950s, when the style of local, culture-conscious 'realism' in which she specialized – folksy anecdotes, stereotypical character sketches, romantic landscape descriptions and melodramatic rhetoric – was confronted by an emergent literary modernism with internationalist aspirations to aesthetic quality. John Docker's *In A Critical Condition* (1984) and Modjeska's *Exiles At Home* have studied the selective historical amnesia entailed by this shift in notions of literary value in Australia during the Cold War period, and their analyses would certainly apply in general to the disappearance of Ernestine Hill.

However, Hill did not share the commitment of many literary figures of her generation to organized social change, and she did not belong to the kind of identifiable political milieu which interested socialist and feminist historians in the

1970s. While her texts are preoccupied with problems of race, environment and, to a lesser extent, gender, she despised and avoided politics as she understood the term (parties, petitions and unions), preferring to trust to nature, poetry and 'humanity' for improving people's lives.[15] In the framework used by John Docker to analyse the literary debates of the 1950s, Hill could not be located either as a radical nationalist (affirming Australian culture from the left of politics) or as a metaphysical internationalist (affirming universals of art from the right). She would probably have to be called a metaphysical nationalist, and so placed beside the point of that debate.

To speculate on the reasons for Hill's exclusion from literary history is not necessarily to argue for a revaluation of Ernestine Hill as a neglected artist or to plead for a more expansive conception of literature. Since she was a very good writer who manifestly helped to shape the national imaginary of her time, both of these projects could feasibly question the politics of prevailing criteria for aesthetic durability (as feminists have done) and/or redeem for literature the general field of what is now called 'popular culture'. However, another possibility is to accept, rather than contest, the historical tension between these terms, and to look at Hill's disappearance as part of the history of the constitution of popular culture in the twentieth century. This would assume that the shifts that brought about her exclusion from the literary canon may be studied – along with her work – as part of the history of media, mass culture and popular fiction in the present.

An interesting example of how these shifts could work, creating divisions that set terms for future debate, is provided in a text by a writer who was also long to be ignored by later academic literary criticism. In an article on 'The Landscape Writers' published in 1952 (just after Hill's major work, *The Territory*), Flora Eldershaw argued that 'three bold stages' make up 'the communal effort called literature': the *folk* stage ('spontaneous, anonymous, and unseparated from the patterns of daily life'), the *co-operative* stage ('in which the sum is more important than the parts') and the *delegated* stage ('in which power so cumulates in a few individuals that they sum up and are accepted as tokens of the whole').[16] Eldershaw insists that these stages do not succeed each other 'like the rungs of a ladder'. The earlier stages persist, sustained by the 'soil' (meaning, a 'blend of earth and social conditions'). This is a model combining natural and political metaphors of literary 'development' to generate great Authors from the anonymous mass – as representative democracy emerges from the people, and the great tree rises from the bushes.

With readings of Fred Blakeley's *Hard Liberty* and Francis Ratcliffe's *Flying Fox and Drifting Sand*, Eldershaw defends landscape writing as a renewal of the old bush-folklore element in Australian literature. In an interesting move, she stresses that it must be understood not only as a return to mythic bush origins ('a Back to Bool Bool festival'), but as a confrontation with the difference made to the bush (and thus to the myth of origins) by new technology and improved communications. Much of the nostalgia of the landscape books was about *confronting* a loss of old myths, rather than a simple dependence on them; Eldershaw explicitly places landscape writing in a context of modernization. Then, at the end of the article, a tension suddenly appears between her metaphors of development. The text switches from explaining the value of landscape writing to calling it a danger to 'truly creative work'. Her reason for anxiety is economic (and ecological); namely, a scarcity of resources in 'the present depression in Australian publishing'. Landscape writers were then outselling self-consciously literary authors. So the logic of Eldershaw's metaphors suggests in the end that they were like undergrowth choking the trees – or, perhaps, an uprising from 'below'. This popular-rebellious possibility (which Eldershaw does not explicitly consider) is the embarrassing one for the text. Without discussing the comparative failure of 'delegated' artists to mobilize popular support, she resolves the tension in her model by switching from earth to water for a natural figure to put landscape writing in its proper political place: it should be both 'tributary' and 'source' for truly creative work.

The river/empire pun reconciles natural and political hierarchies, but it also allows Eldershaw to eliminate the possibility of rethinking 'truly creative' literature in relation to modernization. Literature happens in a space not directly affected by the changes in technology or communications – and in the function of old Australian myths – that she had discussed with so much acuity and foresight in her analysis of landscape writing. Her manifesto for creative writing bears no trace of such 'modernist' concerns or their attendant themes of loss, fragmentation, dispersal, new myth-making and experiment. Instead she looks forward to a literature 'in which man and his environment can be *completely fused and interpenetrated*' (my emphasis). In this moment Eldershaw returns Australian *literature* to a mythic 'source', and confines it to being a 'tributary' creek to that vast imperial river, nineteenth century English Romanticism. The task of dealing with modernity is left to the popular, now not truly 'creative', field of landscape writing.

Reconsidering this text today, it may be tempting to reverse the emphases of Eldershaw's conclusion by making landscape writing a precursor of the creative visual forms of contemporary Australian culture and relegating the literature she admired to the minor field of nostalgia. But the difficulty of playing such border-games – and of definitively placing Ernestine Hill's work now as *either* literature *or* popular culture – is suggested by a commodity, rather than scholarly, category which still easily encompasses both: 'Australiana'. In general bookshops today, especially those without a specialist literature section, the Australiana shelf can run from undisputed literary classics to coffee-table books to wildlife magazines and politicians' memoirs. The term can be used dismissively ('big tacky picture-books'), but it is more often used commercially as a non-polemical description.

What it describes is not a random collection of books contingently about Australia, but a public space set aside for portable (and competing) mythologies. 'Australiana' openly allows for a *promotional* concept of reified Australian identities: it admits that producing images of Australianness is a commercial activity, a mode of entertainment and a genre of cultural practice. So it subsumes (and still sells) the old categories of 'landscape' and 'descriptive' writing. It embraces cross-media products (novelizations, picture-books about films based on literary texts, the video of the live TV coverage of the Invasion Day festivities in 1988) and, as a term in general use, 'Australiana' easily extends to media events like *Australia Live*.

Beginning from this context it is useful to reflect back on the historic confusion noted by Margriet Bonnin about the genre to which Ernestine Hill's work once belonged. In the 1940s and 1950s, 'landscape', 'travel', 'descriptive' and 'frontier' were terms emphasizing different aspects of roughly the same vast corpus of texts. These were books by people who went to 'remote' parts of Australia, travelled round, and wrote stories for city people about why they went bush, what they saw and how it mattered. The term 'travel writing' for this activity is perhaps the best today: unlike 'landscape' or 'descriptive', 'travel' allows for the narrative of movement and the movement of narrative. Unlike 'frontier', it leaves room to consider conflicting as well as changing concepts of space, time and motion. It can link *The Great Australian Loneliness* historically not only to *Australia Live*, but to Robyn Davidson's *Tracks*, Bruce Chatwin's *The Songlines*, *Reading the Country* by Kim Benterrak, Stephen Muecke and Paddy Roe, and to Sally Morgan's *My Place*.

It is also a term which faded from the vocabulary of discriminating Australian criticism precisely during the period in which Hill's reputation declined. One of the signs of an advancing modernism in even the most traditionalist Australian criticism after the 1950s was an increasingly reductive concept of literary form. To move from H.M. Green's *A History of Australian Literature: Pure and Applied* (published in 1961, but written over many years) to *Australian Literature 1950–1962* – a 1963 supplement to Green's history published after his death by the poet A.D. Hope – is to pass, in one fell swoop, from the baroque to minimalism. The expansive catholicity of Green's elaborate classification scheme gives way in Hope's booklet to a mere eight categories, one of which is 'Background', and another 'Miscellaneous'. To pass from Green via Hope to the modernistically spare triad Novel/Poetry/Drama in Leonie Kramer's edition of *The Oxford*

History of Australian Literature (1981), is to pass, with a skip and a jump, from the sublime to the ridiculous.

Descriptive and travel writing still had a conceptual place in H.M. Green's panoramic scheme of literary history, as well as in Eldershaw's arborescent one. But a criticism defining literary value through formal minimization and analytic reduction (the literariness of literature, the qualities of quality) could provide few concepts capable of making sense of travel writing as a practice at all. Modernist criticism, with its interest in establishing and demonstrating *purity* of form, was particularly ill-equipped to do so. With a narrative usually motivated in some way by some notion of the voyage, travel writing tends to move towards a discovery of, and an encounter with, an experience of impurity. Or, to shift the terms away from the historical problematics of modernism (and modern racism), travel writing is about difference, incoherence, mixity and transformation. It is hard to settle the limits or fix the borders of a genre which is usually only recognizable in the first place from a story of crossing borders, defying and redefining limits (geographic, but also experiential, cognitive, cultural, political and aesthetic). It is also difficult to divide a travel writing 'text' from a historical and political 'context'; in the effort to do so, criticism is left struggling with panoramic (and 'metaphysical') concepts like 'movement', or 'voyage', or 'quest'.[17]

Ernestine Hill's work is certainly travel writing in this broader sense. All of her work is organized by narratives of conflict between movement and containment, nomadism and projects for settlement, exotic drive and centralizing force. She was fascinated not only by the theme of crossing (by 1951 she claimed to have been 'twice round Australia by land, clockwise and anti-clockwise ... three times across it from south to north, many times east and west, and once on the diagonal'[18]), but also by the theme of encirclement. Matthew Flinders' circumnavigation of the continent was one of her great historical passions, and an experience she 're-enacted' as part of her research for *My Love Must Wait*. An encounter with mythic others *en route* – most often Aboriginal people, but also Afghans, Chinese, Malays and thrillingly suspect Whites – was not only a major selling-point of her journalism and the theme of most of her stories but also allegorically inscribed in her texts as the condition of her activity: she repeatedly represents herself sitting by a lamp 'writing history' as strange 'characters' drift by with a tale to tell.

At the same time, Hill's passion for the primal scenes of travel writing was combined with a commitment to a vision of Australian modernity, though not a stylistic modernism. Like the writers discussed by Eldershaw, Hill was not only fascinated by the bush *mythos* recycled and reappropriated so often in Australia since the 1890s, but by its intersection with the new vistas opened up by technological change. Her work can now all too easily be dismissed as outback nostalgia by a critical tradition still sufficiently obsessed by the rural component of the 'Australian legend' to keep proving its mythical status. In fact, *Water Into Gold* can equally be described as a case-study in the history of industrialization, *Flying Doctor Calling* as a profile of an experiment in extending public health and medical technology, and both *The Great Australian Loneliness* and *The Territory* as early studies in the politics of tourism. Throughout her career Hill was interested in, and on the whole an ardent exponent of, almost every aspect of what is now casually called 'development'. That she placed her fables of modern-ization in a largely arcadian bush setting, and wrote them as travel stories draw-ing on all the conventions of popular romance and the 'streamer special', makes her work very difficult to locate – indeed, invisible – for critics defending (or deconstructing) various versions of 'the city or the bush', 'art or mass culture', 'modernism or the great tradition'.

Ernestine Hill was far from being the only writer of her time with these preoccupations, and she was not the only one to fade from literature. Margriet Bonnin argues that descriptive writing was a way, especially in the 1930s, for a great many writers (Ion Idriess, Dora Birtles, Frank Clune, William Hatfield and Francis Ratcliffe, among those still read today) to foster a broad public debate that was less about landscape in any simple or nostalgic sense than it was about exploring competing scenarios for a future and usually 'high-tech' Australian society. While many cherished arcadian myths (the noble bushman, the 'vanishing' tribes, the fertile desert ... water into gold),

in one sense the writers were not romantics. They advocated a new civilization based on modern technology, which would take advantage of the economic and spiritual benefits that they felt the interior had to offer. They sought to prick the consciences of Australians in the hope that action would be taken on the preserva-tion of the natural environment.[19]

They were also, Bonnin notes, popularizers of 'scientific and humanitarian inter-est in the Aborigines among the general public'.[20] In other words, descriptive and travel writing was a way of creating connections between otherwise disparate elements of Australian life, of reinterpreting past and present in constructivist fictions of the future, and of trying to *mobilize* people to enact those fictions in reality. It is in these respects, rather than in simply sharing a heritage of nostal-gic folklore and white male pioneer myths, that Ernestine Hill's travel writing can be read as pre-figuring the media landscapes, 'live' panoramas and space-festivals of today.

Ghost writing

> For the sixth time in fifty years, a settlement in North Australia was fading down into jungle mould.

> 'The Olaf not having arrived, we are unable to print our serial, *The Skeleton in the Closet*, announced the N.T. *Times*. A local author was writing a novel, *The Doomed House, or The White Ants' Revenge*. For the rest, they talked snake yarns, gold and the dead.

> Ernestine Hill, *The Territory*, 1951

Broadly speaking, Ernestine Hill was in all her ventures an imperialist, a casual white supremacist and a patriot. *The Great Australian Loneliness* was dedicated 'to the men and women of the Australian outback, and to all who take up the white man's burden in the lonely places'. This emphasis was never substantially modified during the most productive period of her life, which ended with *The Territory*. By the time she put *Kabbarli* together from a lifetime's notes in the early 1970s, she had seen the passing of the genocidal myths of the 'dying race' and the 'half-caste menace', and she was able to regret (mostly by way of a critique of Daisy Bates' beliefs) her own part in their re-elaboration for the receptively racist climate of white Australia and Europe in the late 1930s.

Her major works were unquestioning of orthodox social Darwinist assumptions that Aborigines were doomed to extinction, and that racially mixed people incarnated an unholy transgression of the border not only between black and white but between nature and culture, the dark past (primitive origins) and the bright future (civilized destiny) and, ultimately, between death and life; only when each remained Other to the other could there be a certain love and respect. At the same time, Hill fiercely protested atrocities committed by whites against traditional Aboriginal people. She described massacres, kidnappings, rapes, beatings, forced removal from the land, starvation, slave labour and death camps (in particular, Bates' camp at Ooldea Soak).[21] Most of these stories are presented as local history, complete with names, places and dates. But their significance is usually engulfed in her texts by a meditation on the myth (and the fate) of the Other, and in this way they confirm rather than question a taken-for-granted imperial truth. Her books are full of laments for the 'sylvan', 'woodland' people of the 'authentic tribes' (sometimes 'fauns' and 'hamadryads'), mixed with scorn for 'detribalized' Aborigines (atrocities against whom she occasionally justified), and pity for the 'prison' of the 'dark mind'.

There is nothing exceptional about the phantasmatic structure of the frontier landscape of Hill's travel writing. The most one can say is that it is particularly comprehensive – a compendium of imperial paranoia. If, in Stephen Muecke's terms, 'available discourses' for mythifying Aborigines can be classified as Racist,

Romantic and Anthropological, then Hill's work displays and deploys them all.[22] Furthermore, she extends the romantic and anthropological treatments to the 'fast-disappearing' *white* society of the outback. Nearly all of Hill's 'characters' are presented as emblematic of a 'type' of life dying out. She saw herself not only as a historian but as an anthropologist collecting data while there was still time to do so.

So it is interesting that Hill's texts assume that on the one hand there is something vital about the travel writer's quest to describe human life (catch it while you can) yet, on the other, something morbid, even doomed, about description. It is an assumption shared by many classic accounts of literary realism, and also by theories of the visual media as a vast descriptive regime for destroying (and for Baudrillard, replacing) reality. Roland Barthes summed up this persistent critical anxiety with a maxim: '"capturing life" really means "seeing dead"'.[23] 'Capturing life' is not necessarily a good description of description: it is, however, the way that Ernestine Hill (like many media realists today) understood her basic project.

The Great Australian Loneliness, My Love Must Wait and *The Territory* can all be read as narratives of a quest to capture life and as studies in its failure. Hill's narrators and heroes have a classic empirical mission. They are journalists, explorers, scientists, map-makers: they set off to see everything, to observe, record, chart, name and 'characterize' all the peoples and places encountered *en voyage*, and bring it all back home as entertaining and useful knowledge. Yet in each case, the quest is at least partly thwarted. *The Great Australian Loneliness* ends with a lament that the pioneer culture it has idealized is 'swiftly slipping away' because of 'the aeroplane, the radio and the motor-car' that brought the narrator out West in the beginning and took her stories back out to the cities. One of the first landscape tableaux in the book is a panorama of the country from Perth to Carnavon, as seen from an aeroplane: the technical possibility of beginning the text is a portent of doom to come. In this case, the journalistic voyage regretfully participates in the murder of its object.

In *My Love Must Wait*, Flinders' dream of circumnavigating Australia completely – charting every nook and cranny, renaming each beach and crag – is frustrated by contingencies of nature, politics, war and human caprice. Even his home-coming to publish his discoveries is botched. Class disadvantages, poverty and illness conspire to cheat him of his final triumph. In *My Love Must Wait*, the death of the map-maker's referent is taken for granted ('to embrace these natives was to embrace death', the narrator bluntly declares[24]). The real regret this time is that the relentlessly bellicose society from which the voyage for the ultimate map is launched then incessantly interferes with its realization. Flinders fails to salvage his descriptive dream from the nightmare of history that makes it possible.[25]

In *The Territory*, Hill 'describes' a relationship between the history of space (rather than 'mapping') and death. While the book is full of jocular anecdotes, wry humour and edifying tales of endurance, its tone is overwhelmingly elegiac. Her 'territory' is a landscape of perpetually decaying and disappearing settlements: towns blow away, stations are deserted, boundaries are engulfed by the jungle, washed away by flood or effaced by the sand, while the phases of Darwin's history are variations on a (Darwinian) theme of decay. This space is inhabited by corpses, ghosts, phantoms, skeletons, vanishing tribes, 'riders in mirage' and spectral defenders of a 'freehold in illusion'. Recurring images of death are eerily superimposed: originary scenes of Aboriginal people being murdered and dispossessed by white settlers are overlaid by allegories of a perpetual fading of white colonization – destroyed by nature, by Aboriginal resistance, by the indifference of the rest of the country. If 'capturing life' may theoretically imply 'seeing dead', the life that Hill sought to capture in *The Territory* was represented as already lived in a gorgeous charnel-house.

So a very strong relation is established in these texts between death and the historical mission of travel writing (narration as well as description). This is partly a matter of their chosen landscape: death is a dominant figure in the scenic history of a colonizing struggle to conquer the land, the sea and the natives. In their expansionist commitment to Australia's brave white future, Hill's texts are not apparently concerned with any intimations of an absolute 'death of history', except for Aboriginal people. Hers are histories of death: not only because of the colonial scene, but because history is conventionally represented by Hill as a narrative of the dead, that is, of the past and the 'passing'. One of Hill's favourite metaphors of narration is 'making history come alive': *My Love Must Wait*, for example, is an allegory of history-writing as an act of necromancy. Flinders himself promised that 'if the plan of a voyage of discovery were to be read over my grave, I would rise up, awakened from the dead!', and the final chapter of Hill's novel, 'The Dead Awakes', explains that this is what the narrator has hoped to do for his 'graceful shade' by rewriting his voyages.[26]

Perhaps the most lurid allegory of death as a condition of colonial empirical narration occurs not in Hill's texts, but in *The Passing of the Aborigines* by Daisy Bates. In an extraordinary passage at the end of the first chapter, 'Meeting with the Aborigines', Bates stands by as a group of 'natives' falls upon the body of a dying man, scuffling to inhale his last breath: 'The man was of course dead when we extricated him, and it was a ghastly sight to see the lucky "breath catcher" scoop in his cheeks as he swallowed the "spirit breath" that gave him double hunting power.'[27] The passage has the intensity of a dream-narrative in which the dreamer figures as a voyeur in the scene of her own dreaming. Placed at the beginning of Bates' chronicle of her own life with Aboriginal people, it works as an uncanny account of the moment in which she receives her life-vocation as 'last-breath catcher' to the race she believed to be dying, and whose culture she would see herself as writing down and 'preserving' as history. In the logic of this scene, the field of the Other is not only deathly but *oral*: 'writing' is really the border that finally separates white from black, life from death, and history from oblivion.[28] It also defines a vampiric moment that inverts and accompanies necromancy. In *Kabbarli*, Hill would claim in turn to have had this same benevolent vampiric relation with Daisy Bates. Too frail, too ill and too old-fashioned to submit to the constraints of modern journalism, the fading Bates gave her life-story to Hill in the form of an oral narration: 'We decided that she would talk, and I would write'.[29]

However, none of Hill's texts are histories of death in any unmediated sense. Her narrators traverse imperial spaces already given and mythologized. They are pioneer sight-seers, rather than battling pioneers, of Empire. Touristic and imperial ways of seeing converge, and sometimes conflict. Even Flinders is a hero of a quest for vision, rather than of a struggle for possession: his disastrous imprisonment by the French is determined by sordid political and personal conflicts over 'territory' that he, pure seer, can barely understand. Hill's narrators claim a certain distance from the deaths they define as history: they are reporters coming after the event, spectators still haunting the scene. Yet they are not irresponsible or innocent: death figures in various ways not only as a condition but as a *consequence* of their mediating – and media – activity.

The least lugubrious of Hill's life-catchers is the gay, slightly giddy journalist of *The Great Australian Loneliness*. As H.M. Green pointed out, she is unusually unobtrusive in her story given that its unity derives only from her experience of the voyage.[30] Unlike many other outback quests, Hill's does not lead to a discovery of personal identity, or a brush with the meaning of life. She often dramatizes herself, in a light-hearted way, as silly, or predatory, or both. She is also a repertoire of mass cultural fictions: the book begins with the naive city journalist fantasizing, in a Western mode, that she needs a gun to 'brandish in moments of peril' in the outback. When she is rebuked by an experienced traveller ('it would be a ridiculous insult to the finest people in the world, and you would be the joke'), the first utopian myth of the Loneliness as a safety zone in a hostile world is created.[31] So is the narrator's role: she is to be the learner against whose prejudice and limitations the hinterland is defined. The book is in part a *bildungsroman*, but it is as a flighty urban sensibility, rather than as a questing individual soul, that our tour guide will be (re)educated.

She is sometimes exposed as most brittle and shallow in her perceptions precisely when she poses as securely representative of her urban readers' assumptions. In 'Strange Case of Mrs Witchetty', Hill hunts down a white English woman who had married a traditional Aboriginal man and remained in camp, after his death, with his people. Hill's excitement is swiftly exposed as prurience:

> 'How did he propose?' I asked, indelicately, but, knowing the social limitations of the aborigines, amused and curious.
>   'He asked me to be his wife,' said Mrs Witchetty with dignity ...[32]

At the same time, the manipulation here directed at the reader is marked in the text as one of the narrator's more dubious activities as she 'scents' a story with her 'uncanny nose for news'. Hill's newshound is a conscious stylist, both of the outback as a represented-world ('"the soft pedal on romance", said my better journalistic self'), and of her own persona intervening in it ('I promptly interviewed the captain personally ... and brought all my innocence and naive earnestness into play').[33] The Loneliness as a reservoir of Australian authenticity is not always clearly distinguished in the text from Hill's presentation of it as a space of special-effects. The tele-visual theme of desert mirage ('everything is exaggerated in that unreal light ... All men are giants, moving in a kind of crystallized slow motion') is one way in which the inventiveness of her landscape description can be both affirmed and denied.

As these throwaway lines accumulate, two issues about journalism emerge as puzzles that persist without being resolved by the text. One is the way that media stories not only style the local realities they claim to report, but have effects at a distance that may travel back around in a different form to disturb their original location. The transmission of a story creates an ethical dilemma: as news travels faster and further than the newshound, she no longer covers the distance between a story and its significance. For example, during the writing of this book Hill was involved in beating-up an unfortunate streamer special, the media creation of a wild gold rush to the Granites in the Northern Territory in 1932. Reading the reports of gold discoveries in desert country, Depression-ravaged men headed for El Dorado, found nothing, fell ill in appalling conditions, and had to be taken home at government expense. In an innuendo-laden preface entitled 'She Started It All', Eric Baume in *Tragedy Track: The Story of the Granites* specifically blamed Hill for the incident, implying that Hill's reports were favoured by the powerful newspaper proprietor Robert Clyde Packer (rumoured to have been the father of Hill's son Robert, born in 1923).[34]

The Great Australian Loneliness admits to some responsibility for the Granites fiasco ('we translated gold fever into headlines, and some of their copy was much more feverish than mine') but claims that the fiasco 'served its purpose in focusing the eyes of Australia upon the far-away, unknown Centre'.[35] The interest returned in the form of technical improvements. Isolation and hardship were broken down by 'the motor car, the wireless and the telephone'; that is, by the enabling conditions for more journalism, and, according to Hill herself, for the decline of the old locales. In this way, the Granites episode becomes an allegory of the text that contains it: *The Great Australian Loneliness* was effectively a Depression consolation dream of a 'far-away, unknown Centre' where economic problems might be solved by an inrush of population, and a bit of modernization. The text admits, therefore, that reportage is not descriptive in the realist sense, but polemical, and visionary. Like the greater good, description is an alibi allowing anxiety about the *effects* of media vision to be shunted around in a circle.

The second problem about morbidity and media is related to the problem of destructiveness, but it cannot be dismissed by invoking a greater good. It follows from the idea that writing, and journalism in particular, involves turning human beings into *copy*. Most of Hill's metaphors of writing assume a 'translation', or 'transcription', not only from one order of reality to another, but from the animate to the inanimate; 'life' becomes 'printer's ink', as 'fever' becomes 'headlines'. In the quest to capture life, somehow human living is eliminated and only the medium remains. At one level, Hill's use of these metaphors is merely a reiteration of nineteenth century aesthetic clichés now so dispersed in everyday culture that they function automatically. But they do function: the aporia of the theory that writing 'captures' life – and so must be in some sense separate from, and perhaps inimical to, that life – works in Hill's text not only to disavow the effects that journalism produces in the real that it reports (the descriptive alibi), but also to ensure that writing can be guaranteed a perpetual, impossible quest for the perfect description, the full story, the 'living' characters of history. 'Copy' re-motivates travel.

Casual acceptance of these commonplace assumptions has a complex resonance for the politics of Hill's writing, given the colonial context that she travelled. An example is her portrait of Mrs Witchetty in the Aboriginal camp: 'with no housework to do, she spends all her days in reading hair-raising thrillers, blissfully unconscious that *she is the most hair-raising thriller of the lot*' (my emphasis). Rather than ink or headline, Mrs Witchetty has become a living genre-piece. As a result, Hill's use of her 'case' to admit the possibility of a happy crossing of barriers is partly cancelled in the end by the generic re-coding of the story as a 'hair-raising thriller' – and of Mrs Witchetty as reader potentially consuming herself as commodity.[36]

This is one of many instances in which the search for the real story, the living history, and the true character in Hill's journalism ends in the (re)production not only of a media stereotype, but one which is formally recognized as such. 'Lubra – A Heroine in Charcoal' is another. A heroic story of a particular Aboriginal woman ('Jane'), is subsumed by a formal race portrait ('Lubra ... in Charcoal').

Colin Johnson has pointed out that when pity inspired some whites ('after the back of Aboriginal resistance was broken') to attempt biographies of Aboriginal people, 'these meatless things often had some point to be proved and the authors were not interested in depicting human beings with all the frailties of human beings'.[37] His comment applies with particular intensity to Hill's skeletal stories of Aboriginal lives, but it also applies to her general narrative method, her portraiture and its motivating aesthetic. On the one hand, particular stories had ethical or political points: Aboriginal people were racially doomed to disappear, Aboriginal people should individually be respected. On the other hand, the point of the stories was always the same: 'the medium is the message'. In the last line of 'Lubra – A Heroine in Charcoal', the ethical, racial and formal messages converge: 'for such as Jane are history'.

The anxiety about journalism in *The Great Australian Loneliness* concerns *after-effects*. People and places can be harmed by spreading the word about them, and a journalist's 'philosophy' ('the worse it is, the better it is') tends not only towards morbidity but towards reducing all living beings to by-products of media, or 'copy'.[38] It is a mild anxiety: Hill is very far, both in space and in time, from imagining the apocalyptic modes of high-tech paranoia today. However, her formulation of the question of media responsibility, small-scale and insouciant as it may be, makes explicit one assumption of the paranoid scenario that later versions often suppress. In all her scenes of vampirism, necromancy and copying, it is taken for granted that the objects of the deadly arts cannot speak, or write, for themselves. There is only one place, one scene, of media action: the border between the writing and the written-about, the newshound and her prey, is fixed and absolute.

If Aboriginal people are used as privileged emblems of the Other side of the writing frontier, it is Mrs Witchetty – ' hair-raising' transgression that she is – who can articulate it in the text. Immediately after being called a thriller, Mrs Witchetty says of her life, 'it has been an experience ... and I am alive to tell the tale'. But then, 'I am afraid my book will never be written. I have become lazy and contented like my husband's people.' The dream of Mrs Witchetty writing a book is both a trace of wishful thinking (the autobiography of a thriller would be lively indeed) and a fable of the inevitability of her destiny as copy and as commodity. The fact that her Aboriginal 'affinity' ('lazy and contented') condemns her to be an object, and not a subject, of the quest to capture life suggests how easily racist and realist theories could meet in Hill's 'doomed house' of travel writing.

In *The Territory*, a spectacular solution is provided to the morbidity of capturing life. Unlike the sharp urban operator of *The Great Australian Loneliness*, and the bookish magician of *My Love Must Wait*, the narrator of *The Territory* has, in some mystical way, crossed over a barrier to the other side. She is 'a pilgrim' among ghosts: an all-seeing, all-knowing, yet still restless phantom – present at every scene, hearing every voice, familiar with every patch of ground and every vanishing character in her 'freehold in illusion'. She isn't an indifferent or transcendent God, but she is sometimes an archaic figure returning in her own text ('like Jacob for Rachel I waited seven years for this story') and sometimes an epic poet 'singing' the Territory's people. She includes her past self as a ghost among the ghosts, claiming only the privilege of a greater authority to tell tall tales ('Gold-Mine in the Sky'), and a place in legend as the 'Legacy Lady' ('Vikings of the Arafura'). Even her prose strives for ghostly effects: phrases recur from passage to passage and chapter to chapter, with increasing insistence until the finale is a chorus of echoes lingering on from the rest of the story.

The image of the ghost in Hill's writing generally invokes ideals of indomitability and persistence, as well as the disturbing possibility of the past returning in the present, or of unhealthy incursions from some 'other' zone in space. It is in part a Darwinian (and Ibsenesque) anxiety about a deathly interlocking of heredity and inheritance: the taint of 'bad blood' and bad deeds reappears in the present to forecast the death of the future. So it is sometimes also a placatory appropriation of the Aboriginal 'white ghost' theory that the invaders were dead Aborigines, returning to their own land. Hill was well aware of this theory, and it could be used not only to explain as painless the displacement of Aborigines from their land, but also mythically to efface the history of conflict. Aboriginal owners and white invaders alike could conveniently be considered, after death, as white ghosts.[39]

However, the theme of the ghost in *The Territory* does have a more complex function than simply to admit white Australia's 'skeleton in the closet' and to signify white guilt (both of which it serves to do). The haunting of *The Territory* is also part of Hill's plan to 'capture' the resistant imagination of urban Australians for the North. The book is part Western saga (especially in chapters like 'Bradshaw's Run' and 'The Diamond Eighty-Eight'), part tropical romance ('Vikings of the Arafura', 'A Lantern in the Scrub'), part horror story ('Chokey') and part traditional bush folklore, as well as a ghost story. It made a calculated appeal to the urban popular culture of Hollywood cinema, comics, pulp paperbacks and magazines. Where *The Great Australian Loneliness* offered Australians in the 1930s a space of splendid isolation, the achievement of *The Territory* was to translate the old outback motifs into the busy pop imaginary of the early 1950s.[40]

The Great Australian Loneliness imitated an actual voyage that could be marked on a map. *My Love Must Wait* observed a chronological model of a human life, from childhood to death. In *The Territory*, there is no longer any attempt at mimetically respecting a realist model of the traversal of space and time. In the history of Port Essington ('Phantoms of Failure'), decades pass in a succession of present tenses so swift that the narrative becomes almost incomprehensible. Other chapters (like 'Dots in the Map') survey vast spaces by spending a few lines in places here and there, then flying on to the next. There is no attempt to narrate the progressive *experience* of travel, and no sense of the voyage as *bildung*. All places and times are simultaneously and instantaneously available to the ghost narrator, their significance known, and moralized. It is a tour of the Empire of the dead, and a tour of a series of genres from 'Winged Victory' at the beginning (a 'war story' of Darwin's history through all the phases of its 'nine lives') to the quoting of outback-nostalgia in the final chapter, 'The Last Bushman, or HMS *Coolabah Tree*'.

The Territory is an imaginary landscape in which normal laws of human experience are suspended. In this, it is a classical European interpretation of the Australian outback. With its 'living history' written as a narrative of the dead, it is also a classical justification of White invasion as a natural process with sad, but inevitable, consequences. However, in its panoramic myths of movement (without the time of the voyage), survey (without the traversal of space) and Progress (without *bildung* or progression), *The Territory* also represents those classical traditions pushing against their limits. If the figure of the ghost involves transgression of frontiers, it is perhaps the confines (rather than the funereal logic) of descriptive travel *writing* that *The Territory* contests. The ghost-narrator's tour does not imitate an actual voyage, but it is none the less mimetic of a certain dream of travel: being everywhere, seeing everything, in an instant. A writerly myth of vision drives the narrative of *The Territory*: in its vast, haunted landscape, all art, indeed all knowledge, aspires to the triumph over distance that is the (imaginary) condition of television.

Or so a paranoid reading could easily suggest. However, Hill's theme in *The Territory* was an epic failure of imperial settlement. The Territory was a land of 'living ghosts', because 'so much worth while in empire-building was thrown away'.[41] The rhetoric of death, like the *threat* of a death of history, is used as a point of departure for a stirring, 'yet another effort' polemic. The tour of the dead aims to inspire shame and regret in the living as well as nostalgia and longing, but above all to solicit commitment to further investment and enterprise. Travel writing becomes an allegory of the need for mobilization.

In *The Great Australian Loneliness*, a survey of schemes for improving and populating the outback was a casual part of the tour. One of the most futuristic was a programme of genetic engineering by a certain Dr Cook, who proposed that Aboriginal babies could, unlike 'the Asiatic' and 'the Negro', be bred 'white' in a few generations without any fear of 'throwbacks'.[42] The direct implication was that Aboriginal women could be used systematically to populate the North with the babies they couldn't keep. Hill was sceptical about these racial engineering visions, and the text is in general more concerned to exploit the oneiric attractions for urban readers of an empty space 'far from the rhythm of the "big machine" and the sameness of cities'.

In *The Territory* fifteen years later, however, there is more urgency and defensiveness invested in the project of population. There is not only the recent memory of war with Japan, but a curious new sense of pressure from an emerging and Americanizing urban consumer culture. This time, suburban white women are targets of experiment: populating the outback is becoming a 'home duty' for white wives and mothers. In one passage, a bushman accuses city women of putting the country at risk because they 'can't see no further than the powder on their noses', and goes so far as to define 'half-castes' sympathetically as children cruelly 'turned down' by the white mothers they should have had.[43] As powdered emblems of consumerism, suburban women are also responsible for the economic, as well as sexual, exploitation of Aboriginal women by white men. Another bushman tells 'the story of the "Lochinvar"': how white men would round up Aboriginal women, kidnap them, teach them to ride, and sell them to drovers and station-owners at 10 pounds a head as 'the world's best stock-boys'. For Hill, the moral is not only the injustice to the black women who 'colonized the country', but the imperviousness of urban consumers: 'while the cities of Australia were spreading over smug suburbs, universities, parks, picture shows and chain stores, such were the little dramas of progress enacted in the wild and wide'.[44]

Given the tour of pop genres performed by the text, the tele-visual narration and the proliferation of references to 'picture show' and 'chain store' culture – to the point of using Walt Disney as a source for outback landscape descriptions – there is a circuitous but unmistakable appeal in *The Territory* to suburban women to forsake their smugness and come to the *real* pop territory to be found in the 'wild and wide'.[45]

III. BIG PICTURES

With its sands and seas teeming with wealth, and hills and deserts that hold the secret of every known mineral and metal, some day soon, perhaps, this country will begin to realize its destiny. What is needed in the initial stages is the faith and work of the Australians who have forgotten it, with men who know its vagaries at the head of affairs, but, above all, people, people, people.

Ernestine Hill, *The Great Australian Loneliness*, 1937

Here they come wading in over the sodden golf-course in their Dryzabones and
Wellingtons ... there are now more people here than at Gandi's funeral. Thank God
you've come.

Clive James at The Ultimate Event, Sanctuary Cove 1988.[46]

The Missouri, Sydney Cove

In *Australia: The Last Experiment*, Eric Willmot suggests that 1802 rather than
1788 should mark the beginning of modern Australia. In that year, Aboriginal
people on the coast of Arnhem Land saw Matthew Flinders' ship arrive in the
bay, as well as the usual Macassan fishing boats, and 'the Europeans, the Asians
and the Australians all meet on the shores of the Southland'. It is also the year
in which the Eora warrior Pemelwuy was beheaded by the British.[47] Only then
is the scene set 'for all the actors of modern Australia'.

In a similar way, though in relation to a different scale of events, I think that
the media Bicentennial scene was set not by any of the nation-wide events on
January 1, or the Sydney-based spectacle of the First Fleet Re-enactment on
January 26, but by the visit of the nuclear warship USS ('Dial-A-Sailor')
Missouri to Sydney Harbour for Christmas, 1987. The *Missouri's* significance
was not simply to prepare symbolically for the Invasion Day arrival of tall ships
sporting flags for Coca-Cola, and Australia Post/Intelpost – although it was a
preview of just how sentimental a blind to the situation of contemporary
Australia the Anglocentric celebrations would be. The main aspect of its visit was
expounded by a photo in the *Sydney Morning Herald*, headed 'Making a splash ...
how to arrest a suspect on a surfboard'.[48] A policeman in wetsuit and booties was
taking a fabulous dive through the air – soaring, arms outstretched towards the
water, like any joyous Sydney person on a fine summer's day – to nab a surfing
peace-protester. The anti-nuclear flotilla was out as usual, and the report said
that tugboats helping the US ships to dock were flying anti-nuclear flags. The
benevolence of the scene and the sensuality of the policeman's dive predicted
exactly the way that the televisual pageant of the Fleet on January 26 would
work: state politics, popular protest and partying all making a splash together at
the harbourside water-sports carnival.

Wending its way through seas and islands lovely as a dream, the nuclear ship
is a banalized nightmare. No streamer specials are provoked by the routine
ghastly cargo. The focus of human interest is the life of the ship: its fabulous size,
the sailors, American-Australian romances, the familial yearnings of young
mariners so far away from home, and the money. The rhetoric of death is part of
the landscape: protests, warnings, threats, scenarios and disaster-hypotheticals

enhance the event as background, or flash briefly into prominence as features of a locale. The *Missouri's* visit, like Invasion Day, was primarily a spectacle of mass *attendance*, a display of the power to mobilize crowds. There seems to be no room here for 'critical distance'. These are festivals of confluence, and critical proximity.

But they are not 'post' or 'anti'-historical, even at the level of a shallow media memory. The policeman's soar was suspended between the family album's summer-holiday snaps, a *Good Living* supplement and a single, spectacular image from the *Missouri's* previous visit – an anti-nuclear surfer paddling up to the ship, then maniacally riding the prow. As a great moment in the history of proximity, his ride created that intimate, fluid space into which the policeman dives, years later, as a tactical response, his posture heroizing, his position (like his booties) absurd. This is a space of accompaniment and sensational fellow-travelling, where distance imposed by power is critically defied – and the Law, ephemerally, left floundering.

Those who stayed back on the shoreline in mundane traditional protest were not, however, 'completely ineffective' (to recall Jameson's phrase) in their moral denunciation. At the very least, they defined a context in which the surfer's action made political, as well as avant-garde, sense. To become decor, to become ambiance, to become setting, to become *stereotype*, is not necessarily to be out of the picture. On the contrary: a living stereotype can always historicize, as well as appear in, the media image of any event. It stubbornly refers to the social conditions of its own appearance in space, and endurance through time; that is, to repetition, perpetuation and the possibility of change. As an indomitable trace of a *past* in representation (how many times have I seen that banner, those slogans, before?), a stereotype is the critical accompaniment, and the insistent historical shadow, of simulation as Baudrillard understands it. Like Mrs Smith in *Australia Live* or Mrs Witchetty for Ernestine Hill, the traditional protester in media today acts as a mark of genre, that is, of a persisting, negotiable and collective cultural product. As such, we stereotypes can act as a 'historic' reminder – well or ill performed, more or less successful according to contingencies – that unlike God, the media-simulacrum cannot produce and multiply reality in its singular image alone.

'Back to Bool Bool'

It is easy to say that the numerous space-festivals, landscape-displays and national-identity programmes competing to cover Australia for 1988 were producing, even simulating, the places they 'depicted' and the histories they 'portrayed'. It is now a familiar theme for many modes of criticism much less morbid than Baudrillard's that traditions may be invented, communities imagined and spaces generated. The critical problem in any one instance is, so what?

For some critics – such as Russell Braddon in his ABC television series *Images of Australia* – it is enough to reveal that myths are based in fiction, not in historical authenticity. By kindly humanists no less than for an apocalyptic postmodernism, some kind of symbolic death is assumed to follow from acts of invention, whether a death of a truth about the past (Braddon), or a demise of the very possibility of 'real' reality (Baudrillard). Either way, the basic premise remains that if it's fictive, it doesn't exist. Criticism's job is to banish the phantom by demonstrating its lack of reality. Thus Braddon's first programme revealed that most Australians are not and never have been hardy bush pioneers, that we aren't all white or male, and that Ned Kelly was a criminal.

Revelation of this kind has a ritual quality. The critique is as venerable as the 'Back to Bool Bool' mythology to which it belongs, and yet it remains silent about its own historic status and offers itself as irreverent. This is perhaps the kind of denunciative activity that Jameson has in mind as ineffective. It doesn't question the varying uses of similar myths in different places and times, what happens when they are cherished *as* myths, or the rival myths the criticism itself is recommending. Braddon's series was framed by one of the oldest travel stories in the Australian repertoire, the quest for a 'national identity'. Like any quest, it presupposes a gap between the seeker and object sought-for. So it can only operate *as* quest by reassuring us that the gap is still there, the goal never yet reached, and the search necessitated by 'history' – convict origins, colonialism, immigrant amnesia.[49]

An accompanying *critical* quest may then take the form of a voyage through disillusion. We undergo a progressive dismantling of the available myths, all attributed to credulous Others, and all found wanting as truth. The logical conclusion of the adventure is not the capturing of an identity but the projection of a big picture; in this instance, a vision of a *future* Australia in which a true 'identity' may at last be seized. Braddon's picture had familiar features: a pluri-racial, double-gendered, multicultural society with Japanese as a second language, the three Rs reimposed in schools, a healthy debate about republicanism and a high-tech economic outlook. The future produced by unmasking past myths turned out to be (give or take a touch of eccentricity), a widely current policy-guide for a programme of modernization. The quest for identity is a metaphor of a polemic about the present.

One problem is whether the ritual unmasking of historic national myths in favour of such domestic home truths can effectively address the entrepreneurial logic of a TV Bicentennial. Braddon's demystification of bush myths, for example, barely works now as a critique of *The Great Australian Loneliness*, or *The Territory*, to which it might seem immediately applicable. In Hill's use of pioneer legends, the 'Loneliness' and the 'Territory' are names for dreams of *generating* (rather than celebrating) a substantive sense of nation. They are utopian as well as commemorative programmes: far from suggesting that we are all white male bush pioneers, they deeply regret that we're *not*. If a plan to restyle a population in the image of a revamped old ideal is certainly open to criticism, criticizing the ideal requires a strategy different from triumphantly proving the plan's very premise that it is not based on actual fact.

Revamping is an event that changes materials as well as their meanings, and also a process that may continue till no trace of origins is left. Ignoring material and formal changes is perhaps more surely to take a nostalgic road than those involved in revamping. Thus Braddon watched people staring at the 'amateur theatrics' of violence and gore at re-enacted convict whippings, and saw a loss of historical reality. In another series, *Aussies*, Jack Pizzey looked at similar footage, and re-derived the 'hardness' of Australians from the founding events of the past. Neither considered that in at least one order of reality today, such pantomimes may be enjoyed not only as digests of *The Fatal Shore*, but also as comic reductions of the special effects in any splatter video.

Taxi to Fantasia

In one of the brochure-modernistic passages of *The Territory*, Ernestine Hill assured her readers that 'Walt Disney with his flying crayons never conjured a gayer fantasia in natural history than those evanishing jungles that fade from arsenic green to sulphur yellow and crackle away in fire'.[50] For Ita Buttrose writing at Bicentennial time in the popular *Sun–Herald* ('We can't take tourism for granted'), people can't be lured North now with just a sketch of Disney scenery.[51] Recalling a boat trip along the Katherine Gorge, she criticized the service – no water on board, bad English from the guide. Gaiety for today's discriminating tourist is not a sulphur yellow jungle, but a couple of cans of lemon squash.

Ernestine Hill's fantasia was designed for an ethos of settlement, and driven by a 'populate or perish' imperative. Her panorama of the wide open spaces stresses their vulnerability to invasion, and pleads for a kind of strategic closure. The problem is a disparity between rich natural resources and poor supplies of people. *The Great Australian Loneliness* in the 1930s looked to transport as one solution, and racial engineering as another, while two decades later *The Territory* dreamed of luring white women away from the suburbs. Despite the distance and history between them, both books aim at *mobilization*. They are space–*time* fantasias, using 'landscape' to project big pictures of national development that could be realized in the future by moving people around.

Media space-festivals today involve notions of development and techniques of mobilization quite different from those envisaged by the old landscape writers. The demand of the former is for crowds, not population; people are needed to pass *through* a space, and be filmed or photographed, rather than to inhabit it by forming communities. Where imperialism wanted settlers for security, tourism needs visitors for endorsement. One regime values permanence and accumulation, the other transience and turnover; one fears invasion, the other metaphorically solicits it. Threatened by the foreign, the primitive and by 'ghosts', imperialist discourse tends towards closure: it paranoiacally defends the borders it creates. A touristic space must be liberal, and open: the foreign and the primitive are commodified and promoted, ghosts are special-effects; the only barrier officially admitted is strictly economic.

There is also a difference in rhetoric. Hill's was overtly sectarian: suburban white women are targeted as metonymic bearers of the ideal people they should help to create. The appeal of tourist discourse is *universalizing*: rather than proposing to create a nation from one of its elements, it aims to bring the world (including Australians) temporarily to particular spots. The touristic nation already accepts that identities are mythic, plural and obsolescent. But the nation is also addressed by its entrepreneurs as a beneficiary of the flow of people-and-money to be lured through particular spots: nationality is not here the object of a quest but a field of big-business philanthropy. Certain duties follow for the population, who 'profit' from the flow: this is the space of 'our' national debt, 'our' credit rating, 'our' need to please the consumer.

It is easy now to mock the absurdity as well as the fictiveness of a dream of creating an enclosed high-tech paradise by sending people from the coast to the wide open spaces to fence the land, dig holes and have white babies. Yet, today, the image of Australia as panoramic spread of tourist resorts has sufficient credibility in media to pass as a plan for national salvation. Australia is a space wide open: people come in, cruise around, photograph spectacles, and leave their money behind. Nationalism becomes not a quest for identity or repertoire of myths, but a matter of willingness to redesign everyday life as a landscape for rigorous tourists.

Pointing out that tourism rivals meat and wheat as an Australian 'revenue earner', Ita Buttrose suggested a plan to 'get our act together'. It included 'questioning' overtime and penalty rates in the hospitality sector, revised work practices in the service industry and special catering for Japanese tourists. The *pièce de résistance*, however, was a proposed campaign to re-educate Sydney taxi drivers. Besides better 'class', better manners and a better sense of direction, many will need re-education in 'personal hygiene'. Much depends on this politics of bodies in proximity: for if the tourist trade goes elsewhere (Buttrose muses), 'then what will happen to our balance of payments?'

However widely disseminated, discussed and even acted upon, these mediated scenarios are no doubt mere caricatures (or in Peter Robinson's phrase, 'puerile stereotypes') of projections by serious 'big picture' thinkers of national development, whether in our own time, or in Ernestine Hill's. But they are images of our future that circulate in our lives. Part of their power as popularizations is to act as everyday guides that can at any moment be repudiated (in newspapers, on chat shows) as too *local*, too simple, too schematic. For every clear, bold picture offered the public, there is always a bigger one somewhere else, full of details, blanks and messy patches that only expert professionals can read. (A big picture in that sense is a paranoid myth of information, and of the limits of public intelligence). Some philosophers have claimed that this is an age of decline in meta-narratives, the grand stories of humanity's origins and destiny (Progress, Emancipation) that justify local incidents.[52] This seems a strange argument about media (if not the history of philosophy), for what is striking *in* the media is the wild proliferation of grand narratives. There are more of them around, not fewer; 'emancipation' may be an unpopular story these days, but 'development' (like 'doom') is thriving.

So big pictures should still be questioned in the large terms on which they depend. How big is any big picture, what sort of *time* does it imply? Buttrose's image of tourist fantasia seems eternal: vivid scenery, pleasing service-industry figures styled in rigorous detail and, for background, a blur of visitors streaming in from everywhere, nowhere, 'Japan'. How many fantasias are possible? How far does 'fantasia' extend? Why is it the stream of people, not the Territory, that now seems limitless, inexhaustible? One writer in a Northern fantasia, using the same premise as Buttrose ('every week a new museum opens somewhere in the UK, and the museum/tourist business is the 3rd largest money-spinner in the country') suggests a big picture different from hers, yet just as 'Australian' a landscape: 'who is going to do all this touristing? Tourism is supposed to generate employment so that people thus employed may go and play tourist themselves? ... Closed circuits. There is something nice about the idea that today's museums and tourist resorts are tomorrow's ruins and ghost towns'.[53]

Crocodile, Sanctuary Cove

Tomorrow isn't a concept vital to fantasia, or for high-tech paranoid critique. Both rather invest in 'futures', speculative projections based on models of trends today. Tomorrow is more uncertain than the future: it is closer, and yet more distant, somehow right on the *edge* of today. It's not an imaginary space in which anything could happen, but a time in which something will. In Baudrillard's hyperreality there is no tomorrow, no politics of temporal proximity. There is a future (the perpetual present), but in it we will exist, as now, as chronic after-effects. We are now, and now always will be, always already programmed as an effect of what went before. In hyperreality the image, not the Word, is a fiat. At best we can only thwart, overload, or parody the programmes that precede us.

Curiously, big live media events (as distinct from 'images') imply a different kind of temporality. They do envisage tomorrow, not as the predictable space of a future continuous with the present but as a moment towards which calculations tend, but about which nothing is sure. One such event was a Bicentennial side-show: the opening of a residential and tourist resort, Sanctuary Cove (The Ultimate Address), with a concert starring Frank Sinatra (The Ultimate Event). As a private development, Sanctuary Cove formally had nothing to do with the official Bicentennial. But as the product of a legendary deal between its developer, Michael Gore, and a politician (Sir Joh Bjelke-Petersen), it had *status* as a model of how governments can go about doing national business. The January opening, the promise of Sinatra's historic return to shores he had long forsworn, and Gore's own media profile made The Ultimate Event seem just a part of the one big party.

Attendance was poor for preliminary festivities. The media criticized Sanctuary Cove for confusing sectarian and universalizing modes of address in its promotional publicity. A high-priced, high-security, residential 'vivarium' with public leisure enclaves, Sanctuary Cove is a sectarian establishment with an inbuilt populist appeal. But the advertisement for residents forgot about tourism, and revamped the old frontier code of discriminatory closure: 'The streets these days are full of cockroaches, and most of them are human ...'. Critics predicted that crowds might feel already excluded on specious (if not strictly racist) criteria.

When tomorrow came and the vital people materialized, Gore shed tears of relief on television and drew the moral of Sanctuary Cove. At the end of the Event, a young man wanted Sinatra's autograph to take back to his dying father. Sinatra had already gone, so Gore fetched his stool from the stage. Zooming off later down the road, Gore drove past the young man hitch-hiking, stool clasped proudly in his arms. And Gore beheld, in this poor vestige of his crowd, a great and ennobling truth: he, the rich man in his castle, might have thrown the stool away – not questioning, as at last he had, his own life priorities. This was the real value of the Events at the Address: the poor man's gift of enlightenment to Gore was the ultimate endorsement.

Apart from the flood of gratitude that followed any act of effective people-moving, Sanctuary Cove was hooked in to the official space-festival circuit by the anxiety circulating in advance about what people would do on the day – come or not come, give or withhold consent to the Bicentennial, be good or misbehave.

It is as though the people who can, if they will, become crowds, have their greatest power in the time *before* an event, when suspense about tomorrow is at its most intense. Thus some of the most extensive and favourable coverage of Aboriginal politics seen for years on Australian television preceded Invasion Day, or came on in the aftermath of gratitude that nothing had marred the show. There was a convergence of speculation about what *might* happen on January 26, talk about the criticism that *could* be beamed around the world by overseas press in Australia, and preparations *for* the Muirhead inquiry into Aboriginal deaths in custody.

This 'time' of suspense between today and tomorrow is a 'space' for action, organization and invention that simulation cannot precede. As a period defined by anticipation, it is invisible and unthinkable for the myth of the permanent Aftermath that Baudrillard calls 'hyperreality'. A paranoid imaginary of space alone cannot think the media *event*. Ignoring time, movement and agency, it presumes that nothing critical can happen. Where media activism thinks a little time ahead, simulation forever thinks back.

Convergent space-festivals like The Ultimate Event are planned to pre-empt moments of crisis. For live survey shows, however, the possibility of crisis is built into the format to generate narrative interest. With a dispersive, *longue durée* show like *Australia Live*, to hope for unpredicted events is the *only* narrative interest. Several critical moments enlivened *Australia Live*. The most trying was the bad timing of the Russian cosmonauts in space. The promise of a meta-satellite hook-up was the ultimate panoramic fantasy – exchange and feedback between two surveillance-control cockpits, one down here (nuclear) and one up there (orbital). Alas: when the moment came, the cosmonauts were out to lunch, and stayed out for most of the show. The nuclear model collapsed, and with it the conceits of Australia's centrality and the global primacy of our schedule.

Another was a wildly threshing crocodile caught alive in Darwin Harbour – chomping, munching, lashing out and nearly biting its way to freedom. The studio guides had unusual trouble in streaming it in to the show. Clive James, in particular, oozed panic. Decision loomed between missing a vital connection (panoramic catastrophe), or leaving the croc still struggling (narrative disaster). But there was a discursive as well as a technical hitch. James had begun the segment by boasting about his recent crocodile hunt. The raging beast at last subdued, the Wildlife Officer in Darwin had just a split second left to produce, from the shadows of his boat, a minuscule baby croc – James' catch, and the longed-for punchline to his carefully programmed joke.

What haunts the imaginary space of the live is not the dead (history/footage), nor a Baudrillardian zombie horde of living-dead ('live' personalities *in situ*, silent masses at home) but the volatile force of the living. The live, in this frame of reference, has a rather peculiar meaning. Live television is an operation guaranteed, and yet contested, not by an opposite or a negation (the not-live: the pre-recorded, the archival, the simulacrum, the ghostly, the 'dead') but an array of vague possibilities associated with *life*: un-programmed events, breaks in continuity, accidents, missed connections, random occurrences, unforeseen human and technical recalcitrance. The descriptiveness of live television is not that of a theoretical 'still life', or *nature morte*. It doesn't presume an eternal essence of its object once time and movement have been subtracted. It doesn't generate a chronic hyperreality in its own perpetual static image. On the contrary: the live pursues the living for its transient and fugitive potential, its veer towards instability.

The live and the living interact in a mode of hostile complicity. Overcoming and subjecting to schedule the vagaries of the living is the aim of live television. It depends on the spectre of failure and breakdown to prove the rule of its success. So it shuttles between drive towards total control, and desire for the test of catastrophe. For this system the living are not ghostly after-effects of media, as Baudrillard's fables would have it. The living animate the media event by ignoring its critical limits.

Broadway, Kingoonya

It was the live appearance of Mrs Smith that reminded me of Ernestine Hill, the kind of history she wrote, and the problems her texts raise today about imperialism and racism, media and distance, panorama and historical criticism. Hill's work was already what Jameson calls 'pop' history: it invented a past by revamping and sometimes criticizing stereotypes that were already (in the pop sense) historic – last bushmen, sylvan tribes, white women pioneers. To turn casually, as I have here, from a few minutes of live TV creating a current version of one of these, to a few books by a dead woman writer, is to engage, to some extent, in much the same sort of activity. It is televisual activity, where 'seeing at a distance' translates as images available for re-interpretation in idiosyncratic local settings. It is associative activity, putting quite different elements (TV shows, media memories, political events, academic research notes on Ernestine Hill) into 'cultural', or commodity, proximity. It is also a mediated activity, in which people are confused with their image and never directly addressed.

The reviews of Mrs Smith's live 'performance' completely ignored (like this essay) her living existence. They were not written for her: it is as though, despite the reach of the communications industries, separate linguistic worlds are created not only by an academic essay and 'Kingoonya' (a stereotypical distinction) but by Broadway pop critics as well. In each of these worlds we can talk about others as though they will not hear or respond to what we say, or, if they do, will use another language, in a different place. Stress on the gap between 'academic' and 'ordinary' language hides the proliferation of such gaps in everyday culture, which Barthes called the division or 'war' of languages: 'on the scale of the nation, we understand each other but we do not communicate: putting things at their best, we have a *liberal* practice of language'.[54]

Putting things at their worst, it is as though the principle of Hill's writing about Mrs Witchetty is applied on an ever-expanding scale, turned back invasively on the society that produced it until the cohesive myths of a 'society' become difficult to sustain. Yet in this process, as Iain Chambers points out, a 'strong' sense of singular opposition becomes a 'weak' sense of detailed differences. 'The "Other" becomes the "others"'.[55] There is no single 'source' making sense of the world in communication with a captive audience. Complaints about collapsing standards (in aesthetic quality, in reality-values, or in degrees of critical distance) are side-effects of this process. It is not that aesthetic standards cannot be stated, historical reality asserted, or distance maintained (critics do these things all the time), but rather that there is no guarantee of 'a' public who will care to validate the outcome, or be mobilized by the result.

A paranoid border-rhetoric cannot begin to come to terms with the intimate proximities lived today between people and media. There isn't necessarily a happy or liberating proximity; there is depression, boredom, anger, deception, addiction, oppression, indifference and lies. But only by beginning to think of media as accompanying experience, and as time (not just 'space') for action, can criticism respond to an event like the Aboriginal protest march on Invasion Day, and its re-occurrence in subsequent playbacks. The Aboriginal demonstrations – the march, the flags, the boats, the tents, the voices shouting and wailing, and the confluence of different people from all over the country – did mobilize an effective force of 'singular opposition', without enacting a myth of the Other. That historic role was already prepared for Aboriginal people by the First Fleet Re-enactment context (making any Aborigines present play themselves in the European script); by the panoramic telecast (showing them 'on shore' as the ships came in); and by the history of the *form* of Invasion re-enactments. In fact, the simulacrum immediately preceding this one was the 1938 re-enactment, for which a group of Aborigines were kidnapped near Menindee, held captive for a week, and forced to play 'their' part in the Sydney proceedings.

However, the 1988 protest showed that precedents, like simulacra and scripts, can be destroyed as well as revised. Aborigines had already transformed the Re-enactment's significance by proclaiming a Year of Mourning, and by making a formal Landing politically impossible. So proceedings began in open admission that the ceremony was not a factual mimicry of the past, but a political event in the present. Once the basic premise had been altered, the ceremonial present became, for the official script on the day, a field of suspense and evasion. Speech after speech from the dais skipped hastily from mumbling about 'the mistakes of the past' to vague expressions of faith in 'the future'. The *significant* present was elsewhere: with people lying in the sun, having picnics, watching boats and milling about, but above all with the insistent critical accompaniment of the Aboriginal protest. Audible and visible in most telecasts on the day, extending later into media commentary, news items, current affairs shows and the television archive of future Aboriginal images, that protest effectively historicized, on Aboriginal terms, an entrepreneurial 'national' event.[56]

In 'Paranoid Critical Methods', Ross Gibson argues against the nostalgic 'return to nature' involved in seeing mediation as alien to a 'naturally' natural world of hands-on landscape painting. He suggests instead 'a *redefinition* of what is nature *nowadays*'. For Gibson, redefining nature, landscape and environment to include the mass media – and their dangers, and so an ecology of their use – is a way of polemically rejecting the Frontier imaginary, with its spectres of cultural degeneracy menacing from the Other side:

> ... not only sunshine, clouds, landforms and all things 'green', but also the cinema, television, pop music, books, motor cars, magazines and all available mass-mediated images and sounds are part of my nature. All this nature is part of my culture. Such is the environment I perceive and accept as a natural (though mutable) fact.[57]

'Mutable' is the vital term for this polemical collapsing of critical distance between spaces of nature and culture. Mutable media forms can not only be thought of historically, but challenged, and changed, historically. However, like Eric Willmot's revision of the beginnings of modern Australia, this change is only made possible by rethinking temporal, as well as spatial, experiences of mediation – and thus our histories of change.

NOTES

1 Keith Dunstan, 'But what about the country's pimples?', *Sydney Morning Herald* January 5, 1988.

2 These theses are mainly developed in *De la séduction* (Paris: Galilée, 1979) and *Les Stratégies fatales* (Paris: Grasset, 1983). Baudrillard gives a basic outline of the theory of simulation on which his work on television depends in 'The Precession of Simulacra' in his *Simulations* (New York: Semiotext(e), 1983).

3 Fredric Jameson, 'Postmodernism, or the Cultural Logic of Late Capitalism', *New Left Review* 146 (1984): 77.

4 Ibid., p. 86.

5 Ibid., p. 71.

6 Ibid., p. 79.

7 Alice Jardine, *Gynesis: Configurations of Woman and Modernity* (Ithaca NY and London: Cornell University Press, 1985), ch. 4.

8 Andreas Huyssen, *After the Great Divide: Modernism, Mass Culture, Post-modernism* (Bloomington and Indianapolis: Indiana University Press, 1986).

9 Margriet Bonnin, *A Study of Australian Descriptive and Travel Writing, 1929–1945*, PhD thesis, University of Queensland, 1980, p. 2.

10 For an illuminating account of the relationship between these two publications and Hill's role in assisting Bates, see Bob Reece's Introduction to P.J. Bridge's edition of Daisy Bates, *My Natives and I* (Victoria Park and Carlisle: Hesperian Press, 2004), pp. xi–xxxiii. Hill was unimpressed by the edited book version of Bates' narrative: 'to my surprise, when the book appeared as *The Passing of the Aborigines* it was shorn of the earlier chapters, and of her life story very little appeared' (*Kabbarli: A Personal Memoir of Daisy Bates* (Sydney: Angus & Robertson, 1973), p. 154).

11 *The Great Australian Loneliness* was one of the most famous descriptive books of the early 1940s. It was reprinted many times for more than twenty years, sold well in the UK and (as *Australian Frontier*) in the United States, and it was issued as a 'text-book' on Australia for American troops in the Pacific war. *My Love Must Wait* (1941), written with the assistance of the Commonwealth Literary Fund, was a bestseller which long remained the most commercially successful of Australian novels published in Australia. Studied as literature in schools, it was broadcast as a serial (with Peter Finch playing Matthew Flinders) by the Australian Broadcasting Commission.

12 'Story of the State' was published in *The Centenary Chronicle, 1836–1936* (Adelaide: Advertiser Newspapers, 1936). One of Hill's radio plays, 'Santa Claus of Christmas Creek', was published in Leslie Rees, ed., *Australian Radio Plays* (Sydney: Angus & Robertson, 1946). As a schoolgirl she also published a book of verse, *Peter Pan Land* (Brisbane, 1916).

13 Mary Gilmore, George Mackaness and Mary Durack were close friends of Hill, and Henrietta Drake-Brockman, Katherine Susannah Prichard, Xavier Herbert and Eleanor Dark were among her correspondents. See also Hal Porter's pen portrait of Hill at a literary gathering in Adelaide just before her death in his *The Extra* (West Melbourne: Nelson, 1975), pp. 177–179.

14 On the critical reception of descriptive books in general, cf. Bonnin, *Study of Australian Descriptive and Travel Writing* p. 45 f., and on Hill, pp. 72–73. On the feminization of mass culture, cf. Huyssen, *After the Great Divide,* ch. 3 ('Mass Culture as Woman: Modernism's Other').

15 Cf. *The Territory*, ch. XIX, 'On With the Motley'.

16 Flora Eldershaw, 'The Landscape Writers', *Meanjin* XI:3 (1952): 216.

17 A classic study which has trouble differentiating 'travel' from 'narrative' is Percy G. Adams, *Travel Literature and the Evolution of the Novel* (Lexington, KY: University Press of Kentucky, 1983). Other recent studies of travel writing relate its modern forms to the history of imperialism, studying how particular texts use an encounter with difference to construct a problem of 'Otherness': see Michel de Certeau,

Heterologies: Discourse on the Other (Manchester: Manchester University Press, 1986); Mary Louise Pratt, 'Scratches on the Face of the Country; or, What Mr Barrow Saw in the Land of the Bushmen' in *'Race', Writing and Difference*, ed. Henry Louis Gates, Jr, *Critical Inquiry* 12:1 (1985): 119–143; and Georges van den Abbeele ed., 'The Discourse of Travel', *L'Esprit Créateur*, XXV:3 (1985).

18 Cited in William H. Wilde, Joy Hooton and Barry Andrews, eds, *The Oxford Companion to Australian Literature* (Melbourne: Oxford University Press, 1985), p. 341.

19 Bonnin, *Study of Australian Descriptive and Travel Writing*, p. 392.

20 Ibid., p. 240.

21 In *The Territory*, Hill also recognized the pioneer economy's dependence on Aboriginal labour, and in particular the role played by women in the cattle industry. See Ann McGrath, *'Born in the Cattle': Aborigines in Cattle Country* (Sydney: Allen & Unwin, 1987) and Bill Rosser, ed., *Dreamtime Nightmares* (Canberra: Australian Institute of Aboriginal Studies, 1985), available on-line, www.emediaworx.com.au/images/download/echapter.pdf.

22 Stephen Muecke, 'Available Discourses on Aborigines', in *Theoretical Strategies*, (Sydney: Local Consumption, 1982), pp. 98–111.

23 Cited in Michel Beaujour, 'Some Paradoxes of Description', *Yale French Studies* 61 (1981): 47.

24 *My Love Must Wait* (Sydney: Angus & Robertson, 1941), p. 180.

25 The relation between them is highly ambiguous. See Christina Thompson, 'Romance Australia: Love in Australian Literature of Exploration', *Australian Literary Studies* 13:2 (1987): 161–171.

26 *My Love Must Wait*, p. 453.

27 Daisy Bates, *The Passing of the Aborigines* (London: John Murray, 1938), p. 8. This sentence was not written by Hill; in Bridge's edition of *My Natives and I* (p. 21) it is marked as additional text from *The Passing of the Aborigines*.

28 See Henry Louis Gates Jr, 'Writing "Race" and the Difference It Makes', in *'Race', Writing and Difference*, p. 9f.

29 *Kabbarli*, p. 142. Unlike the Aborigines, however, Bates had the chance to read over and correct Hill's 'copy' of her life.

30 H.M. Green, *A History of Australian Literature*, edited and revised by Dorothy Green (Sydney: Angus & Robertson, 1985), Vol. II, p. 1389.

31 *The Great Australian Loneliness* (hereafter *G.A.L*) (Sydney: Angus & Robertson, reprint 1963), p. 17.

32 *G.A.L*, p. 272.

33 Cf. *G.A.L*, pp. 63, 208, 261, 279.

34 Eric Baume, *Tragedy Track: The Story of the Granites* (Sydney: Frank C. Johnson, 1933); cf. Bonnin, *Study of Australian Descriptive and Travel Writing*, pp. 23–26. During this period, too, Hill was active in promoting Daisy Bates' claim that she had saved an Aboriginal baby from being eaten by its mother; Ernestine Hill, 'Black Baby saved from being eaten', *Sunday Sun*, June 19, 1932. She later tried to dissociate herself from the story (*G.A.L.*, p. 254).

35 *G.A.L.*, p. 312.

36 *G.A.L.*, pp. 274–275. The last scene with Mrs Witchetty has her a 'scuttling lubra', shutting her door 'tight against the prowling of the debil-debil'.

37 Colin Johnson, 'White forms, Aboriginal content' in *Aboriginal Writing Today,* eds Jack Davis and Bob Hodge (Canberra: Australian Institute of Aboriginal Studies, 1985), p. 22. 'Colin Johnson' was an early pseudonym of the writer Mudrooroo, who has also published as Mudrooroo Narogin and Mudrooroo Nyoongah.

38 Bonnin points out that 'the power of the popular press in Australia and the ethics of journalists were both subjects of great concern to writers during the 1930s, even ... to those descriptive writers who were also journalists'; *Study of Australian Descriptive and Travel Writing,* p. 20.

39 Ernestine Hill, *Water into Gold* (Melbourne: Robertson & Mullens, rev. edn, 1946 [orig.1937]), p. 19. On the 'white ghost' theory, see Henry Reynolds, *The Other Side of the Frontier: Aboriginal Resistance to the European Invasion of Australia* (Ringwood, Vic. and Harmondsworth: Penguin, 1982), ch. 2.

40 On the deliberate appeal by Hill and other landscape writers at the time to city readers, cf. Bonnin, *Study of Australian Descriptive and Travel Writing,* pp. 39, 235–236, 302–305.

41 Ernestine Hill, *The Territory* (Sydney: Angus & Robertson, 1985 reprint), p. 227.

42 *G.A.L,* pp. 225–232.

43 *The Territory,* p. 392. Bonnin points out that this addressing of discussion about miscegenation to white city women was 'overwhelmingly' common in descriptive books: 'if the empty spaces of Australia were to be populated by whites, it was up to the women to act'. (p. 234). For an Aboriginal history of the context of this discussion, cf. Rosser, *Dreamtime Nightmares.*

44 *The Territory,* pp. 310–312.

45 *The Territory,* p. 18. Cf. Bonnin, pp. 304–305, on Hill's descriptive vocabulary.

46 Cited in 'Today's People', *Sydney Morning Herald,* January 11, 1988.

47 Eric Willmot, *Australia: The Last Experiment,* 1986 Boyer Lectures (Sydney: ABC Enterprises, 1987), p. 33.

48 *Sydney Morning Herald,* December 23. 1987.

49 When national identity is taken to be a condition already achieved, the result is often formulated in that staple sub-genre of imperial travel writing, the 'race portrait'. Thus in Jack Pizzey's programme, *Aussies,* 'the Australian' was sketched (from an English immigrant point of view) in a manner formally improving on Hill's portraits of Aborigines only by the 'courtesy' of a second-person mode of address.

50 *The Territory,* p. 18.

51 *Sun–Herald* February 21, 1988.

52 See Jean-François Lyotard, *The Postmodern Condition: A Report on Knowledge* (Manchester: Manchester University Press, 1984).

53 Paul Willemen, unpublished paper, 1988.

54 Roland Barthes, *The Rustle of Languages* (Oxford: Blackwell, 1986), p. 107.

55 Iain Chambers, 'Maps for the Metropolis: A Possible Guide to the Present', *Cultural Studies* 1:1 (1987): 9.

56 This account conflates different interpretations by different networks.

57 Ross Gibson, 'Paranoid Critical Methods', *Art & Text,* 26 (1987): 63.

3

White Panic or Mad Max and the Sublime

There were no Alpine precipices, no avalanches or volcanoes or black jungles full of wild beasts, no earthquakes … Nothing appalling or horrible rushed upon these men. Only there happened – nothing. There might have been a pool of cool water behind any one of those tree clumps; only – there was not. It might have rained at any time; only – it did not. There might have been a fence or a house just over the next rise; only – there was not. They lay down, with the birds hopping from branch to branch above them and the bright sky peeping down at them. No one came. Nothing happened. That was all.

C.E.W. Bean (1945)[1]

Well, how the world turns! One day, cock of the walk; next, a feather duster. … So much for history. Anyway – water? Fruit?

Aunty Entity, Mad Max Beyond Thunderdome (1985)

Soon, very soon, we will have to … recognize that Australia is an off-shore island in an Asia-Pacific world of very dynamic and fast-growing societies and civilisations. If we continue to turn our backs on them … we are doomed to isolation and insignificance as a nation.

Jamie Mackie (1992)[2]

A recent history of the relationship between immigration and foreign policy in twentieth century Australasia and North America begins by noting that while 'much had been written on the origins of the White Australia Policy, very little had been written on its maintenance'.[3] As in the United States, Canada and New Zealand, new notions of 'race' – linked to rising nationalism and emerging Social Darwinism, useful to the economic protectionism espoused by farmers, manufacturers and trade unions alike – intensified pressure to restrict Asian immigration to the Australian colonies during the later part of the nineteenth century. However, this does not explain how the policy effected by the first Act of the new

Australian Commonwealth in 1901 lasted as long as it did (1973); why Australian governments were vocal in defending it, while other countries with similar policies were much more discreet; nor why and how it was abolished. To answer these questions, Brawley looks to the international context of Australian domestic policies.

I am not a historian, but my abiding intellectual concern is also with 'how and why' questions of maintenance and change. The rhetorics of cultural studies sometimes incline us to give far more weight to the latter (change) than to the former (maintenance); doing so, we too easily rest content with a 'thin' account of the past that underestimates both the resilience of old stories and the complexity of *cultural* change. 'White Australia', for example, was not only a policy valorized by a set of beliefs instilled in people over decades, but a wild array of stories, myths, legends, rumours, images, factoids and ideas not necessarily coherent with the policy's aims or with each other – and always taking on lives of their own. What follows is a short and selective account of the life of one such story, 'the sublime', as it has been maintained, changed, even nudged towards its 'use-by date' in recent years, by Australian films in international distribution.[4]

Tracing a line of allegorical thinking *about* policy logics and popular myths of race that wanders through action and horror cinema in the 1970s and 1980s, I ask how such a calculatedly national cinema as Australia's has dealt with what David Walker calls 'the psycho *dynamics* of whiteness'.[5] For my purposes, John Barrell's study of *The Infection of Thomas de Quincey: A Psychopathology of Imperialism* offers the most useful model of these dynamics. In contrast to the 'apparently exhaustive' binary schemes of self/other, black/white, Eastern/ Western, Barrell describes a triangular dynamic ('this/that/the *other* thing') which better captures the complexity and flexibility of White Australia as a historical formation.[6] Working through that dynamic, action films generically tend not only to experiment technically with 'special effects' of becoming-other but also to experiment rhetorically with the very fantasies of invasion by Otherness that politicians, journalists and intellectuals have invested in puta- tively 'white' popular culture for over a century.[7] I take cinematic thinking to be affective and energetic in character, reading films as events rather than as symp- tomatic statements. So I ask what these films *do with* cultural materials now often simply labelled and denounced as Orientalist, but which have been used as diversely in the past as they are in the present to transform historical clichés and to try out models for a *potential* national narration.

My purpose is less formal than this outline implies. I try to sketch an aesthetic genealogy for the remarkable rhetoric of menace used in recent times by some of the enthusiasts (for there are others, of which I am one) for enmeshing Australia culturally as well as economically in 'an Asia-Pacific world'.[8] Jamie Mackie's ominous pairing of 'Asian' dynamism with Australian 'doom' in the passage cited above is only one example of an authoritative discourse, pervasive in recent years, whereby Australia is 'likened to a malaise that requires resolution'.[9] What follows is an argument against this discourse of doom, and the affective politics of 'white panic' that it exploits – and that the cinema I study explores.

Max and the sublime

In 1979, Dr George Miller ended one of the two main plot lines of *Mad Max* by symbolically exterminating the private sphere. The killing of the hero's wife and child cuts his last links to a dying order that divided social life between spaces of work and leisure, between time for mates (other men) and family demands, between war on the road and uneasy peace at home. In the most famous scene of the film, avenging bikers simply run down Jess Rockatansky (Joanne Samuel) as she flees with her baby down the highway. We don't really see the impact, but we do hear a thump as Jess falls down out of the frame, and then a child's shoe flutters on to the tarmac.

By Australian standards at the time, this was an appalling transgression. *Mad Max* provoked an outcry about violence in the cinema and, as Tom O'Regan recalls, people would 'remember from the film a violence in excess of what was literally there'.[10] No doubt this sort of 'false memory' can arise in reaction to any cleverly edited action sequence that works more by suggestion than showing; our imagination excessively completes the scene. The question still arises, what is being suggested? *What* do we imagine? Memories, versions, readings of any film will differ with the complex histories that spectators bring to a screening and the act of completing a scene. So what made *this* scene articulate so powerfully, for Australians, 'collective neuroses and fears'?[11]

Although we learn in a coda set in a hospital that Jess is not yet dead, the smashing of his family leaves Max (Mel Gibson) free to follow the other plot line – his struggle to *not*-become another crazy in a violently male, indivisibly anarchic world – towards the wasteland. Max survives to become the hero of two more films: *Mad Max 2* (a.k.a *The Road Warrior*, 1981) and *Mad Max Beyond Thunderdome* (1985), the latter co-directed by Miller with George Ogilvie. The trilogy is now famous as a formally influential action epic about car crashes, homosocial subcultures and the end of the world as we know it. Yet while the films attracted attention internationally for their mythical force and strong visual style, Constance Penley summed up the early critical response to them when she dismissed the first two as exemplary of 'recent dystopian films … content to revel in the sheer awfulness of The Day After'.[12]

In Australia, however, the social realist edge and the humour of these films more immediately inflected their meaning: the first film's vision of a bellicose car culture could be seen (by Ross Gibson) as 'predominantly naturalistic', while the formalist *élan* of the second film was grounded (as Stuart Cunningham noted) by insider jokes about Australian popular culture.[13] With the release of *Beyond Thunderdome*, critics soon began to read the Max films seriously as reworking 'Australian historiographical understandings'.[14] It is not hard to see why. Moving from a loss of family to a nomad/settler conflict (*Mad Max 2*), and then the making of a new society partly based (in *Beyond Thunderdome*) on convict labour, the Max trilogy revised the dreams and nightmares of white settler mythology as well as probing fears of a nuclear future. Rhetorics of movement, loss and alienation have often shaped the telling of histories in modern Australia, a nation created by and for trade flows, transportation, immigration and anxious dreams of conquering space.[15] Max is an emigrant with no hope of returning home; his is a story of displacement and traumatic severance, and it serves on many levels as a myth of origins projecting into the future a scene of repetition in which the repetitive ('on the road again', heading for the Unknown) can always be redeemed as a brand new start. However, it is also a story of sometimes violent *contact*. Max's adventures are all about the others whom he meets along the way, and how he slowly changes in response.

Moreover, the trilogy is not a simple 'Day After' story. It has an interesting temporal structure: the catastrophe is not only undramatized but diffused over time. In *Mad Max*, apocalypse is present as a potential of the spectator's present; the film always begins 'a few years from *now*', in a world a little worse than the one we know, and ends, some time later, with Max *en route* to a world worse again. At the beginning of *Mad Max 2*, an apocalyptic Oil War is already in the past, fictively located 'between' the first two films. But this beginning is narrated from the *future* of the events that *Mad Max 2* will go on to depict, and an opening collage of images, evoking a disaster that occurred before the narrator was born, mixes stills from *Mad Max* with archival scenes of war – as though Jess died during, not before, the conflagration. 'The End' is most vividly envisioned in these films as a running down, not a sudden, drastic rupture; time 'after' is clearly marked only in relation to Max's personal tragedy. The temporal setting of *Beyond Thunderdome* is also drifting, vague; it is 'after' *Mad Max 2*, Max is older; society is becoming more complex as a harsh law and politics replace the open savagery that succeeded, in the second film, the degenerative madness of the first; the continent of Australia is once again occupied by several different cultures, if still divided between those with access to power and those without.

As stories of contact, then, these films are also about the tensions between memory and history, personal and public time, repetition and singularity, entropy and dynamism, banal and unprecedented events; at every moment of Max's trajectory from suburban bread-winner to road warrior to reluctant hero of legend, he faces problems of moving and acting between radically different orders of experience. This is one reason why the trilogy, with its narrative emphasis on 'sheer awfulness' and its emphatic poetics of landscape, resonates strongly with the 'plot of the sublime':[16] in modern times, a scenario in which a dynamic self, normalized white and male, is overwhelmingly threatened by a fearsome power of alterity; freezes in astonishment (in Burke's words, 'that state of the soul, in which all its motions are suspended, with some degree of horror'); then bounces back with renewed strength and vigour by making sense of the threatening power, while appropriating some of its force.[17]

Let me say three things about my interest here in the sublime. First, it is limited. The critical revival of interest in Anglo-American Romantic literature (prompted by Harold Bloom and Thomas Weiskel in the 1970s), and in philosophical aesthetics as a discourse on the 'transport' of thought towards its limits (Lyotard) has produced a body of theory so vast and difficult that it has its own sublime effect.[18] I am concerned with popular or *casual* versions of the sublime, which often work with older and less overtly self-reflexive aesthetic ideas. Where serious post-Kantian readings generally think the sublime relationally as a problem of/for a subject caught up in incommensurability,[19] I want to keep hold of the vernacular use of the term to refer, in an 'essentialist' and often humorous way, to something treated *with admiration or respect* (for Burke, 'inferior effects' of the sublime) as the cause of a feeling of shock, amazement, or simply of being 'impressed'.[20]

Now, it is arguable that in an era when advertising ascribes sublimity to ice cream and tourism sells alterity, there is no popular sublime; there is only a theoretical discourse that *represents* the popular in terms of the excess, hybridity and confusion that Alexander Pope called 'bathos' in his 1727 satire on false sublimity, 'The Art of Sinking in Poetry'.[21] However, I prefer Anthony Vidler's emphasis on the inseparability of 'true' sublimes from those ambiguous genres, such as the grotesque and the uncanny, by which sublimity has been popularized and 'falsified' historically.[22] This approach makes it possible to say that popular sublimes corrode the possibility of making purely aesthetic distinctions between critical and popular discourse: their force is precisely to blur the finely differentiated categories multiplied by theories of the sublime, and to *produce* the 'numberless confusions' about the sublime from which theorists must always distinguish our own discourse before performing (as I just have here) another act of critical clarification.[23]

More significantly I want, second, to emphasize the historical variability of the scenario's contents and uses. For my purposes, it matters that the sublime in

Australia has had *practical* force as a story elaborated for a particular form of settler colonialism as it extended across the continent, Aboriginal land, and as immigrants from Europe began to think of themselves as 'close' to the vastness of 'Asia'. It follows that if the concept of the sublime always entails a limit-event of some kind, the now very large number of readings rendering that event variously in terms of modern European and American histories of gender (Patricia Yaeger), sexuality (Lee Edelman), slavery and racial terror (Paul Gilroy), individualism (Frances Ferguson), nationalism (David Simpson) and 'heady imperialism' (Weiskel) may need to be cited with caution in other contexts.[24] In Australian white settler literature, for example, the 'language of the sublime' was, as Peter Otto points out, invoked 'well into the twentieth century … by travellers, explorers and writers as a discourse appropriate for an encounter with an alien land or people', and the 'language' was primarily Edmund Burke's.[25] Britain's invasion and settlement of the Australian continent began in 1788, and *A Philosophical Enquiry into the Origin of Our Ideas of the Sublime and Beautiful* (first published in 1757 and 1759) was widely read by the early colonists; Robert Dixon has shown that they used it as 'a basic handbook – even in the field' for ordering their responses to 'scenery'.[26] However, it is often a *failure* of that language of the sublime, a mismatch between handbook and field, model and experience, that precipitates in settler texts the 'plot' of the sublime; it is from the botching of a first, formal exercise in 'European vision' that a struggle ensues to reconstitute a way of seeing and reappropriate descriptive power.[27]

'There were no Alpine precipices,' writes C.E.W. Bean in *On the Wool Track*, rehearsing with a magisterial eloquence the sublime *topoi* that do not describe 'the country where men have died'. In their place, as Christina Thompson points out, is a 'nothing appalling and horrible' that is itself so appalling and horrible that its power as 'a nothingness which is actually something, an immensely powerful, active force' *is* the thing of which men die:[28] for Bean, it had 'actually done them to death' (p. 2). Practised in this way, the sublime displaces the often bloody human conflicts of colonial history with a pale metaphysics of landscape in which Man confronts the Unknown (forces routinely capitalized at this time). Aboriginal peoples are written out of this scenario as it creates its *terra nullius*, no-one's land; if in North American popular culture the Western genre conceded that violence occurred between settlers and indigenous people, in this country 'there happened – nothing'. Bean's text is subtly explicit on this point, as the 'effects of blackness' that terrified Edmund Burke are set aside with the cliffs and the avalanches: 'There was some danger from blacks – not a very great risk. The real danger was from the country itself' (p. 2).[29]

Bean's extraordinary account of death by thirst in country that was not a desert but 'looked like a beautiful open park with gentle slopes and soft grey tree-clumps' (pp. 2–3) exemplifies *how* a Burkean aesthetic was popularized in Australia: encountering the limits of that aesthetic, white settlers made new clichés; describing a different country, they made national myths. In a book published a year after *On the Wool Track*, Bertrand Russell would rattle off the 'old' European clichés as they were used by the young Kant: 'Night is sublime, day is beautiful; the sea is sublime, the land is beautiful; man is sublime, woman is beautiful; and so on'.[30] Australian writers of a metaphysical bent could be moved well into the 1950s by the *problem* posed to them by this schema: what is 'Man', if little of his world seems beautiful and may prove deadly when it does look beautiful; if the land is more terrifying than the sea; and if the night brings relief from 'the demon dread of day'?[31]

What, then, is 'woman'? The third thing that interests me about the sublime is the way that popular versions tend to complicate rather than bracket (as most recent theoretical treatments have done)[32] a symbiotic relation to the Beautiful understood right up front as feminine, sociable and domestic (in Bean's terms, 'gentle' and 'soft'), but also as *unreliably oppositional* to the sublime; staging a sort of failure of binary thought, popular sublimes may grapple more intensely with problems of similarity, resemblance and convergence than with 'critical' questions of difference. However, migrant nostalgia can introduce a stabilizing element here, whereby the contrastive force of the Beautiful is most securely preserved *in time* as a lost 'home' or 'mother country' accessible only to memory, while persisting in space as an inaccessibly distant place. Graeme Clifford's film *Burke & Wills* (1985) performs this double movement in an instant at the end of the opening sequence, when a scene of gentlemen and ladies playing at being lost in a lovely green English garden maze is displaced by a frame-full of 'nothing' – the endless desert in which the explorers will lose their way, and die.

In this intensely clichéd movement, women disappear; left behind in time as well as space, they too are consigned to the order of memory. The most stable opposition, then, is that which organizes a division between past and present, or between the past and all time *after* an event or a moment that produces this division and renders it absolute. Such a twisting of narrative time into a 'then' and an infinite 'after' has its effects on conceptualizing the future; happy endings, the resolution of a disequilibrium, the achievement of a sociable balance or a 'return' to a state of harmony, become more difficult to achieve.

Inside/outside: phobic narrative

Consider the sentimental or 'bathetic' version of the sublime at work in Hollywood films about aliens. These days, such films often express a desire for reconciliation with 'E.T.': *Close Encounters of the Third Kind* is paradigmatic of this desire, on which the *Alien* trilogy, with its logic of convergence between murderously self-sacrificing human and alien mothers is a perverse variation, and the best rendition I know has a classic figure of sublimity as its title: *The Abyss*. However, optimistic contact allegories of this kind are rare in classic Australian cinema, which emphasizes fantastic animals (*Long Weekend, Razorback*) or supernatural forces channelled by mystic Aborigines (*The Last Wave, Dead Heart*) rather than extra-terrestrials, and avoids happy endings – especially the bellicose triumph for 'our' side reclaimed by Hollywood in *Independence Day* – unless these are legitimized by self-mocking, send-up comedy (*Crocodile Dundee, Marsupials: The Howling III*).

Much more common in the Australian action cinema of the 1970s and 1980s was a double reworking of, on the one hand, the thematics of the colonial natural sublime (deadly space, isolation, 'nothing') with, on the other, that peculiar dread of the future as the *outcome* of an inner decay already menacing the 'race' that has haunted Social Darwinist narratives since the later nineteenth century.[33] This has been by no means a uniquely Australian dread. Significant numbers of intellectuals in most Western countries were obsessed by it until after the Nazi Holocaust; globally popular spin-offs of *Rosemary's Baby* and the *Omen* films continued to exploit its broad folkloric appeal; postcolonial governments, too, have used it to produce their own 'narratives of national crisis'.[34] However, it is hard to exaggerate the influence of the twin scenarios of 'race suicide' (that is, miscegenation between 'fit' and 'unfit' persons and classes as well as races) and 'white peril' (falling birth rates among white Australians as compared with the 'sheer terrifying numberlessness' of the populations of a deliriously totalized 'Asia'[35])that circulated *in* Australia during the very decades at the turn of the century in which the modern nation was shaped.[36]

So it is not surprising that these bizarre, apocalyptic scenarios, obsessed with 'breeding' and 'degeneracy' rather than love or sexual morality and with population 'bombs' rather than pods from outer space, should have fascinated filmmakers creating a new national cinema in Australia after the late 1960s, when Social Darwinism was at last formally discarded as a legitimizing narrative of state. The film revival of the 1970s 'played' in a climate of heady anti-imperialism, sexual liberation, and cultural revolution. Five years before *Mad Max*, Peter Weir's horror-comedy *The Cars That Ate Paris* (1974) used a car-crash allegory to pillory the racist insularity and heterophobia of a nation that had found it logical to go to war in Vietnam to 'stop them coming over here'. A small town isolated in the middle of 'nothing', Paris cannot tolerate change or difference but, in reality, it feeds on strangers. Parisian women do not bear enough children for the town to survive: so, like the mutant cars that terrorize the streets, Parisian patriarchy reproduces by making over the remnants of the car-crashes caused by the men.

This macabre and very funny parable about a paranoid, exclusionary society with a cannibalistic immigration policy opened up a whole series of scary narratives in which a white group or couple is contained in a 'safely' closed space – whether a house (*Shame*, *Phobia*), a remote town or farm (*Wake in Fright*, *Turkey Shoot*), an isolated beach (*Long Weekend*), a boat (*Dead Calm*) – which is invaded by an outsider/other and turns into a trap, or is revealed to be itself a prison that accelerates the community's tendency to degenerate from within. This second nightmare of insularity, an entity's potential for disaggregation by an *internally* proliferating otherness or 'infection', is often forgotten these days by critics of British Australia's obsession with being invaded or 'swamped' by outsiders. However, it is integral to the 'peril' projected by the population sublime. A fear of 'in-breeding' invests the invasion scenario with intense ambivalence, with desire as well as hostility; the fearsome power of alterity is always needed to save us from ourselves.

Correspondingly, problems of control and mastery may be most acutely posed not by 'aliens', but by the go-betweens or *carriers* who exemplify contact between inner and outer worlds and, quite commonly in cinema, between genres.[37] Thus a long tradition of European family melodrama about 'bad blood' informs the horror of Colin Eggleston's *Long Weekend* (1977), in which a corrupt white couple, having sinned against Nature (the man casually kills animals, the woman has had an abortion) is driven mad by 'nothing' – birds, a dugong calling her lost calf – in the bush; the sound of the mother dugong's grief *carries* between the human and natural orders, shattering the woman's brittle urban shell. In action films, peril is more overtly externalized as the enormity of other people: this is the terrain of *Mad Max 2*, in which a weakened, vestigially heterosexual band of white-clad settlers marooned in the wasteland, dreaming of a beach with 'nothing to do but breed', confronts the greater violence of the black-leather queers, sadists and degenerates ravening around their fort. With his 'terminal crazy' tendencies and ascetic post-sexuality, Max himself is the carrier, of violence and salvation, *par excellence*.

These films work with a way of structuring historical materials that I call, 'phobic narrative'.[38] Widely used in the media to frame economic and political debates about Australia's future, phobic narrative constitutes space in a stifling alternation of *agoraphobia* (fear of 'opening up' the nation to an immensely powerful Other, typically now 'the global economy') with *claustrophobia* (fear of being shut away from a wider, more dynamic, typically 'Asian' world): pressure accumulates in this way on the figure of the border between forces pushing in and forces pushing out. History is then caught in an oscillation between *entropy*, a slow running down of closed, communal time, and an explosive temporality of *catastrophe* unleashed by the Other coming from elsewhere. The driving force of phobic narrative is then a pre-emptive desire for avoidance: how to avoid invasion at one pole while avoiding isolation at the other; how to avoid stagnation while avoiding revolution and disruption.

In practice, this repetitive swinging between opposite extremes of anxiety about the future can serve to shape not a quest for national 'identity' in the European sense (invoking an ideal unity of language, 'blood' and territory), but a pragmatic emphasis on solving 'how?' problems of becoming, rather than 'who?' or 'what?' questions of being. Accordingly, there is sometimes a perceived gap between the virulent rhetoric of phobic nationalism in Australia, and the *relatively* low levels of physical violence attending actual conflicts over the nature and future of the nation.[39] For this very reason, however, the question arises of phobic narrative's recurring power to shape those 'Australian historiographical understandings' (in O'Regan's phrase) that came to inform *Mad Max*. Any revision of historical materials creates a remainder, something left over each time; we may think of this as an edge of difference or as an incommensurability, but it can also be something that *returns* as an element excluded from differing versions of a story, securing their similarity.

Phobic narratives of Australian national space clearly worry over the possibility of at least one specific form of historical repetition. The simplest way to render this is to consider that both the colonial sublime of landscape (the 'nothing') and the Social Darwinist sublime of population (the 'numbers') entail invasion scenarios in which white people are victims. In the first, the bush and the desert act as inhuman agents of a depopulation: tales of lone white men dying of nothing in an 'uninhabited' land condense and censor a history of Aboriginal deaths and black resistance to white settlement; responsibility for colonial violence passes to a homicidal land. In the second, the coast is a permeable barrier against waves of *over*-population rolling in from the future ('Asia'). This figure operates most powerfully in a register of paranoid anticipation, and if the scenario it organizes often spatializes the future threat in terms of a particular country (whether China, Japan, Vietnam or Indonesia), its basic structure is able to accommodate any number of ethnic, racial, religious and social prejudices, including a generalized anxiety about the economic impact of immigration itself; it was common for nineteenth century English settlers to express fears of being 'swamped' by *Irish* immigrants, and complaints are heard today from Australians of many ethnic backgrounds that too many New Zealanders are now 'allowed in'. At the same time, this vision of the future carries a pressing mnemonic force that secures a chain of displacement: saying that invaders will come by sea, we admit that it is we who came by sea, and something we did to others becomes something that happened to *us* and could happen all over again; on the beach, we replay our genocidal past as our apocalyptic future.[40]

Daiwei Fu has pointed out to me that this use of the sublime is not exclusively European. Aboriginal people in Taiwan recall an old myth (similar to one attributed to Native Americans in Kevin Costner's *Dances with Wolves*) that predicted a future in which large numbers of Han Chinese would come across the water to the island, and people in Taiwan today have their own fears about overwhelming numbers of people across the water even as TV and tourist promotions pour out images of 'the sublime of mainland China'. This Taiwan-centred comparison helps to clarify the *constitutively* Eurocentric, practical force of the sublime in Australian settler culture, for it is precisely the latter's imperviousness to intimations that its materials might *not* be unique or distinctive which helps to secure a myth of identity based in a lonely, cosmic fear.

'Terror in the Bush', or the Risks of Maternity

Thus it happens that a woman, peacefully sunbathing alone on a quiet, idyllic beach, will raise her head for no obvious reason and look around with an unaccountable sense of unease. It is almost mandatory in action films that a shot of calm, beautiful scenery anticipates terrible events; in Australian film, an idyllic beach scene in particular marks a *premonition* of repetition, running in reverse Burke's 'plot' of delight as the aftermath of danger or pain, a 'tranquillity shadowed with horror' (p. 34). In *Mad Max*, Jess hears seagulls, sees 'nothing' along the beach; the dog has run off, but dogs do that; she gathers her things and heads for home through bush that looks like a beautiful park, with gentle slopes and soft grey tree-clumps.

I am not sure where I first heard the phrase 'white panic',[41] but it always comes to mind when I watch the next scene. As I understand it, this phrase refers not to white bodies *in* a state of panic but rather, by metonymy, to that hallucinatory blurring or bleaching out of detail produced *by* the blinding heat of panic. Such panic is 'white' in that it erases differences from the field of sensory perception; panic motion is clumsy and uncontrolled. Fittingly, then, panic for theoreticians is not strictly a sublime emotion. Panic is a response to an objective cause of some kind, and it is a precondition of the modern sublime that we are not really in peril: for Thomas Weiskel, 'if the danger is real we turn and flee, without pausing for our sublime moment'.[42] At the same time, he clarifies that anxiety is also subjective in that it is retroactive: 'the threatening occasion appears to revive a fundamental fantasy of injury and escape … played out hypothetically (pictured to ourselves) in the phenomenal terms of the occasion before us' (pp. 84–5). In other words, a work of memory is involved when we recognize a danger; we panic when something tells us we have seen this movie before.

Watching a film, any spectator is in a complex, doubled position in this respect. In a cinema, we can certainly savour our sublime 'moment' if what we see stirs feelings of panic; watching a video, we can replay the occasion and 'pause' it as many times as we wish. However, the social '"givenness" of subjectivity' that Rey Chow calls 'pregazing',[43] already caught up as it is in larger historical processes of interpellation and recognition, ensures that such feelings are also *retro*active, and not only in relation to the formal dynamics of identification with a camera, a gaze, an editing principle and so on. However rarely it happens to film-literate people, we can perfectly well be panicked by a non-cinematic fantasy or a memory in some way played out in the phenomenal terms of the cinematic 'occasion before us'.

Mad Max is not the only film to have made me flee the cinema (at a blundering run quite unlike the lucid 'walking out' that signifies distaste), but it is easily the most memorable; the first time, I didn't make it through Jess's headlong flight through the bush. A cut takes us from behind Jess as she leaves the beach to a frontal view of her walking cautiously up the slope through the trees. As noises thicken in her sound-world and chords stir nervily in ours, she hesitates; the camera comes in closer and a strange cry curdles the air; Jess stops, bites her lip and looks around. Abruptly, we see men running behind trees in the distance! – but does she? or do we see them from the perspective of men closing in from the other side? Suddenly, we are behind her: in the most aggressive movement in the film, the camera lunges at her back; she screams, she turns – and from Jess's point of view we see 'nothing', a frame-full of beautiful bush.

From here, the scene plays out what is for many people a powerful *cultural* memory, 'terror in the bush'. As urban souls who see the bush from planes and cars or on a nice stroll in a National Park packed with tourists, many Australians know about this terror while never having felt it. Without warning or reason, a person or a group (it is a highly contagious form of fear) is overwhelmed by a feeling of being watched from all sides, caught in a hostile gaze rushing in around the 360 degrees of a circle; panic flight is a common reaction. This is how D.H. Lawrence described the experience in his 1923 novel *Kangaroo*:

> ... there was something among the trees, and his hair began to stir with terror, on his head. There was a presence. He looked at the weird, white, dead trees, and into the hollow distances of the bush. Nothing! Nothing at all. He turned to go home. And then immediately the hair on his scalp stirred and went icy cold with terror. What of? He knew quite well it was nothing. He knew quite well. But with his spine cold like ice, and the roots of his hair seeming to freeze, he walked on home, walked firmly and without haste.[44]

Often used naively to document how Europeans 'felt' about the Australian bush, this passage is a formal exercise in the sublime. The narrator not only describes his terror of an overwhelming presence, but also the turn of his mastery over it ('firmly and without haste'); control is crucial to the sublime, whereas panic is a feminizing state because it tends to involve a failure of control. Relayed by critics and historians, however, the passage also laid down the canonical literary account of terror in the bush as Lawrence went on to ascribe 'the horrid thing in the bush!' to 'the spirit of the place', assimilating this in turn to 'a long black arm' and then to 'an alien people' watching (again) its 'victim' while patiently 'waiting for a far-off end, watching the myriad intruding white men'.[45]

More mundane explanations can be given of terror in the bush. When I first felt it as a child, playing with a friend not ten minutes run from her house, my father told me it was only sheep or kangaroos peering at us from behind the trees. At the other extreme, it can be theorized away as a purely cultural phenomenon, a 'white guilt' acquired (but how?) in infancy. Despite its racial romanticism, Lawrence's version is at least capable of admitting, like *Mad Max*, that terror in the bush involves not only a response to something powerful in nature *and* a narcissistically bounced, accusatory historical gaze, but also a fear of the actions of other human beings. 'Panic' is a good name for this compound sort of fear; in Greek mythology, Pan was a hybrid creature, half-human, half-goat, who made noises in the woods which terrified people.[46]

Pan was also a lustful god. Like the 'obscurity' and 'darkness' prized by Burke as productive of the sublime, woods and 'low, confused, uncertain sounds' (p. 83) carry special terrors for women and vulnerable men.[47] Rational fear of rape and murder saturates the scene of Jess's terror: three more times we see her see 'nothing' as we see the bikers come closer while the cries grow louder and unmistakably human and male; she falls, and her beach-wrap flies open up to her waist. This scene terrified me because the editing 'joined' my own vivid memory of terror in the bush to the knowledge all attentive spectators will share that 'the horrid thing in the bush!' is, in this instance, not a 'spirit' or 'a long black arm' but a bunch of crazy white men.

Clearly, the chase scene splits along gendered lines the white Australian 'we' I have been using to this point. If *Mad Max* portrays a society disintegrating into two groups, hunters and hunted, this is the scene in which the feminized side of that dichotomy is elaborated paradigmatically (Jess crashes into a bird, then the corpse of her dog, and then a lumbering, childish man). Routinely splitting the narrative image of woman from the movement of the narration,[48] it induces in at least this female spectator the sense of externalization that makes most rape scenes alienating. Yet something else drifts across this division, holding Jess's image as woman in the historical field of *white* panic composed by the articulation of the natural with the population sublime.

For me, this 'something' is neither a memory nor a 'fantasy of injury and escape', but a trace of a knowledge acquired from other texts and stories and brought to bear, retroactively, on the scene. Jess in *Mad Max* is not simply a woman. Jess is a *mother*, her abstract status affirmed by the generic name 'Sprog' (a colloquial term for offspring) that she and Max have given their child. Only in the beach-bush-house sequence is Jess a woman alone; in every other situation of danger, she carries Sprog in the posture of an iconic 'mother with child'. This sequence in fact mediates between two other chases in which a child is menaced: near the beginning of the film, the Nightrider tries to run down a toddler on the road; near the end, the Nightrider's mates run down Jess and Sprog. At this level, the narrative is organized by a triptych of victim figures: child, woman and mother-with-child.

What happens if we see Jess in these scenes as black? If we hallucinate her as an Aboriginal mother, fleeing terrified with a gang of white men in pursuit?[49] As well as restoring a still often suppressed dimension of sexual violence in Australia, we retrieve a scene of racial terror crucial to national history but almost never dramatized in mainstream national cinema.[50] At various times, most intensely between the 1920s and the 1960s, all Australian states forcibly took children away from Aboriginal families, placing them in state 'homes' or in white foster care, with the aim of assimilating them to white society. Inspired by utopian-futurist forms of eugenics, extreme proponents of this policy hoped it would result in the 'biological absorption' of Aborigines by white people in a few generations.[51] While this genocidal programme was unrealized, failing at the time to win public support, its monstrous fantasy of exploiting black women and children to build up White Australia's 'numbers' against the *external* threat of the future/'Asia' passed rapidly through the media into popular lore about the population 'problem', and the children were no less cruelly taken from their mothers.[52]

Once their stories of terror and privation are not only included but made central in 'Australian historiographical understandings', we might one day be able to see the ferocious pursuit of the mother in *Mad Max* as an allegory which, at the beginning of a period of profound transformation in Australian society away from the twentieth century model of racist mono-culturalism, comple- mented and partially revised Bean's elegy for the white men dead in the bush. These passages complement each other not when we notice that Bean wrote a history of Man while *Mad Max* opened a space for the experience of women and children (in this they diverge), but when we can see both as enacting the displacement that founded the 'national culture': Jess is, of course, white, but more significantly there are no Aboriginal people anywhere in her world. However, the dystopian futurism of *Mad Max* changed the traditions it drew on – and deeply shocked its first audiences – by projecting a mythic landscape and a (future) past in which *something* happened (telling in fiction a terrible historical truth), while showing us unequivocally that 'the real danger' for all in this land-scape was not, as Bean imagined, from 'the country itself' at all.

Nobody, somebody: women of the future

From this premise, different stories can begin to be told. If the future remains an object of dread, it is less predictable; open to change by human actions, endings become an object of experiment and even happiness a narrative option. I have space here only to suggest some directions for further discussion by jumping over to the images of the future in *Beyond Thunderdome*.

By the third film, new peoples are creating themselves by alliance and impro-visation; there is no nation, and no state to administer a population. Presumably, the Northern Tribes who set off for Paradise at the end of *Mad Max 2* are still breeding away on the coast. In the desert, a White Tribe of children is living in a lush lost valley, the 'Crack in the Earth': looking like ragtag extras from a Hollywood jungle movie, their style of life is adapted from Tom Cowan's *Journey Among Women* (1977), a lesbian-influenced film about a new society founded by women convicts, and their 'fecund haven concealed in the blasted interior' is an old motif of Australian fantasy literature.[53] Then there's Bartertown: a wild, hard-trading, frontier city, formally invoking the Hollywood biblical or Roman epic with its pell-mell costume clichés ('African' warriors, 'Roman' soldiers, 'Arab' souks, an 'Asiatic' despot), with 'British' colonials and global media icons tossed into the mix, but threaded together by the East Asian motifs – a headdress here, a tattoo there – that make Bartertown unmistakably a desert descendant of today's fantastic, hyper-capitalist Pacific Rim.[54]

Each group is developing a distinct political system. The Northern Tribes are patriarchal. The White Tribe is a sexually egalitarian gerontocracy (older children lead) and Bartertown is dominated by a single woman, Aunty Entity (Tina Turner). While always signifying herself, 'Tina Turner' is styled here as 'Cleopatra-esque', and thus is coded, in the old Hollywood manner, as an Oriental woman of beauty, ferocity and power; ruling by public rituals of punishment ('the Law') and behind-the-scenes intrigue, Aunty uses a deft com-bination of forced labour and environmentally sustainable technology to build Bartertown on a Pharaonic scale.

Max, ever the go-between, provokes an encounter between those two futures. From the crossing of White tribalism with entrepreneurial multiculturalism emerges a third future, the mixed society that salvages the city of Sydney

('Home') at the end of the film. Unsurprisingly, Home offers the best of both worlds. Like Bartertown it is innovatory, but it remains egalitarian like the Crack in the Earth. Unlike the Crack in the Earth, it is technologically based. Unlike Bartertown, subject to the violence and spectacle of the Law, Home is made socially cohesive by a communal practice of narration and memory. Home's leader, Savannah Nix (Helen Buday), is a white woman who embodies the best of both sexes. A warrior *and* a mother, Nix is a compulsive historian: she makes the people recite their history every single night of their lives.

It is easy to produce a series of binary oppositions between Nix ('Nobody') and Entity ('Somebody'); the film invites us to do so. Nix is to Entity as white is to black, innocence to sophistication, idealism to pragmatism, memory to forgetfulness; and also as history is, not to nature (a dualism made meaningless in *Mad Max*), but to *economy*. Aunty Entity is a business woman. If her view of history broadly resembles Henry Ford's ('history is bunk'), as she explains her approach to Max it more exactly recalls a philosophy associated with the late Fred Daly, a much-loved Australian Labor politician: 'one day, cock of the walk; next, a feather duster'. However, for Aunty, history's *content* is not a struggle for justice but a random play of individual survival and opportunity: 'on the day after, I was still alive. This Nobody had a chance to be Somebody. So much for history.'

Yet there is a double historical displacement going on around the charismatic figure of Tina Turner. She is a black ruler in the Outback, in the place of the Aboriginal women who never figure in this epic (a displacement which provoked some controversy in Australia when the film was released). She is also a woman in charge of an Oriental-multicultural trading zone in which, despite its lavish iconic diversity, the only woman from Asia in sight is tattooed on the Japanese sax-player's back. So if we decide to read *Beyond Thunderdome* as a significantly Australian film, there is a sense in which we can say that troubling issues of race and gender in representation are *peripheralized* by the figure of 'Tina Turner'. I mean this literally: all through the trilogy, glimpses of other stories (the Feral Kid with his boomerang in *Mad Max 2*, the saxophone player himself) flash by in the 'peripheral vision' of the narrative. At the same time, this whole saga of the destruction and rebuilding of society is all about those peripheralized figures, and the roles they play in other stories of depopulation and repopulation, war and migration, historical dominance and economic power.

If we stay with the opposition between Nix and Entity, it is clear that the film sentimentally resolves their conflict in favour of the brave new world built in Sydney by Nix. Hers is the good way forward, and it leads to the future that the Australian Labor government of 1983–1996 promoted in its utopian moments: an open, tolerant, enterprising, 'clever' society, creating new industries or recycling the debris of the old, welcoming people from everywhere, while retaining the *good* old white Australian values of collectivism, historical consciousness and care for social welfare. These are virtues distinguishing Home from brutal Bartertown, where atomized, competitive individuals must fight for their lives without a safety net.

If this is a sentimental resolution, it is also a phoney one. As a happy ending, it didn't take; *Thunderdome* was the most costly and the least successful film of the trilogy. At the level of the economic allegory of survival always subtending the national cinema, Tina Turner's presence is primarily a sign of the global distribution and massive budget of the film; she is 'in place' for marketing purposes. And on screen, Aunty is a lot more fun than Savannah Nix. Aunty has wit, sexiness, style, humour and a real affinity with Max; she exudes a lively cynicism more in tune (I venture to assert) with Australian popular culture than Nix's tense, puritanical fervour; a media creature, Aunty inhabits the big-screen spectacle of *Thunderdome* with grace, consistency and ease. In contrast, Nix, for all her social *bricolage* and home-spun historiography, is perhaps less a portent of the future than a nostalgic reminder of the more primitive technical conditions in which the first *Mad Max* was made.

When we ask how Max mediates the dyad of black and white heroines, the happy ending is more ambiguous. Max cannot join the maternally nurturing utopia of Home any more than he could really live in an infantile lost valley; cut off from Nix's future by the searing knowledge of his past, Max admits the spiritual congeniality of the un-maternal Aunty by staying in the dystopia where each has thrived: Max, by devolving from lawman to 'Nobody' ('The Man With No Name'); Entity, as a Nobody enabled to become the Law. To the end, then, something *grates* about the figure of the white mother-and-child.

Something always did. Even in *Mad Max*, only Jess and Sprog truly live the inhibiting ideals of normality, order, control; almost all the other characters are already, one way or another, social 'feather dusters', except Max's mate Goose (Steve Bisley), the road war's first casualty. Max himself is a waverer, afraid of becoming one of the crazies he is meant to control – which is exactly what he needs to do in order to survive. As O'Regan points out, the death of his wife and child *makes* Max; once 'Mad', he can avoid the ' "vegetable" fate of his mate', survive the apocalypse and enter the new world.[55] This has often led feminists to take a dim view of the films, particularly since casting white women as 'God's police' – moral guardians of community, enforcers of social law – is an old colonial tradition.[56]

Yet Jess herself is a lot more fun than Savannah Nix, to whom the 'guardian' cliché better applies. We are not incited to rejoice at Jess's fate, and so *Mad Max* is all the more shocking for the directness with which it offers a cure for the 'psycho dynamics' of white settler history: imagine a future, even narrate the nation, without recourse to the biological mother-with-child. This opens another series of questions about the impact under colonialism of the concept of population. If we read allegorically for ways in which the iconography of white Motherhood displaces other histories of sexuality and race in the national frame, it is crucial also to attend historically to this icon's luminous negativity in much Australian popular culture; consider Barbara Baynton's cry of outrage at frontier society in her horrifying story 'The Chosen Vessel', first drafted in 1896, about a young bush mother murdered in front of her baby.[57] Why is the 'private sphere' of reproduction (in Burke's terms, the white Beautiful) so often cast as an obstacle to the emergence of a brave new world?

One approach would consider the practical force of a more complex aspect of the sublime than the basic themes I have set out here. It is useful to bring Lyotard's analysis of 'the event' and the terror of death in Burke's sublime to bear on the anxiety about mothers in phobic national narratives, and on the apocalyptic hyperbole of the narration. Lyotard argues that Burke's sublime is 'kindled by the threat of nothing further happening'; he reads Burke as a theorist of the event and 'the question of time' ('*Is it happening?*'), for whom the greatest terror is that '*It*' will stop happening in the ultimate privation, death.[58] This is why the sublime is a revitalizing experience: since a healthy soul is an agitated soul, ever ready for the next event, the 'exercise' of the sublime (Burke, p. 136) simulates and overcomes a fear of being 'dumb, immobilized, *as good as dead*' (Lyotard, p. 205; my emphasis).

It is clear that the unhealthy lassitude threatening the 'nerves' for Burke (and the power of art for Lyotard) is a feminizing 'evil' (Burke, p. 135) associated more readily with bourgeois home life than with war or rebuilding a city. Equally, it is clear that Lyotard shares Burke's disinterest in the eventfulness of *birth*; for neither thinker does the concept of 'labour' (or terror) have maternal connotations. In eugenic mythology, however, the event of a birth can bring into the world the most dreadful of deaths, slow, collective, inexorable: one can never be sure exactly what a woman is 'carrying', or whether a threat to the future of a family, community, nation, or 'race' will successfully be contained.

In this context, Lyotard's account does get at something crucial about the myth of the mother-as-carrier reworked by the *Mad Max* trilogy. Herself a go-between who bodily mediates (in this discourse) inside and outside worlds, the mother can be a bearer of a 'peril' from the *past* as well as of hope or fear for the future. Sweet, suburban Jess errs on the side of an inadaptive inheritance; with her, a whole way of life that is no longer viable is destroyed. Futurist Nix, in contrast, is able to reconcile the dynamism of free trade Bartertown with the commemorative hyper-activity of the protective Crack in the Earth, where the White Tribe fends off 'slackness' (their term for cultural degeneracy) by telling agitated stories of an apocalyptic event.

Again, a historiography is invoked by these tales of dynamism and slackness, one whereby the sublime organizes 'othering' tropes into a vision of Australian society as a catastrophe waiting to happen – if not in a collision between (their) powerful and (our) feeble energies, then as an inner Nothingness spreading unopposed. Consider D.H. Lawrence, writing in *Kangaroo* about an Englishman's perception of Australian urban democracy: 'The *vacancy* of this freedom is almost terrifying. … Great swarming, teeming Sydney flowing out into these myriads of bungalows … like shallow waters spreading, undyked. And what then? Nothing' (pp. 32–33). Again, Lawrence was not the only writer to find Australians suffering a deficit of the spiritual vigour that comes from a bracing exposure to terror; in this highly selective account of history, popular culture was constituted for decades as an oscillation between stupor (for example, Ronald Conway's *The Great Australian Stupor*, 1971) and nihilism (Manning Clark's 'The Kingdom of Nothingness', 1978).[59]

Fictively remedying what is only a deficit in critical vision, no longer thinking history 'through' the body of the mother, the *Mad Max* trilogy tries to transcend this culture of futility and its compensatory, ennobling stories of 'heroic failure' – stories at the heart of the conquistador vision of Man confronting 'the land'. *Beyond Thunderdome* may fail because it does strain for transcendence, while leaving Max in the wasteland as a hint that there might be a *Mad Max 4*. However, as Gibson says, it is significant that Max doesn't die, that the land doesn't kill him, and that he, unlike Bean's victims, succeeds 'in *living*, rather than escaping … into apotheosis'.[60] For my purposes, it is equally important that the vitality of the 'Home' Max can't desire is signified by the child Nix holds in her arms as she tells the city's survival stories, and by the image of a mother assuming the power of historical narration.

Going outside

This is only a story, one of many to use lucidity and humour to salvage something from twentieth century Australia's 'waning myths', and do something different with them.[61] However, stories do know a thing or two about the power and resilience of myth that scholars and politicians often seem to miss. If panics over immigration from Asia seem to be recurrent in Australian public life, how surprised can we really be – when so much official rhetoric of 'Asianization' addressed to us over recent decades has been marked by the very same panic, prompted now by economic rather than racial anxiety about the future?

When, for example, Jamie Mackie issues the stern warning I cited at the beginning of this chapter – 'soon, very soon, we will have to be capable of meeting

[Asians] on their terms' – a truth is told with good intentions. In some ways Australia is indeed 'an off-shore island in an Asia-Pacific world of very dynamic … societies', and yet this mundane truth is told by reanimating White Australia's menacing Asian sublime. To whom is this lesson addressed? Surely not to Asian-Australians. What is wrong with living on an off-shore island, and what power does Mackie assume 'we' have had, that we should find this humbling? What is an 'insignificant' nation? In whose terms is drawn this distinction between significant and insignificant nations? Whose gaze is being invoked? Must significant relationships be defined at the national level? What sacrifices are we asked to make by this invocation of an overwhelming 'other' power, on whose 'terms' we are asked to remake ourselves? Are these not, in fact, *Australian* terms, through and through?

It is remarkable how this imaginary simply has no room for the ordinary; for banal, friendly, unsensational contact, everyday mixed experience, the event of a routine birth. Everything happens in a frenzied and apocalyptic register. One of the best films to deal with this material, John Dingwall's *Phobia* (1988), imploded its conventions brilliantly by allowing the agoraphobic migrant heroine (Gosia Dobrowlska) to walk outside with no appalling or horrible consequences; her fear has been created by her Australian husband (Sean Scully) harping about her strangeness in an 'alien' land. Renate's discovery of the outside as an everyday, negotiable reality is lethal to the hyperbolic drive of phobic narrative, in which all events are on a grand scale and every encounter over-determined.

Going outside means talking *to* the people – in Renate's case, Anglo-Australians – cast as 'Them' in phobic narrative. This, too, is something scholars and politicians could learn from filmmakers, obliged as the latter are to tell stories for an irrevocably diverse world. Responding to the book that Mackie introduces, Alison Broinowski's *The Yellow Lady: Australian Impressions of Asia*, Foong Ling Kong points out that this text, intensely critical of the past and present limitations of settler Australians, assumes that Asian women 'exist in a one-dimensional space and listen as they are spoken about; they do not hear themselves'.[62] In the process, it reconstitutes in its mode of address as well as its title the cultural closure it berates. Excluded from the field of 'Australian' impressions of 'Asia', Kong's writing as a woman who 'shuttles' between Kuala Lumpur and Melbourne is consigned by *The Yellow Lady* to the peripheral vision of history – another tattoo.

However, new modes of address are hard to develop and practise, failures are ordinary and helpful examples are sparse. I have been interested here in how one work of cinema, firmly based in the most uncompromisingly masculine myths of the white Australian tradition, changes them in definite ways. A study of the *Max* films, however, should above all provide a context for valuing the achievement of less widely distributed, more evidently experimental films about action, domesticity and 'contact' made by women in recent years: Tracey Moffatt's *Night Cries: A Rural Tragedy* (1987), about an Aboriginal daughter caring for her dying white mother in a glowingly aestheticized desert; Pauline Chan's *Traps* (1993), in which a British Australian couple, absorbed in their professional and marital everyday, stumble into the beginning of an insurgency they can barely comprehend in French-occupied Indochina in 1950; Margot Nash's *Vacant Possession* (1994), where a white woman returns after her mother's death to her home at the 'national birthplace', Botany Bay, to face a father crazed by the Pacific War – and the family of her Aboriginal lover, whom her drunken father shot.

Such films are often relegated by critics to the worthy periphery of national cinema, as 'independent', 'feminist', or 'multicultural' films. Certainly, they mark the limits of the national cinema project classically understood; centred on the experience of women and children shuttling or shuttled around the world, they internationalize local knowledges of national tensions rather than helping to build a cohesive population in one place. However, I believe they are also creating, without panic or hyperbole, historiographical understandings for the future.

NOTES

1 C.E.W. Bean, *On The Wool Track* (Sydney and London: Angus & Robertson, 1945), pp. 2–3. Further references are in parentheses in the text.

2 Jamie Mackie, 'Foreword' in Alison Broinowski, *The Yellow Lady: Australian Impressions of Asia* (Melbourne: Oxford University Press Australia, 1992), p. v.

3 Sean Brawley, *The White Peril: Foreign Relations and Asian Immigration to Australasia and North America, 1919–78* (Sydney: University of New South Wales Press, 1995), p. 1.

4 See David Carter, 'Crocs in Frocks: Landscape and Nation in the 1990s', *Journal of Australian Studies* 49 (1996): 89–96.

5 Walker, David (1995) 'White Peril', *Australian Book Review* September 1995, p. 33.

6 John Barrell, *The Infection of Thomas de Quincey: A Psychopathology of Imperialism* (New Haven, CT and London: Yale University Press, 1991), pp. 10–11. I deal here only with a twentieth century triangulation, 'white/Aboriginal/Asian', as projected from the enunciative position (my own) of 'white' as 'this'. However, Australia has always been a multi-racial society, and other ways of triangulating social space have shaped its history, such as (in the nineteenth century) 'English/Irish/Aboriginal', and sometimes (during panics about Fenian terrorism in the colonies), 'English/Aboriginal/Irish'. For analyses of how the stakes of discourse about Australian history shift when the 'this' of Australian enunciation is not projected as 'white', see Ghassan Hage, 'Anglo-Celtics Today: Cosmo-Multiculturalism and the Phase of the Fading Phallus', *Communal/Plural* 4 (1994), pp. 41–77, and Foong Ling Kong, 'Postcards from a Yellow

Lady' in *Asian & Pacific Inscriptions: Identities, Ethnicities, Nationalities*, ed. Suvendrini Perera (Melbourne: Meridian, 1995), pp. 83–97.

7 This does not mean that only people who identify as 'white' respond to these fears and fantasies, or enjoy films experimenting with them; nor does it mean that all or even most white people do so identify and enjoy. I am not concerned here with the problem of how we can know what different people and differing audiences 'make' of texts. Rather, I am interested in the related historical issue of what filmmakers 'make' of the materials of previous films, and studying this entails, in my view, a positive description of the recurring tropes of culture.

8 I owe my awareness of this rhetoric to Suvendrini Perera, 'Representation Wars: Malaysia, *Embassy*, and Australia's *Corps Diplomatique*' in *Australian Cultural Studies: A Reader,* eds John Frow and Meaghan Morris, (Sydney and Chicago: Allen & Unwin and University of Illinois Press, 1993), p. 17.

9 Kong, 'Postcards from a Yellow Lady', p. 91.

10 Tom O'Regan, 'The Enchantment with Cinema: Film in the 1980s' in *The Australian Screen*, eds Albert Moran and Tom O'Regan (Ringwood, Vic. and Harmondsworth: Penguin Books, 1989), p. 126.

11 O'Regan, 'The Enchantment with Cinema', p. 126.

12 Constance Penley, 'Time Travel, Primal Scene, and the Critical Dystopia', *Camera Obscura* 15 (1986): 67.

13 Ross Gibson, *South of the West: Postcolonialism and the Narrative Construction of Australia* (Bloomington: Indiana University Press, 1992), p. 159; Stuart Cunningham, 'Hollywood Genres, Australian Movies' in *An Australian Film Reader,* eds Albert Moran and Tom O'Regan (Sydney: Currency Press, 1983).

14 O'Regan, 'The Enchantment with Cinema', p. 127. Along with those by Gibson and Cunningham such readings include Susan Dermody and Elizabeth Jacka, *The Screening of Australia: Anatomy of a National Cinema*, Vol. 2 (Sydney: Currency Press, 1988); Meaghan Morris, 'Fate and the Family Sedan', *East–West Film Journal* 4:1 (1989): 113–134, also http://www.sensesofcinema.com/contents/01/19/sedan.html; and Jon Stratton, 'What Made *Mad Max* Popular?', *Art & Text* 9 (1983): 37–56. Later readings with a national-historical emphasis include Delia Falconer, '"We Don't Need to Know the Way Home": Selling Australian Space in the *Mad Max* Trilogy', *Southern Review* 27:1 (1994): 28–44, while Mick Broderick develops the reading of the trilogy as a global postmodern myth that is favoured by George Miller himself: 'Heroic Apocalypse: Mad Max, Mythology, and the Millennium' in *Crisis Cinema: The Apocalyptic Idea in Postmodern Narrative Film*, ed. Christopher Sharrett (Washington, DC: Maisonneuve Press, 1993).

15 See Geoffrey Blainey, *The Tyranny of Distance: How Distance Shaped Australia's History* (Melbourne: Sun Books, 1966).

16 Peter Otto, 'Forgetting Colonialism (David Malouf, *Remembering Babylon*)', *Meanjin* 52:3 (1993): 545–558.

17 The citation in parentheses is from Edmund Burke, *A Philosophical Enquiry into the Origin of Our Ideas of the Sublime and Beautiful*, ed. J.T. Boulton (Notre Dame and London: University of Notre Dame Press, 1968), first published 1757 and 1759. Further references are in parentheses in the text.

18 See, respectively, Harold Bloom, *The Anxiety of Influence: A Theory of Poetry* (Oxford: Oxford University Press, 1973); Thomas Weiskel, *The Romantic Sublime: Studies in the Structure and Psychology of Transcendence* (Baltimore and London: Johns Hopkins University Press, 1976); Jean-François Lyotard, 'The Sublime and the Avant-Garde' in *The Lyotard Reader*, ed. Andrew Benjamin (Blackwell: Oxford, 1989), and *Lessons on the Analytic of the Sublime,* trans. Elizabeth Rottenberg (Stanford: Stanford University Press, 1994).

19 For example, Peter de Bolla, *The Discourse of the Sublime: Readings in History, Aesthetics and the Subject* (Oxford: Blackwell, 1989); Frances Ferguson, *Solitude and the Sublime: Romanticism and the Aesthetics of Individuation* (New York and London: Routledge, 1992); and Neil Hertz, *The End of the Line: Essays on Psychoanalysis and the Sublime* (New York: Columbia University Press, 1985).

20 Burke, *A Philosophical Enquiry*, p. 57.

21 Alexander Pope, 'The Art of Sinking in Poetry' in *Selected Prose of Alexander Pope,* Paul Hammond, ed. (Cambridge: Cambridge University Press, 1987).

22 See Anthony Vidler, 'Notes on the Sublime: From Neoclassicism to Postmodernism', *Canon: The Princeton Architectural Journal* 3 (1990): 165–191; and *The Architectural Uncanny: Essays in the Modern Unhomely* (Cambridge and London: MIT Press, 1992).

23 The phrase 'numberless confusions' is from Paul De Man, 'Hegel on the Sublime' in *Displacement: Derrida and After*, ed. Mark Krupnick (Bloomington: Indiana University Press, 1983), p. 139.

24 See Patricia Yaeger, 'Toward a Female Sublime', and Lee Edelman, 'At Risk in the Sublime: The Politics of Gender and Theory' in *Gender and Theory: Dialogues on Feminist Criticism,* ed. Linda Kauffman (Oxford: Blackwell, 1989); Paul Gilroy, *The Black Atlantic: Modernity and Double Consciousness* (Cambridge, MA: Harvard University Press, 1993); Ferguson, *Solitude and the Sublime*; David Simpson *Romanticism, Nationalism, and the Revolt Against Theory* (Chicago: University of Chicago Press, 1993); and Weiskel, *The Romantic Sublime*, p. 6.

25 Otto, 'Forgetting Colonialism', p. 548.

26 Robert Dixon, *The Course of Empire: Neo-Classical Culture in New South Wales, 1788–1860* (Melbourne: Oxford University Press, 1986), p. 48.

27 Bernard Smith, *European Vision and the South Pacific, 1768–1850* (Oxford: Oxford University Press, 1960).

28 Christina Thompson, 'Romance Australia: Love in Australian Literature of Exploration', *Australian Literary Studies* 13:2 (1987): 164.

29 See Burke, *A Philosophical Enquiry*, pp. 147–149.

30 Bertrand Russell, *History of Western Philosophy* (London: Allen & Unwin, 1946), p. 679; see Immanuel Kant, *Observations on the Feeling of the Beautiful and Sublime,* trans. John T. Goldthwait (Berkeley: University of California Press, 1960 [1763]), pp. 46–48.

31 Otto, 'Forgetting Colonialism', p. 549. Otto is citing J. W. Gregory's account of his travels at the turn of the twentieth century, *The Dead Heart of Australia* (London: John Murray, 1909). Writers with these concerns in the 1950s include Ernestine Hill, Randolph Stow and Patrick White, while David Malouf's novel *Remembering Babylon*, which Otto reviews, was published in 1993 (Sydney: Chatto & Windus). For readers

unfamiliar with these texts I should stress that they represent only one strand of Australian literature. While landscape metaphysics has been valued highly by critics and historians of national culture, it has never been the only or even the dominant preoccupation of writers in Australia's predominantly urban society.

32 The most influential contemporary polemic against Beauty is Lyotard's *The Postmodern Condition: A Report on Knowledge*, trans. Geoff Bennington and Brian Massumi (Minneapolis: University of Minnesota Press, 1984), pp. 71–82. Significant exceptions to this tendency are Jeremy Gilbert-Rolfe, *Beauty and the Contemporary Sublime* (New York: Allworth Press, 1999), and Dave Hickey, *The Invisible Dragon: Four Essays on Beauty* (Los Angeles: Art Issues Press,1993).

33 See Octavius C. Beale, *Racial Decay: A Compilation of Evidence from World Sources* (Sydney: Angus & Robertson, 1910).

34 Geraldine Heng and Janadas Devan, 'State Fatherhood: The Politics of Nationalism, Sexuality and Race in Singapore', in *Nationalisms and Sexualities*, eds Andrew Parker, Mary Russo, Doris Sommer and Patricia Yaeger (New York and London: Routledge, 1992), p. 343.

35 Barrell, *The Infection of Thomas de Quincey*, p. 5.

36 See Lynette Finch, *The Classing Gaze: Sexuality, Class and Surveillance* (Sydney: Allen & Unwin, 1993); Neville Hicks, *'This Sin and Scandal': Australia's Population Debate, 1891–1911* (Canberra: ANU Press, 1978); and Rosemary Pringle, 'Octavius Beale and the Ideology of the Birthrate: The Royal Commissions of 1904 and 1905', *Refractory Girl* 3 (1973): 19–27.

37 See Ross Chambers, 'Fables of the Go-Between' in *Literature and Opposition*, eds Chris Worth, Pauline Nestor and Marko Pavlyshyn (Monash University: Centre for Comparative Literature and Cultural Studies, 1994).

38 Morris, 'Fate and the Family Sedan'.

39 On this phenomenon in controversies over Chinese immigration in the nineteenth century, see Andrew Markus, *Fear and Hatred: Purifying Australia and California, 1850–1901* (Sydney: Hale & Iremonger, 1979).

40 See Meaghan Morris, 'On the Beach' in *Too Soon Too Late: History in Popular Culture* (Bloomington and Indianapolis, Indiana University Press, 1998), pp. 93–199.

41 An obvious source of the concept, as distinct from the phrase, is the chapter on 'The Whiteness of the Whale' from *Moby Dick*: 'It was the whiteness of the whale that above all things appalled me ... for all those accumulated associations, with whatever is sweet, and honourable, and sublime, there yet lurks an elusive something in the innermost idea of this hue, which strikes more of panic to the soul than that redness which affrights in blood.' Herman Melville, *Moby Dick* (London and Glasgow: Collins, 1953 [1851], pp. 169–170.

42 Weiskel, *The Romantic Sublime*, p. 84; see Burke, pp. 40 and 46.

43 Rey Chow, *Woman and Chinese Modernity: The Politics of Reading between West and East* (Minneapolis: University of Minnesota Press, 1991), pp. 19–27.

44 D.H. Lawrence, *Kangaroo* (Harmondsworth: Penguin, 1950 [1923]), p. 19.

45 See John Carroll, ed., *Intruders in the Bush: The Australian Quest for Identity* (Melbourne: Oxford University Press, 1982); Manning Clark, *Occasional Writings and Speeches* (Melbourne: Fontana/Collins, 1980), pp. 46–47.

46 On the modern sense of 'panic' as a contagion which 'spreads' or is carried between people, taking on a political dimension in contexts of social crisis, see Homi K. Bhabha, *The Location of Culture* (London and New York: Routledge, 1994), pp. 198–211.

47 My thanks to Min-Jun Gu for bringing home to me the importance of this aspect of this scene.

48 On this splitting, see Teresa de Lauretis, *Alice Doesn't: Feminism, Semiotics, Cinema* (London: Macmillan, 1984).

49 I gratefully borrow the notion of reading as 'hallucination' from Naifei Ding.

50 The breakthrough film in this respect was *Rabbit-proof Fence* (2002), directed by Phillip Noyce.

51 Anna Haebich, *For Their Own Good: Aborigines and Government in the South West of Western Australia, 1900–1940*, 2nd edn (Nedlands: University of Western Australia Press, 1992), pp. 316–325.

52 See, for example, Ernestine Hill, *The Great Australian Loneliness* (Sydney: Angus & Robertson, 1963 [1937]), pp. 225–232.

53 Gibson, *South of the West*, p. 162.

54 Bartertown also looks back, like the Crack in the Earth, to Australian popular fiction in the 1890s when Orientalist tales of a 'lost civilisation' in Central Australia enjoyed considerable success; see John Docker, *The Nervous Nineties: Australian Cultural Life in the 1890s* (Melbourne: Oxford University Press, 1991).

55 O'Regan, 'The Enchantment with Cinema', p. 127.

56 Dermody and Jacka, *The Screening of Australia,* Vol. 2, pp. 177–178; see Anne Summers, *Damned Whores and God's Police: The Colonisation of Women in Australia* (Harmondsworth and Ringwood, Vic.: Penguin, 1975).

57 Barbara Baynton, 'The Chosen Vessel' in *Portable Australian Authors: Barbara Baynton,* eds Sally Krimmer and Alan Lawson (St Lucia: University of Queensland Press, 1980), pp. 81–88.

58 Lyotard, 'The Sublime and the Avant-garde', p. 204.

59 Ronald Conway, *The Great Australian Stupor* (South Melbourne: Sun Books, 1971); Manning Clark, *A History of Australia,* Vol. IV: *The Earth Abideth For Ever, 1851–1888* (Melbourne: Melbourne University Press, 1978), *passim.*

60 Gibson, *South of the West,* p. 175.

61 Ibid., p. 175.

62 Kong, 'Postcards from a Yellow Lady', p. 91. 'The Yellow Lady' is the title of an erotic etching from the 1920s by the painter Norman Lindsay, an enthusiast for White Australia. Reproduced on the cover of the first edition of Broinowski's book (Melbourne: Oxford University Press Australia, 1992), this intensely 'othering' image was meant to define the book's object of study, not reiterate Lindsay's values. However, reproductions do reproduce; Kong's 'Postcards from a Yellow Lady' is an analysis of this problem.

Beyond Assimilation: Aboriginality, Media History and Public Memory

It is a bad idea to give an academic talk straight after a screening of Tracey Moffatt's *Night Cries* (1989). The effect is 'grating', as the director has said of her use of the song 'Royal Telephone', which shatters the mood at the end of the film, its cheesy message 'unwelcome and inappropriate' after the mother's death.[1] *Night Cries* moves most people very deeply. I have watched it in several countries, with people engaged by the racial dimension of Moffatt's 'rural tragedy' and with others indifferent to it, and in both cases a distress verging on speechlessness is a response that women particularly, though not only, express.

Not often do we see a film exploring a daughter's ambivalence about her mother – let alone her hostility towards a frail, old, pain-racked and helpless mother – without the mother being portrayed as *bad*, as a bad mother who deserves our anger. *Night Cries* is not *Mommy Dearest*. The mother in Moffatt's film is not a wicked, selfish woman, or a cruel stepmother: she has been a loving mother; her whiteness is not a fault or a personal crime, and the nation-building history that has forced these women's lives together has also created bonds of love and dependency at the core of their shared existence. Even in the beach flashback, when the daughter remembers a childhood crisis of loss and abandonment (and perhaps comes close to remembering an earlier crisis, the loss of her black mother), all that the white mother has done, really, is leave the child's field of vision for a moment. That happens to babies everywhere at some time. *Night Cries* confronts us directly with this mix of tenderness with a violent, angry feeling with no special fictional pretext, no narrative justification, to make it okay.

Not everyone finds this wrenching. Some people register a 'so what?' reaction to another glossy, good-looking short film. At a 1992 screening of *Night Cries* in Taipei, where young women wrestling with the relationship between feminism and Confucianism in their lives were stricken (they said later) by the immediacy for them of the mother–daughter relationship in the film, the 'so-what' response was eloquently framed by Fred Chiu, an anthropologist from Hong Kong Baptist University.[2] Expressing a sense of bemusement that I recognize very well, he suggested that if one lacks some sense of the historical and cultural background of *Night Cries*, one sees only the generic: a maternal melodrama, and an arty use of signs of cinematic modernism slicked over with a pomo, MTV-Day-Glo gloss.

There are many other ways of responding to *Night Cries*. I pick these extremes to begin with because both engage directly with crucial aspects of the project of the film. Tracey Moffatt has said that she would like to think:

> ... that my film is universal, that it isn't particularly about black Australia and white Australia. It's about a child's being moulded and repressed – she is very sexually repressed. It could be the story of anyone stranded in the middle of the desert having to look after their ageing mother.[3]

At the same time, *Night Cries* has also plausibly been described as 'an autobiography of a whole generation of Aborigines';[4] those who, like Moffatt herself, grew up under the official policy of assimilation most intensely pursued across Australia between the late 1930s and the mid 1960s.

It is important to remember that assimilation was indeed a *policy* in this period, thus part of our historical and cultural formation as Australians, and not simply a process or, to borrow Fred Chiu's phrase, a 'generic' effect of any old kind of colonization, an ideology that is vaguely always around. A policy is the outcome of discussions and decisions that could have gone another way; it has precise, practical consequences for people's lives. Those of us who in the past knew little of Australian history are beginning to learn that what happened to various Aboriginal people in different regions and under different state governments during the assimilation period varied greatly.[5] Most of us know, however, that all states of Australia at various times both encouraged and forced black mothers to give up their children for fostering or adoption by white families; we cannot not know now that the extermination of Aboriginality – culture, identity, kinship – was the aim of assimilation. 'Assimilation' in this context was understood in the bodily sense of the term: it did not mean (as it could have) working for social and economic equality and mutual enrichment between Aboriginal and European peoples, but rather the swallowing up, the absorption, of the former by the latter.[6]

Ruthlessly authoritarian forms of social engineering were not imposed by Australian governments on Aboriginal families alone. In my home town in the 1950s, white children, too, were 'taken by the welfare' (as we would say, accepting this as a sad but normal thing), and childish bad behaviour was often met with threats that 'the welfare' would get us. State child theft was not practised only from the 1930s to the 1960s, and it did not happen only in Australia; a poignant ABC-TV mini-series, *The Leaving of Liverpool* (1992), tells the story of the children (many of Irish descent) who were 'stolen' in Britain during this period and sent to charity 'homes' resembling labour camps in Australia.[7] But we cannot not know now that the policy's application in Australia to Aboriginal people had a calculatedly ethnocidal and a systematically racist purpose; and we cannot not know that the taking of Aboriginal children was practised on a horrifically large scale.[8]

Only in recent years, however, has some notion of the scale of the trauma and disruption that this policy created begun to filter through to the *white* Australians in whose idealized name it was practised. Or, rather than speaking of an 'idea' filtering through, I should say that only recently have we begun to develop a collective capacity to comprehend, to empathize, to imagine that trauma and disruption. This is a matter of a politics of remembering. It is important to clarify that many (I would guess most) white Australians 'were not "aware" of what was happening' *not* because we did not *know* it was happening (we did) but because we were unable or did not care to *understand* what we knew; we could not imagine how Aboriginal people felt. So we whites have not 'just found out' about the lost children; rather, we are beginning to remember differently, to understand and care about what we knew. This politics of memory has been initiated largely by Aboriginal uses of film, television and music – media work – in the past three decades.

Anyone who reads about Australian films in magazines will know that Tracey Moffatt herself was fostered, voluntarily, by her *murri* mother; she was raised by an older white woman, but grew up knowing her black mother as well as her white foster mother. However, other aspects of her life are also important to the making of *Night Cries*. Alongside its universal (child/parent) and Aboriginal (black daughter/white mother) dimensions, *Night Cries* is also a cultural autobiography of a whole generation of Australians who grew up between the late 1950s and the 1970s 'glued' (as Moffatt says of herself) 'to the television', and with a love of American popular culture ('a diet of very commercial cinema through to avant-garde films') that often divided us from the cultures of all of our parents.[9] Out of this aesthetic love, Moffatt studied filmmaking and film history at the Queensland College of the Arts, from which she graduated in 1982. She exhibits as a photographer, and along with her feature film *beDevil* she has made several short films besides *Night Cries*: some for television, like her work for the SBS series about positive representation, *A Change of Face*, some for community use, like her film on HIV-AIDS for the Aboriginal Medical Service, as well as her experimental *Nice Coloured Girls*, and a music video for INXS ('Apocalypse').

So if we choose to look at *Night Cries* as autobiography, we need to respect the place of art and media history in Tracey Moffatt's life, and the place she gives it in the collective experience that her film recalls and literally *stages* with its image of the desert 'floor', that shiny stage the daughter walks between the house and that old Australian icon, the 'dunny' (toilet) out the back. The film is doubly coded at the formal level of Moffatt's work as an artist, just as it is on the personal and social levels; it is both international and 'Australia-specific' in its *aesthetic* frame of reference.

For film-conscious people, *Night Cries* is most easily accessible at first in its internationalism. The opening quotation of Rosalind Russell in Joshua Logan's *Picnic* (1956) and the dagger titling place the film in the 'generic orbit' of the 1940s–1950s Hollywood family melodrama and the woman's film, on the one hand, and horror films on the other (an association reinforced at the beginning by screaming sounds recorded during a voodoo ceremony in Haiti in the 1930s).[10] Other details intensify this cinematic familiarity: the beautifully minimal decaying railway platform, visible in many Australian towns but also recalling countless Westerns (especially Sergio Leone's *Once Upon A Time in the West*) along with Ted Kotcheff's *Wake in Fright* and George Miller's *Mad Max 2*; and the reflective desert floor, which Moffatt borrowed from one of the stage effects of *bhutto* theatre via Paul Schrader's film *Mishima*.

Whether we notice them and can name them or not, these details nudge *Night Cries* into a broad image economy, a global circuit of cultural reception. At the same time, other images and sounds can make watching the film a memory-saturated experience for anyone who grew up in rural, poor, or simply ordinary Australian houses in the 1950s and 1960s: the outdoor toilet, the galvanized iron, the creaking and banging screen door, the tin of Golden Syrup on the table, the mother's music box, the washboard and, for me, the most devastating memory-trigger – the one that really *gets* me, though it's one of several moments that interrupt and block my own no doubt very complex impulse to identify wholly with the black daughter in this scenario – the mosquito net. Of all the interrupters in the film (such as the close-ups on Marcia Langton's face as she looks 'off' into her own fictive memory space in the shots preceding each flashback), the one that forces me wholly into the last place I want to be, the *mother*'s space, is the scene of her anguish in bed; it brings back stifling childhood memories of being sick, hot and feverish under a mosquito net, struggling with this nightmarish webby thing entangling your limbs and smothering your face.

So we could simply say that *Night Cries* matches its international generic reception markers with a national, historical iconography – global media images, national and local domestic memories. However, once again there is a third term here, one that mediates the other two and makes the word *national* more difficult to use (unless we ask what we are going to mean by 'national') by recalling another history of black/white relations: a *media* history, not only of European image-makers representing Aboriginal culture, but also of Aboriginal image-makers and mediators representing European culture and trying to engage in dialogue with it.

I say 'trying' because a dialogue presupposes that both parties equally recognize the other's right to participate. A refusal to do this is at the core, not just of colonialism in general, but of the particular media history recalled by *Night Cries*. Moffatt's film refers not only to Hollywood films and to 1950s Australian domestic culture but to the work of three cultural mediators of race relations in Australia. One is the white filmmaker Charles Chauvel, director of the film *Jedda* (1955), from which the setting of *Night Cries* and its two women characters are developed. The other two are Aboriginal mediators: Jimmy Little, the singer we see and hear in the film, and Albert Namatjira, the painter whose work is commemorated in the art direction.

These are the stories of mediation on which I want to focus. First, though, let me sum up and reframe what I've said by introducing the theoretical perspective on 'dialogue' provided by Marcia Langton (who plays the daughter in the film) in her essay, *'Well, I heard it on the radio and I saw it on the television ...'*, in order to recall some of the themes of critical discussion around *Night Cries* when it first appeared in Australia.[11] I began by asking if *Night Cries* is a film about something universal, or an autobiography of a generation of Aborigines. It seems easy to say that it is both, and a third thing besides. Yet what disturbs some critics about work like this is that it does lay claim to a power to universalize, an experimental power to venture generalizations about women's relations, even cross-cultural *human* relations, rather than exclusively stressing the 'radical difference' of black Australian women's experience. This issue has resonances with debates elsewhere around race and culture, especially in the United States, and when people in Australia bring those debates directly to bear, without regard for particular (and differing) histories, the playing out in *Night Cries* of some *positive* emotions in the social economy of assimilation, even of a certain black–white emotional 'complicity', as one critic (Geoffrey Batchen) aptly and admiringly puts it, is construed as a problem.[12]

For others, especially those influenced by the critical avant-garde and documentary aesthetics inspired by social movements in the 1970s, the big cinematic ambition of *Night Cries* – that beautiful, breath-taking gloss – is also a problem. Truly political films, some still feel in an age of many mediums as well as of multimedia, should be gritty, rough-grained and 'realistic'. This can link up with a tenacious European belief that authentic Aboriginal cultural production should never be tainted with worldly success or, as Stephen Muecke bluntly puts it, with money.[13] Perhaps it is in response to this kind of censorious feeling, this demand that a poor-looking realism signify true Aboriginality, that Moffatt has said: 'Yes, I am Aboriginal, but I have the right to be avant-garde like any white artist'.[14]

This intense opinionation about what Aboriginal artists and performers should and shouldn't do has its own media history, as a viewing of *Jedda* may remind us. As a form of stereotyping, it falls into one of the three broad categories of intercultural relations that Marcia Langton identifies as ways of creating Aboriginality. For Langton, '"Aboriginality" is a social *thing* in the sense used by the French sociologist Emile Durkheim' (p. 31). A social 'thing' is a social *fact* which is like a material thing in that it cannot be known through introspection alone. For Durkheim, 'social *things*' come to be known through observation and experiment.[15] In this spirit, Langton argues that Aboriginality is 'a field of intersubjectivity in that it is remade over and over again in a process of *dialogue*, of imagination, of representation and interpretation' (p. 33; my emphasis). Aboriginality is not a fixed thing. It 'arises', she says:

> ... from the subjective experience of both Aboriginal people and non-Aboriginal people who engage in any intercultural dialogue, whether in actual lived experience or through a mediated experience such as a white person watching a program about Aboriginal people on television or reading a book. (p. 31)

Including *mediated* experience in the field of intersubjectivity then allows Langton to construct 'three broad categories of cultural and textual construction of "Aboriginality"': one where an Aboriginal person is interacting with other Aboriginal people in social situations largely located within Aboriginal culture; one in which Europeans who have never had substantial first-hand contact with Aborigines engage in 'the stereotyping, iconising and mythologizing' of Aboriginal people; and one in which Aboriginal and non-Aboriginal people engage in actual dialogue, testing and adapting 'imagined models of each other to find satisfactory forms of mutual comprehension' (pp. 34, 81). The inclusion of mediated experience is vital here, because, as Langton says (putting forward a model of 'Europeanality'):

> The most dense relationship is not between actual people, but between white Australians and the symbols created by their predecessors. Australians do not know and relate to Aboriginal people. They relate to stories told by former colonists. (p. 33)

From my own experience, I would add that part of the density of the mediated relationship for white Australians is an experience of learning, often from Aboriginal media work, how selective were the symbols created by our predecessors and how unforthcoming the colonists when telling their stories. This sort of learning does not necessarily lead to the third form of intersubjectivity, actual dialogue. But it can help. This is one reason why the aesthetic *work* of a film like

Moffatt's is so important for the ways it encourages us all to revise our inherited stories intimately, to remember our own childhood or 'maternal' experiences differently, and to do this *inter*-subjectively, in a collective or public way.

Let me recall a scene from *Jedda*, one of the stories that *Night Cries* brings in to the present and changes. *Jedda* was released in 1955 amidst a ferment of debate about the assimilation policy and theories of culture contact. This debate is staged in *Jedda* between the white adoptive mother, Sarah McMann (Betty Suttor) and her husband Doug (George Simpson-Little), in the form of an argument about whether Aborigines could or should be Europeanized. She thinks yes, he thinks no. She is a would-be reformer and an interventionist. He is more tolerant of Aboriginal tradition and has some respect for its antiquity. She is an idealist, in a thin-lipped way; he is a robust pragmatist interested in making the best possible use of the labour of Aboriginal stockmen. The Aboriginal characters take no part in this debate, although we sometimes see them in the frame (for example, a woman working at the kitchen stove) as the argument is played out between the whites; here, there is no inter-cultural dialogue in Langton's sense.

In one famous scene, however, this 'white' argument is played out *in* Jedda's body (as Jedda somatically becomes the vehicle of the argument) and *through* Ngarla Kunoth's performance of hysteria as she plays the piano in front of an Aboriginal 'shield' which is hanging as an art-work (or a trophy) on the homestead wall. The set here, with its large back window and door, is the one recalled in *Night Cries*. Jedda has just tried to explain to Sarah her wish to go on walkabout with her people; laughing and scolding Jedda's desire away (or so she thinks), Sarah tells her the only walkabout she needs is a nice trip to Darwin, then leaves Jedda alone at her piano lesson. As Chauvel narrows down space to three points or blocs of reference – the piano, the shield, Jedda's body – two musics begin to interfere with each other in Jedda's 'head': the European music that she plays, and an Aboriginal music she hears swelling from the shield. Jedda is overwhelmed, stops playing and bangs her head on the piano.

Everything happens here according to a logic of split identity projected as the dividing of an Aboriginal woman's body and mind. This logic is also organised by a scenario of heterosexual desire: Jedda's helpless dizziness at hearing an Aboriginal music 'inside' prepares for the scene in which she first sees her 'Nemesis', Marbuk (the unassimilated, wild black man from the bush) but she is saved, temporarily, by the appearance at the door of Joe (the assimilated, not-so-black man). In its intensely melodramatic emotional saturation, this scene is the most explicit allusion in the film to the *white* hysteria about race and population that possessed intellectuals and policy-makers from the late nineteenth century to the 1960s (and which staged an uncanny return, just as Aboriginal music does to Jedda, in Australian public life in the 1990s).

Despite appearances in this scene, however, Chauvel apparently believed in the assimilation of Aborigines by Europeans through intermarriage.[16] Jedda is supposed to marry Joe (Paul Reynell), the head stockman. Joe, we're told, is the son of an Afghan teamster and an Aboriginal woman, but he is *sonically* identified, through his accent on the soundtrack, as 'British' – more British, in fact, than Doug. In the historical reality to which the film's fiction alludes but could not name, Joe could plausibly have had a European father, perhaps Doug McMann himself. The piano scene is inserted between two dialogue scenes, one between Sarah and Jedda, one between Doug and Joe, in which a strong mother/daughter, father/son parallelism is formally established. All three scenes are about who or what has the power to determine Jedda's identity and, therefore, her future.

Of course, the intermarriage scenario is threatened by the figure of the unassimilated Marbuk (Robert Tudawali). Marbuk is literally *unassimilable* for the intermarriage scenario, which is not projected as in any way 'dividing' a *white* woman's body; the scenario reserved all the women for white and 'nearly-white' men. Chauvel solves the Marbuk problem by making him a criminal against Aboriginal law: as Langton puts it: '*Jedda* rewrites Australian history so that the black rebel against white colonial rule is a rebel against the laws of his own society. Marbuk, a "wild" Aboriginal man, is condemned to death, not by the white colonizer, but by his own elders. It is Chauvel's inversion of truth on the black/white frontier, as if none of the brutality, murder and land clearances occurred' (pp. 45–46). At the same time, Tudawali's was the most powerful screen presence in *Jedda*, and this led Colin Johnson to claim that in allowing Marbuk to 'steal the show for the Aboriginal male', Chauvel had made an Aboriginal text in spite of himself.[17] Langton, in turn, speculates that white women might have formed a 'secret identification' with Jedda, the black daughter, because of Marbuk's seduction, 'so much more exciting and dangerous than the Rock Hudson type of seduction in the Hollywood romance?' (p. 48).

Night Cries explores a third possibility. Setting aside the 'split identity' model of Aboriginal modernity, it focuses on the women's relations and moves us into the more ambiguous cultural space of a shared but unequal *dependency* between identities with uncertain borders between them. This dependency is one experienced by both the European and the Aboriginal characters: there is not only the European dependency on Aboriginal labour (a structure of economic exploitation which we witness in both films), but also the emotional dependency of the white mothers on their black daughters, as well as of the daughters on their mothers – which we also witness in both films, but which we see more intensely in *Jedda* after *Night Cries*.

Moffatt's scenario produces this intensified vision by testing out a new narrative possibility: what if Jedda had rejected both men and just stayed home with mother? This is how *Night Cries* links *Jedda* to *Picnic* (1956), a film about a family of women bored senseless in small-town Kansas until a socially outcast male (William Holden) comes and lures Kim Novak away. What if *Kim Novak* had just stayed home with mother? What kind of story would that make? She could have become a stifled, repressed, hysterical and very funny spinster like the Rosalind Russell character in *Picnic*. She might also have been just like the angry, stifled daughter in *Night Cries*.

In *Night Cries*, the men are gone; the rural economy has changed, the house has decayed, the windows are grimy and patched, and the space of settlement has contracted.[18] The pebbled path which in *Jedda* led from the house to the gate of a vast cattle empire with sheds, barns and stockyards opening on to a property of thousands of square miles, leads now directly to the galvanized iron toilet (which, with its huge external bolt, also looks uncannily like a police lock-up). In *Jedda*, the world of the 'woman's film' is mainly confined to the interior; the exterior offers the generic world of action, adventure, nation-building, high drama and jumping off cliffs. In *Night Cries*, however, the domestic *interior* has become a 'frontier'. It is not really a frontier between two radically different cultures; the identities of mother and daughter are too blurred and shifting, too interdependent, for that. This frontier is the one where state policy impacts on the psyches of black and white women in a continuous, prolonged abrasion.

From the 1950s to the 1980s, between 'Chauvel' and 'Moffatt', the daughter's objects of desire have changed. Moffatt's daughter dreams of little black dresses, train trips and tourist resorts rather than of 'walkabouts' (though she'd love to leave home) and corroborees (though she'd love to be able to party). But the strain on her is much the same as for Jedda, and it is enormous. Moffatt's daughter does not only hear 'two musics' but rather all kinds of sounds and songs and cries, including a train – that train which is perhaps not really coming as she lies with her mother's body on the platform. With this contraction of Chauvel's bifurcated world (interior/exterior, woman's film/action film) to one continuous space, *Night Cries* subjects state policy to the temporality of the everyday, domestic life in which policy's consequences are lived out. Moffatt's 'woman's film' puts domesticity, rather than great events, at the core of national history. With its more muted representation of the daughter's bodily hysteria (Langton's performance of breathlessness is more restrained than the crisis that Chauvel draws from Kunoth), Moffatt's film tells us that this is how the burden of history actually feels, and where it falls, most of the time.

Moffatt also transforms Chauvel's way of working as an Australian filmmaker struggling to survive in an international economic space. Chauvel was busy mixing Australian themes and settings with Hollywood styles and conventions in the 1950s, yet *Jedda* was the only Australian narrative feature produced in those years.

Moffatt has pointed out that the set in *Jedda* (the window with a badly painted mountain range for backdrop) was quite un-Australian to begin with. Australian outback station homes are not like American ranch houses, and *Jedda*'s interior is weird – part 1950s suburban, Australian-style 'California bungalow', but above all, as Moffatt says, 'very *Bonanza*'.[19] Moffatt herself is working in a well-established tradition of cinematic hybridization, one that includes the films of Chauvel. However, she makes two significant changes to the *Jedda* model.

One is to do with landscape. Like many white Australian image-makers, Chauvel believed passionately in The Land, or 'the spirit of place', as a source of national identity. This was a Romantic appropriation of Aboriginal tradition, or an image of such tradition, intended to give European-Australians a way to resolve our own supposed 'split identity' (which this discourse claims we experience). Chauvel's version of this has been called 'locationism'.[20] He would travel around looking for fabulous landscapes, then write a story and find actors (often 'characters' playing themselves, as the bit parts do in *Jedda*), to match the landscape. *Jedda* was deemed sensational on its release because Chauvel had found untrained Aborigines who were capable of acting – a discovery solemnly debated as proof that they could be assimilated. Even Tudawali's untimely death was later conscripted (as negative evidence) to this debate, rather than to a broader story of what happens to people plucked out of their ordinary lives, turned briefly into stars by the media, then dumped.

In an inversion of Chauvel's approach, *Night Cries* uses two unknown white actresses alongside two of the best known Aboriginal public figures in Australia – Marcia Langton and Jimmy Little. Against Chauvel's aesthetic of authentic locationism, *Night Cries*' vision of landscape is passionately artificial ('the faker the better', Moffatt says); she describes her own preferred landscape as 'a studio apparition'. So given the history I've just outlined, perhaps Moffatt's assertion of 'the right to be avant-garde' against both the realism *and* the Romantic 'locationism' of classical Australian cinema is as much a critique of a certain Europeanality (to use Langton's phrase) in art as it is an assertion that Aboriginality can include growing up glued to *Bonanza* as well as having two mothers – and listening to Jimmy Little's interpretations of American gospel and country and western music.

This brings me to the first of the two Aboriginal mediators invoked in the film. Most middle-aged Australians, and many younger and older, know Jimmy Little's version of 'Royal Telephone' by heart. I don't know why: whether you like it or not, it is one of those songs that stick. It was a huge hit when I was about 13. There was a big fuss about Little himself as 'the first' Aboriginal pop star, but that faded (although he continued to sing, like many stars of the 1960s, on the club and cabaret circuit, until his fame was renewed in the wake of Moffatt's film). Always, the song, and the memory of his voice, remains. Many people believe he wrote the song, which is in fact American. Moffatt's use of Jimmy Little is unsettling, even macabre, at times; he's miming 'Love Me Tender' during the scene in which the daughter is cracking the whip and the mother is shuddering and sighing, with pain or pleasure, we can't be sure. Little himself is part of an 'unsettling' cultural history in a broader sense; as an evangelical Christian, his first media role was in a Billy Graham film made in Australia in the early 1960s. So he has been part of a transformation of Aboriginal religious life, and thus of the role of art in society. Moffatt does not mock Little's Christianity or his music. She makes the mood around him *fluctuate*, by the way she cuts his image in and out of other scenes, fragments his body, silences and releases his gorgeous voice; his presence phases between soothing and sinister, corny and uncanny; 'like something familiar which turns into something horrible'.[21]

In '"Love Me Tender, Love Me True, Never Let Me Go ...": A Sri Lankan Reading of Tracey Moffatt's *Night Cries – A Rural Tragedy*', Laleen Jayamanne asks what the figure of Little is *doing* in this film; what his role is as the male but somehow 'not phallic' third term intervening between mother and daughter in the most intense scenes (the whipping, the beach flashback), and as the figure whose body and music, at the beginning and the end, frames the film. Jayamanne speculates that Little performs and voices something troubling, something mediating the public history that joins the private lives of mother and daughter: 'with style and panache he embodies cultural assimilation'.[22] If this is so, Little's role is crucial since, according to Jayamanne, the film is not only about 'the politics of imitation and assimilation', as Batchen suggests, but 'perhaps also about an aesthetics of assimilation'. By recalling Jimmy Little, she says, 'Moffatt is making an enabling tradition for herself to work in'.[23]

If Jimmy Little was acclaimed by white Australians as 'the first' Aboriginal pop star, he was not our 'first' Aboriginal post-war culture hero. That was Albert Namatjira, the memory of whose work saturates the colouring and the light of the film. Namatjira was not 'the first' Aboriginal artist to paint in a European style – Marcia Langton has some acerbic things to say about our obsession with 'firstness' – and he was certainly not the only Aboriginal artist of his time to paint naturalistic landscapes.[24] But he did become uniquely famous for doing it. As early as 1946 a film about his life, *Namatjira – The Painter*, was sponsored by the Commonwealth Department of Information.

Ian Burn and Ann Stephen have given us a way of understanding Namatjira's life by relating it not to the discourse of 'split identity', but to art history and the history in the art.[25] Namatjira was born in 1902, and he grew up in the area of the Lutheran mission established at Hermannsburg in 1877. For people in this region of Southern and Central Australia, the years of Namatjira's youth and early adulthood were a time of rapidly accelerating social change. Here are some orienting dates: in 1928 there was a massacre of Aborigines at Coniston Station; in 1929 the railway, and thus, eventually, tourism, reached Alice Springs; in 1932 the white landscape painter Rex Battarbee and others visited Hermannsburg; and it was probably in 1935 that Albert Namatjira made his first watercolour paintings (although these were not, Burn and Stephen stress, the only kind of art that he practised).

Namatjira was enormously successful. He became the most popular Australian painter of his time, perhaps the most popular painter, period, in Australian history. Non-Aboriginal Australians loved his landscapes. As the making of the 1946 film suggests, the government took an interest in promoting him as a 'star' of cultural assimilation – he was used as living evidence, once again, that the policy could work. The reasoning seems to have been that if Aborigines could learn to paint 'accurately' – that is, master European perspective conventions (and many white people argued that they couldn't) – then they could and therefore *should* become European.

Let's remember that apart from a few ethnographers and eccentrics, Europeans knew almost nothing fifty years ago about Aboriginal art: we were ignorant of its range across different media, its diversity across the continent, and the complexity and richness of its conceptual basis. Unlike Polynesian and Oceanic art, Aboriginal art was not taken up in the wave of primitivism that sustained so much aesthetic modernism early in the twentieth century.[26] Only in the 1950s were small samples of Aboriginal art, mostly bark paintings from Arnhem Land, beginning to be collected and exhibited, and these came rapidly to define 'the look' deemed authentically Aboriginal by intellectuals and the discriminating art public when Namatjira was at the height of his popular fame.

He was presented to the Queen in 1954, and went on a tour of the cities. By 1958, media and public enthusiasm about him was so great that there was an outcry when it was discovered that neither of the major state galleries in the East owned even one of his paintings. Sylvia Kleinert records that one trustee of the National Gallery of Victoria responded to the furore by calling Namatjira's watercolours 'absolutely frightful, real potboilers'.[27] This judgement, with its high modernist scorn for an apparently accessible, naturalistic art in a 'low', 'amateur' medium (watercolour), largely held in art circles until the mid-1980s, when there was a wave of interest in the contemporary acrylic elaborations of Western Desert ground and rock paintings which came from an area much closer to Namatjira's country than had the Arnhem Land barks.

These days, those acrylics probably define 'the look' that many non-Aboriginal Australians equate with 'Aboriginal art'. As the art historians from whom I have learned these things have noted, the Western Desert movement has greatly changed the intellectual climate in which Namatjira's work is evaluated. Yet from a 'European point of view', I think there remains something troubling about Namatjira's aesthetics. I can express this best with a postcard available all over Sydney. It has a black border surrounding a dots-and-roundels image described, on the back of the card, as 'The Map', and attributed to 'Aboriginal Artist Reggie Ryan'. The left hand border of the card says 'Aboriginal Art', and then 'Australia' appears in the bottom right corner. I don't know anything more about Reggie Ryan or his painting than this card tells me. What the *words* on the card suggest most immediately, as Ryan's image sits among the others, mostly photos of Sydney, in any standard tourist rack, is that here I have the essence of 'Australian Aboriginal Art'. However, after reading Langton, Kleinert, and Burn and Stephen on the history of debates about cultural identity in Australia, I have a feeling that this postcard really offers me an essence of 'Europeanality' understood as a *particular way of framing* 'Aboriginal art': a way that uses a singular instance 'generically', in Fred Chiu's sense, to contain in one abstract gesture an entire complex culture.

That much is easy. However, I then try to imagine a similarly labelled postcard having a Namatjira 'gum-tree and mountain-range' image in place of Reggie Ryan's dots and roundels; I try to imagine a generic 'Namatjira' being sold to tourists in Sydney as 'Aboriginal Art – Australia'. The effect would be quite different, but it isn't easy to say exactly why. Perhaps it is just that 'European' Australians still don't quite know what to do with Namatjira's art today, in spite of the excellent scholarship now available to us. There really is something unassimilable in the way that these utterly familiar paintings send a historical image of 'our' own visual culture back to us, instilling doubt about our new second-hand fluency in discussing 'Aboriginal Art' using the conceptual tools of post-modernism. There is also something unassimilable about ourselves *to* ourselves when we ask *why* it might seem odd to package a Namatjira painting today as an emblem of 'Aboriginal Art', and what would need to change in Australian society for that sense of oddness to vanish.

I have two comments to make in conclusion about the issues *Night Cries* raises by reminding us of these histories of mediation. First, this 'right to be avant-garde'. What can that mean in Australia now? I understand Moffatt to be using 'avant-garde' in its popular sense; she is generally claiming the right to do something new, to innovate, to change the rules of the genres she works in, and she is also assuming that 'avant-garde' is an established, even a commercial genre of cultural practice. But this invites the question, innovate in relation to what? Let's remember that for 'European' Australian artists, modernism usually has been understood 'generically', as an imitative (and often also derivative) practice. To put it bluntly, modernism here was a set of stylistic effects and cultural postures, produced in Europe and the United States, that Australian artists *copied*. The Modern, as David Bromfield argues, was something that had already happened somewhere else; 'an extensively known history created through endless images from elsewhere and transmitted through the cinema and illustrated magazines'.[28] Given this framework, Namatjira's famous and massively reproduced painting *Ghost Gum* could now be perceived as a remarkable experiment with the rules for painting his country that mattered to Albert Namatjira. But it could not be perceived as avant-garde by white art critics in the 1950s and 1960s because it did not look like a Jackson Pollock, and it did look like our own conservative nationalist tradition of pastoral painting. No dialogue, on these terms, was possible.

Further questions of history arise if we turn to scholarly work on the literally 'European' avant-gardes: for example, Peter Burger's argument that the avant-garde movements tried to overcome the institutional separation of art from life, whereas the institutionalizing process of modernism acted to divide them all over again.[29] It is clear that, by these criteria, Namatjira's response to the cultural dislocations lived by the Arrente people in the 1950s would have a far better claim to be avant-garde than most of the non-Aboriginal art being produced in Australia at this time. Yet his was an art that ordinary people loved. As Kleinert as well as Burn and Stephen make clear, one reason his art was devalued was that it was an art that people could *live with*, an art working in close proximity to the cultural values of home decoration as well as to the tourist industry. My childhood home did not have an Aboriginal shield hanging above a piano like the homestead set in *Jedda*. It had a reproduction of Namatjira's *Ghost Gum* hanging above the wireless – and later, above the television.

Like Jimmy Little's music, Namatjira's art really did change the way white Australians perceived Aboriginal people, and thus the way we perceived ourselves; he helped to make it possible for us to think differently about our place in the country we had come to live in. This is a history at stake in Jayamanne's suggestion that, by recalling Jimmy Little and Albert Namatjira, Tracey Moffatt is 'making an *enabling* tradition for herself to work in'. This tradition is not – despite, or because of, its big aesthetic ambitions and Moffatt's well-deserved personal success – easily assimilated by Australians today. To commemorate Namatjira is to remember something about the place of art in *his* life that requires us to make a connection between the delight white Australians take today in Aboriginal culture, and/or our images of it, and the ways in which our social and economic practices still affect Aboriginal lives. In the year that Namatjira met the Queen (1954), he was charged with drinking wine – then a crime for 'registered' Aboriginal people, who had no civil rights until 1967. The case was dismissed, and in 1957 he was given special exemption from discriminatory legislation by being granted citizen status. But in 1958, he was sentenced to six months hard labour for sharing alcohol with friends and relatives, as his own law said he must. He served two months, he was released, and he died in 1959.

My second comment is that as we continue to discuss the role of culture in the social conflicts and injustices of the present, aesthetic work such as Moffatt's is developing a tradition which is enabling for others as well as herself. This tradition is not one of 'forcing us to confront the past' in a polarizing, polemical way, but more subtly making it less attractive, less *interesting* to go on telling the same selective stories as our predecessors than it is to remake our national histories in a spirit of inclusiveness, justice and truth. Langton explains that the creation of Aboriginality as a social *thing* is a process for which personal reminiscence is insufficient. It is neither here nor there for me to say of Europeanality, 'We had a Namatjira in our house!' But in its insufficiency, it can help create the possibility of a field of intersubjectivity where a different form of public memory may take shape.

There is an extraordinary painting about this field by another Aboriginal artist, Robert Campbell Jnr. It's called *Roped Off at the Picture II* (1987). It mixes perspectives, literally: embedded in Campbell's own 'picture' is an obliquely angled version of the Renaissance perspectival tradition that ordinarily organizes an audience's relation to a film image on screen in a theatre, impossibly combined with an 'Aboriginal' aerial perspective; the painting's little black and white figures, including the usher in the theatre and the cowboy on the screen are, like the audience bodies, actually facing us (those seated, with a leg splayed out), as though we, the viewers, are hovering above them.

In this remarkably twisted space, at least two things are happening. On the screen a white cowboy, not a black stockman, is riding around in the cultural space (the *mise en scène*) of a Namatjira 'gum-tree and mountain-range' landscape. In the social space of the cinema, the picture is not so mixed; the black spectators are roped off from the whites in the three worst rows in the cinema, right up under the screen.

As a child around 1957, I saw *Jedda* in an informally segregated theatre, a lot like this, at the height of the debate about cultural assimilation. There was no rope, as I recall, in the Tenterfield Lyric Theatre, but there was always an usher with a torch prowling round up front to keep 'rowdy Aborigines' in line.

As a film critic, I must say that an image of Campbell's painting (which I have only seen in a book)[30] always pops into my head these days when I find myself expected to talk about theories of reception and spectatorship in cinema studies. Like *Night Cries, Roped Off at the Picture II* brings history right into the field of aesthetic experience and cultural debate, and asks questions about the present. The ropes and even the ushers are gone from picture-theatres now, but the painting has a powerful capacity to make one wonder what else has changed in the social and personal field of relations it recalls – and what role the effort to keep 'Aboriginal art' in line has played in the history of those relations.

Afterword

When I wrote this paper as a public lecture for a largely non-academic audience in Hawai'i in 1993, I called this an open question as well as a hard one; I was (and I still am) truly uncertain about how to answer it. Going over what was for many people in the audience an unfamiliar history so as to *reach* that open question was basically the point of the talk; I did not set out to offer a new or original interpretation of *Night Cries*, but rather to pass on something of the complexity of the things that had already been said about it, to put it in a historical and cultural context, and to share my sense of why it mattered. I wanted to interest people in *Jedda*, Marcia Langton's book, Jimmy Little's music, Laleen Jayamanne's essay, Namatjira's painting, and the book that I drew on so substantially, *The Heritage of Namatjira*.

While I have a long-running interest in the relationship between the 'avant-garde' and the 'ordinary', and in the question of history in cinema, much of the history I learned by studying *Night Cries* was unfamiliar to me too. Since I was sharing enthusiasms and 'teaching myself in public' (that dreadful crime for scholars), I never intended to publish the talk. I feel differently about this now. Since the election of John Howard's government in 1996, disavowal and sheer ignorance about Australian culture and history have acquired a respectability that was unthinkable only three years before his election; there is renewed fervour for 'roping off' the past and pulling rowdy Aborigines into line; there is, once again, white debate about assimilating Aborigines, and a growing disinclination to hear stories about mothers and the children parted or thrown together by policy in the past.

We are being asked to forget about the past few years of remembering. Personally, I have no intention of doing this. It has been far too interesting, too *involving*; Moffatt's films, Langton's essay, books like *The Heritage of Namatjira* have engaged me in *my own* history as an Australian to a degree that I never thought possible (brought up as I was on a historiographical tradition of sheep, damned sheep and explorers). My personal intentions are of little consequence. However, as Australian artists and intellectuals accustom ourselves again to working in a world where vicious speech is honoured for its 'freedom' and redneck radio sets the standard for serious public debate (it takes me back to my childhood, really), there is at least something academics can do to resist the new institutional separation of art from life, the roping off being imposed on us.

We can start teaching ourselves in public more often and more persistently; we can repeat as often as possible the things we know or are learning about the past, and try to share this knowledge around as much as possible; we can tell other people about books and films that have given us ways of understanding ourselves as well as others. At the moment, every second newspaper column I read is calling for a 'new' approach to politics from the left of Australian opinion, or just from the decent centre – a right and proper demand. However, I suspect that in the small and, for the moment, fairly powerless sphere of cultural criticism, the way towards a new *approach* lies in reducing our need for intellectual novelty.

Writing from an American experience of resurgent racism and political correctness panic, Michael Bérubé points out how 'thoroughly conditioned' academics have been by the legacy of modernism (rather than the avant-garde) to criticism, 'the imperative to say something new'.[31] I think he is right to say that to play any role at all in public debate these days, we have to unlearn this imperative to signify the (mostly illusory) newness of what we have to say: writing and speaking in public, 'we have to be willing to restate other people's work and forego the pleasure of producing the new, and we have to give examples'.[32] My only disagreement is that I don't see this as forgoing *pleasure* – a pleasure of which the 'enabling tradition' of experimental artists like Little, Namatjira and Moffatt provides a powerful historical example.

NOTES

1 Scott Murray, 'Tracey Moffatt, *Night Cries: A Rural Tragedy*', *Cinema Papers* 79 (1990): p. 22.

2 Discussion at *Trajectories: Towards a New Internationalist Cultural Studies – An International Symposium*, sponsored by The Institute of Literature, National Tsing Hua University (Hsinchu), Taipei, Taiwan, July 1992.

3 Cited in Murray, 'Tracey Moffatt', p. 22.

4 Geoff Batchen, 'Complicities', *Artful*, College of Fine Arts Students Association (October 1990), n.p.

5 See Anna Haebich, *Broken Circles: Fragmenting Indigenous Families, 1800–1990* (Fremantle: Fremantle Arts Centre Press, 2000).

6 On the digestive aspect of assimilation in Moffatt's later film *beDevil*, see Mary Zournazi, '"The Queen Victoria of Bush Cuisine": Foreign Incorporation and Oral Consumption Within the Nation', *Communal/Plural* 4 (1994): 79–89.

7 For information, see http://www.abc.net.au/programsales/s1123499.htm.

8 See Coral Edwards and Peter Read, eds, *The Lost Children: Thirteen Australians taken from Aboriginal families tell of the struggle to find their natural parents* (Sydney: Doubleday, 1989), p. ix; and *Bringing Them Home: Report of the National Inquiry into the Separation of Aboriginal and Torres Strait Islander Children from Their Families*

(Sydney: Human Rights and Equal Opportunity Commission, 1997). http://www.hreoc.gov.au/bth/index.htm.

9 Cited by Patricia Mellencamp, 'An Empirical Avant-Garde: Laleen Jayamanne and Tracey Moffatt' in *Fugitive Images: From Photography to Video,* ed. Patrice Petro (Bloomington: Indiana University Press, 1995), p. 178.

10 Ingrid Periz, '*Night Cries*: Cries from the heart', *Filmnews* August 1990: 16.

11 Marcia Langton, *'Well, I heard it on the radio and I saw it on the television ...': An essay for the Australian Film Commission on the politics and aesthetics of filmmaking by and about Aboriginal people and things* (North Sydney: Australian Film Commission, 1993). Further references are in parentheses in the text. The quotation that Langton uses for her title ('Well, I heard it on the radio and I saw it on the television') is the opening line of 'Treaty', a hit song by Yothu Yindi.

12 Batchen, 'Complicities', n.p.

13 Stephen Muecke, *Textual Spaces: Aboriginality and Cultural Studies* (Sydney: University of NSW Press, 1992); see particularly chs 7 and 8.

14 Cited in Murray, 'Tracey Moffatt', p. 21.

15 Emile Durkheim, *The Rules of Sociological Method* (New York: The Free Press, 1964 [1938]), pp. xliii f.

16 On Chauvel, see Stuart Cunningham, *Featuring Australia: The Cinema of Charles Chauvel* (Sydney: Allen & Unwin, 1991).

17 Colin Johnson, 'Chauvel and the Aboriginal Male in Australian Film', *Continuum* 1:1 (1987): 47–56. 'Colin Johnson' was an early pseudonym of the creative writer Mudrooroo; see ch. 2, n. 37 above.

18 Periz, '*Night Cries*', p. 16.

19 Moffatt, personal correspondence; see also Murray, 'Tracey Moffatt', p. 22.

20 See Cunningham, *Featuring Australia: The Cinema of Charles Chauvel.*

21 Moffatt, cited in Murray, 'Tracey Moffatt', p. 22.

22 Laleen Jayamanne, '"Love Me Tender , Love Me True, Never Let Me Go...": A Sri Lankan Reading of Tracey Moffatt's *Night Cries – A Rural Tragedy'* in *Feminism and the Politics of Difference,* eds Sneja Gunew and Anna Yeatman (Sydney: Allen & Unwin, 1993), p. 78. This essay is also in Laleen Jayamanne, *Toward Cinema and Its Double* (Bloomington and Indianapolis: Indiana University Press, 2001), pp. 3–12.

23 Jayamanne, '"Love Me Tender ..."', p. 76.

24 See Peter Sutton, ed., *Dreamings: the Art of Aboriginal Australia* (Ringwood, Vic.: Viking, in association with the Asia Society Galleries, NY) and *The Heritage of Namatjira: The Watercolourists of Central Australia,* eds Jane Hardy, J.V.S. Megaw and M. Ruth Megaw (Melbourne: William Heinemann Australia, 1992). On Namatjira, see 'The Extraordinary Life of Albert Namatjira', *The Koori History Website*: http://www.kooriweb.org/foley/images/history/albert/albertdx.html.

25 Ian Burn and Ann Stephen, 'Namatjira's White Mask – A Partial Interpretation' in Hardy et al., *The Heritage of Namatjira,* pp. 249–282.

26 However, Burn and Stephen stress: 'A notable exception occurred in 1917 at the Cabaret Voltaire, the centre of Zurich Dada, when Tristan Tzara sang three Central Australian "songs" in French as part of his cycle of "Poèmes Nègres", which subsequently appeared in the journal *Dada.* By this appropriation, these Aboriginal oral

traditions briefly became a Dada readymade pulled from the obscurity of *Die Aranda- und Loritja-Stamme in Zentral-Australien*, the work of Carl Strehlow produced at Hermannsburg and published in Frankfurt between 1907 and 1920': 'Namatjira's white mask', p. 260.

27 Sylvia Kleinert, 'The Critical Reaction to the Hermannsburg School', in Hardy et al., *The Heritage of Namatjira*, p. 241. This judgement is shared (in a feminizing mode) by Lévi-Strauss, who 'describes Aranda painting as: "the dull and studied watercolours one might expect of an old maid"'; Kleinert, p. 235.

28 David Bromfield, 'Making the Modern in the Newest City in the World', *Aspects of Perth Modernism, 1929–1942* (Perth: Centre for Fine Arts, 1988), p. 2.

29 Peter Burger, *Theory of the Avant-Garde,* trans. Michael Shaw (Minneapolis: University of Minnesota Press, 1984).

30 Jennifer Isaacs, *Aboriginality: Contemporary Aboriginal Paintings and Prints* (St Lucia: University of Queensland Press, 1989), p. 15.

31 Michael Bérubé, *Public Access: Literary Theory and American Cultural Politics* (London: Verso, 1994), p. 167.

32 Ibid.

PART TWO

Translation in Cultural Theory

5

The Man in the Mirror: David Harvey's 'Condition' of Postmodernity

Difference is a misreading of sameness, but it must be represented in order to be erased. The resistance to finding out that the other is the same springs out of the reluctance to admit that the same is other.

Barbara Johnson, *A World of Difference* (1987)[1]

Autobiography of a reading

Reading David Harvey's *The Condition of Postmodernity* was an estranging experience for me. At first contact, I was struck by what Foucault calls 'the stark impossibility of thinking *that*':[2] how could anyone see practices that for me are quite distinct – feminist art, post-structuralist philosophy, architectural postmodernism, genre cinema, 'roots' community movements and radical difference politics – as somehow similar in their 'reflection' of a 'fragmented', 'ephemeral', 'chaotic' condition of life? Projects which I have been involved with for twenty years (and which I take to be coherent, ongoing and fairly stable in their concerns) thus became, in Harvey's reading, unrecognizable. For Foucault, the encounter with an alien taxonomy is a comic and wondrous experience. But I was not amused: in the name of a 'survey', I saw conceptual distinctions blurred, political difference denied, conflicts ignored and histories of struggle (most spectacularly, feminism) erased by this image of a fractured postmodern 'other' in flattering need of the remedy of wholeness that Harvey's Marxism might then provide.

Then I did see the humour of it. What is wonderful about the moment of alterity for Foucault is that we apprehend, in an 'exotic' system of thought, 'the limitation of our own'.[3] The critical and cultural practices that Harvey reduces to the same may constitute a world of difference to me, but they also set practical limits to my everyday working environment, give or take a few forays into economics and social theory. So extensive and complex has the international field of cultural studies become that I, absorbed in its conflicts, had come to argue not just that critics moved to celebrate the postmodern city should do some political economy first, but that the once enabling mistrust of 'totalizing' theories and of economism inscribed in much of our work was now an anachronism; no Marxist, I thought, *really* claims that sort of mastery any more.[4] In *The Condition of Postmodernity*, I came face to face with my own parochialism: 'if there is a meta-theory with which to embrace all these gyrations of postmodern thinking and cultural production, then why should we not deploy it?' [5]

This prompted a more self-critical discovery. In my bemusement at Harvey's use of polemically hysterical passages from Terry Eagleton as true descriptions, or at his uncritical acceptance as 'daring' of the most orthodox determinist features of Jameson's 1984 thesis on postmodernism as a 'logic' of late capitalism (*Condition*, pp. 9, 53, 63, 117), I was confronting a mirror image, on a grander scale, of my own past use in cultural studies of Harvey's economic geography. I had invoked his authority, offered his *Studies in the History and Theory of Capitalist Urbanization* as more or less 'true' to my students, and discounted most of his critics as too 'specialized' for me.[6] No wonder I was shocked by Harvey's interdisciplinary reading habits; my own had been, in many respects, the same.

I begin with this rather personal allegory in order to frame what follows as a partial reading of *The Condition of Postmodernity* – one deriving its questions from the historical project, rather than the 'field', of cross-disciplinary feminist enquiry. I do not attempt a complete or impartial account of the book; this is to admit to ignoring much that gives an ambitious text its appeal. The point of my partiality is not to defend my turf against incursion: I am neither an exponent of affirmative postmodernism nor an opponent of Marxism, and I do not race to rescue theories from the perils of popularization. Graeme Turner has written eloquently of 'the ambiguity of the position occupied by those who attempt to present academic knowledges to popular audiences'.[7] The broad interest aroused by *The Condition of Postmodernity* is testimony to the value of risking that ambiguity.

This is a book with academic concerns – postmodernism, post-Fordism – but it also addresses a general reader who wants to know what happened (or became more obvious as happening) in Western societies during the 1980s: why some places boomed while others suffered, why yuppies flourished while poverty and homelessness increased, why conservative regimes came to power, and what all this had to do with *Blade Runner*, pink and blue buildings, Lyotard, Cindy Sherman and a crisis of representation. I can share that reader's desire. 'What happened?' is a narrative question, and Harvey is a good storyteller. He gives us a double narrative, and a narrative of doubling: on the one hand, a gripping account of the political-economic transformation of late twentieth century capitalism, on the other a sweeping saga of the European experience of time and space since the Enlightenment. Linking these, a major sub-plot occurs in the present tense: a battle between Marxism and postmodernism to determine the nature of the relationship between the other two.

It's a great read. But there are many ways of telling, and using, stories. As Doreen Massey points out, the moral of Harvey's tale (and his resolution of complex problems of causality and influence) is all too often 'time–space compression and flexible accumulation' or, more classically, 'capital and labour'.[8] His narration, epic yet meticulous in describing the intricate moves of capital, is profoundly reductive in impulse. For me, this is the pleasure of his text. For all the grimness of Harvey's vision of a gaudy and turbulent world, there is something reassuring about the confidence of his grasp on its 'gyrations', and a comfort in his return to what Angela McRobbie calls 'a simpler and more direct notion of determination. What happens in the economy has a direct effect on what happens in culture'.[9] The sense of homecoming that this arouses need not be restricted to those of Harvey's readers who grew up on the Left. It has a similar affective appeal to the contemporary discourse of those charismatic leaders and nostalgia films which have played such a crucial role in Marxist formulations of postmodernity.[10]

This is not an inappropriate way to read a text which is not a novel, but a manifesto for 'a renewal of historical materialism and of the Enlightenment project' that calls for a 'counter-attack of narrative against the image' (*Condition*, p. 359). Nor is this just a covert way of dismissing Harvey's concerns. On the contrary: how stories are told, and why; who tells them, to whom, for whose benefit and in which contexts; how stories circulate, how their force and value change; what we *do* with other people's stories, what happens if we retell them in different ways – the problem of narrative (not the same thing as 'fiction') has motivated feminist research in and across many disciplines for decades. It has engendered the study not only of those 'exclusions' that guarantee the coherence of any given discourse but of the positive force of *other* stories, and different narrations of the same story, which may not be so much untold as rather unheard, ignored, or unreceivable in dominant disciplinary terms – terms that include the institutional criteria of what may count, for a given knowledge, as a proper and plausible yarn.

However, Harvey's understanding of 'narrative' simply *opposes* it (in 'counter-attack') to 'the image' (*Condition*, p. 359). It follows, then, that Harvey cannot recognize Cindy Sherman's famous *Untitled (Film Still)* photographs as images charged with narrative tension. Sherman's series – pictures of a woman (always played by Sherman herself) poised as though between gestures in diverse film scenes and settings – help Harvey to define postmodernism. They are among the few works by women figuring in the book. But instead of seeing them as engaged with the historically specific *relationship between* images and stories producing 'woman' (and desire) in Western cinema,[11] Harvey can only see in them a vaguely metaphysical insistence on 'the plasticity of the human personality through the malleability of appearances and surfaces' (*Condition*, p. 7). This translation of the historical and female (Sherman) as metaphysical and human (Harvey) is ensured by the indeed metaphysical assumption, pervasive in Harvey's book, that image is to narrative as 'surface' is to depth, 'appearance' to reality, *shallowness* to *complexity*, and space – at least, aesthetic space – to time. These slippages also ensure that images cannot be read as *actions* in 'counter-attack'; Sherman's story about the story of femininity in cinema is unreceivable.

For feminist criticism, then, *The Condition of Postmodernity* offers itself as a back-to-basics occasion. Harvey's story has been criticized by feminists working diversely in geography [12] art[13] and sociology,[14] and this is not surprising. In defence not only of 'meta-theory' but of economic determinism, *The Condition of Postmodernity* offers a reading of culture that depends on a massive exclusion of feminism rather than critical dialogue with it, and so assumes the Marxist primacy that it claims to argue for. It uses 'women' to signify 'white' and 'straight' in an open set of Mixed Others ('women, gays, blacks, ecologists, regional autonomists, etc.') whose concerns are described as 'local' (*Condition*, pp. 47–48). It assumes that these are 'place-bound', and that their resistance tends inexorably toward fragmentation, pastiche or traditionalism (*Condition*, pp. 303–305). No evidence is offered for this assessment: there is some mention of fascism, but none at all of debates *about* the question of difference; one 'condition' of Harvey's discourse is a culture where Homi Bhabha, Stuart Hall, bell hooks, Paul Gilroy, Gayatri Spivak, Eric Michaels, Trinh T. Minh-ha, Craig Owens or Michele Wallace have not yet written.

Yet the occasion has been valuable insofar as feminist responses have not gone back to basics, but have engaged in critical debate from a present in which there *is* now no way back from relational thinking about gender, race and class to a simpler, more direct, class fundamentalism. It is from this present that I am immediately uncomfortable with my own exclusionary gesture in opposing 'our' relational thinking to 'Harvey's' fundamentalism. It uses the same scare tactics as Harvey does in associating new social movements with 'the Heideggerian trap' (*Condition*, p. 304). It also ignores the puzzling fact that Harvey wants to *contribute* to thinking difference. Near the end of the book, there is a plan for developing historical-geographical materialism. Its first point is that 'difference and "otherness"' should not be 'added on' to Marxist categories but 'omni-present from the very beginning in any attempt to grasp the dialectics of social change' (*Condition*, p. 355). 'Difference and "otherness"' here is shorthand for concerns 'other' than class, and analyses that 'differ' from Marxism ('writers in the tradition of Fanon and Simone de Beauvoir, as well as ... the deconstructionists'; *Condition*, p. 355). Why, then, does Harvey pay scant attention in his own text to any but the major white male theorists of postmodernity – and none at all to postcolonialism (subsumed as 'geo-politics')?

There is a deep ambivalence in the argument here, which cannot be reduced to a quantitative problem of representation or solved by adding references. My reading is also ambivalent. Coming after such a combative text, Harvey's plan is like the conciliatory offer that follows an ambit claim: his materialism will take difference, discourse and image production seriously in return for a recognition of 'real' as well as 'metaphorical' spaces of power, and a cessation of hostilities against 'meta-theory' defined as 'an attempt to come to terms with the historical and geographical truths that characterize capitalism both in general as well as in its present phase' (*Condition*, p. 355). I am sympathetic to the gist of this, and tempted not to niggle at its letter – for example, the reality/language opposition subtending the remark about spaces. Yet the reductive spirit of the rest of the text suggests that the letter can be trusted. For Harvey can *only* analyse postmodernity by first rewriting as 'the same' all the differences that constitute it for him as a topic for debate in the first place.

My reading explores that ambivalence; this is its partiality. First, I discuss an example of Harvey's rewriting of one of his major theorists (Lyotard), in order to analyse the assumptions that can generate the possibility of 'thinking *that*'. This is a way of examining one of the 'conditions' enabling Harvey's postmodernity to take the form that it does. Then I respond to Harvey's rhetorical question, 'if there is a meta-theory ... then why should we not deploy it?' (*Condition*, p. 337), in order to argue that Harvey's fractured 'condition' is more local in its provenance than his text suggests that it is. This is a conventional move these days in the discourse genre called 'postmodernism'. Here, it is also a feminist claim that there *is* no such meta-theory, and that there are good reasons why we should not pretend to deploy one.

Postmodernism, with mirrors

The Postmodern Condition (1984) by Jean-François Lyotard is an important reference point for *The Condition of Postmodernity*. Harvey's title mirrors, by reversing, Lyotard's title, while his subtitle (*An Enquiry into the Origins of Cultural Change*) specifies the difference in genre from Lyotard's text (subtitled *A Report on Knowledge*) that this reversal entails. Harvey never confronts Lyotard's thesis *about* postmodern knowledge; instead, he treats *The Postmodern Condition* as a symptom *of* the postmodern condition, using fragments of Lyotard's discourse to create his own image of postmodernism-as-a-whole. Thus Lyotard's 'grand narrative' and 'metadiscourse' merge in Harvey's 'meta-theory', and the 'specificity' that Lyotard accords to 'language games' (referring to the socio-historical status of rules differentiating practices) is converted by Harvey (who reads *specific* as *local*) into a 'fetishism' of 'impenetrable', 'opaque otherness' (*Condition*, p. 117). 'Meta-theory' and 'otherness' then represent major stakes for Harvey's critique of postmodernism via, respectively, a defence of a totalizing Marxism, and an attack on particularism. In the metonymic style of all good caricature, 'Lyotard' stands for *The Postmodern Condition*, which stands for postmodern philosophy. The hostile figure of Lyotard, then, is crucial to Harvey's text.

So who is Harvey's Lyotard and what is his postmodernism? In a discussion of 'Postmodernism in the City', Harvey identifies Lyotard with the avowedly postmodern architecture critic Charles Jencks:

> 'Why' [says Jencks] 'if one can afford to live in different ages and cultures, restrict oneself to the present, the locale? Eclecticism is the natural evolution of a culture with choice.' *Lyotard echoes that sentiment exactly.* 'Eclecticism is the degree zero of contemporary general culture: one listens to reggae, watches a western, eats McDonald's food for lunch and local cuisine for dinner, wears Paris perfume in Tokyo and "retro" clothes in Hong Kong.' (*Condition*, p. 87; my emphasis)

Harvey sources neither of these quotations, but even a reader unfamiliar with either may doubt the exactness of the echo between the 'natural *evolution*' – a form of progress – of Jencks' 'culture with choice', and the 'degree *zero*' – a condition verging on entropy[15] – of Lyotard's 'general culture'. Doing so, the reader might sense, though Harvey does not, the sarcasm of Lyotard's text.

The sentence from which Harvey has quoted is not a casual echo of Jencks, but an explicit critical reference to his work. It is part of an attack on the '"postmodern" (in Jencks' sense) solution' that accommodates art to capitalism:

> Eclecticism is the degree zero of contemporary general culture: one listens to reggae, watches a western, eats McDonald's food for lunch and local cuisine for dinner, wears Paris perfume in Tokyo and 'retro' clothes in Hong Kong; *knowledge is a matter for TV games.* It is easy to find a public for eclectic works. By becoming kitsch, art panders to the confusion which reigns in the 'taste' of the patrons.

Artists, gallery owners, critics, and public wallow together in the 'anything goes', and the epoch is one of slackening. But this realism of the 'anything goes' is in fact that of money; in the absence of aesthetic criteria, it remains possible and useful to assess the value of works of art according to the profits they yield.[16]

It is hard to read this as echoing Jencks' 'sentiment', even if we mistake the stringent Lyotard for a fan of quiz shows and kitsch. All the pandering, wallowing and slackening here imputed to 'the epoch' demands a view of eclecticism ('confusion') that not only differs from but *opposes* Jencks' celebration. Indeed, Lyotard's censorious remarks about the culture of 'anything goes' are actually 'echoed' by *Harvey*: 'Postmodernism swims, *even wallows*, in the fragmentary and the chaotic currents of change as if that is all there is' (*Condition*, p. 44; my emphasis).

This is not an isolated glitch but a compositional method: in another example, Harvey directly assimilates Lyotard's pragmatics to Richard Rorty's pragmatism (*Condition*, p. 52) despite the *debate* on this very issue between Lyotard and Rorty.[17] Following an image by Barbara Kruger, Deutsche calls this method 'mistaken identity', the representation of difference as sameness; mistaken identity is one of the ways in which the subject of a totalizing discourse secures its own sense of wholeness by relegating 'other viewpoints – different subjectivities – to invisible, subordinate or competing positions'.[18] In some instances, Harvey revises others' positions to make them support his own: thus Giuliana Bruno's well-known essay on the film *Blade Runner* becomes for Harvey an essay by *Giuliano* Bruno – a sex change which for Deutsche corresponds to the way Bruno's essay loses in Harvey's retelling its feminist critical dimensions.[19] Here, conflating Lyotard's arguments with those of two of his adversaries is a gesture of rivalry rather than subordination; it allows Harvey to compose and confront a single 'postmodern' position *competitive* with his own.

No doubt this simplifies greatly the critical task of Harvey's 'survey' (*Condition*, p. xviii). However, there is more similarity between Lyotard and Harvey than Harvey's text can admit. Both are concerned with the problem of value. Both insist on the nexus between art and money. Both take an agonistic view of knowledge as social practice: in dismissing Lyotard's concept of justice as 'pristine' and 'universal', Harvey ignores an affinity between that concept and the text from Weber on struggle that opens Part I of his book.[20] Both Harvey and Lyotard, unlike Jencks, endorse (different) aspects of the project that Harvey, following Habermas, calls 'modernity' (*Condition*, p. 12), and that Lyotard, opposing Habermas, calls 'the Avant-Garde'.[21] For Harvey, 'there is much more continuity than difference between modernism and postmodernism'; the latter is 'a particular kind of crisis within the former' (*Condition*, p. 116). For Lyotard the postmodern is 'undoubtedly a part of the modern'; it is 'not modernism at its end but in the nascent state, and this state is constant'.[22] Lyotard's model of recurrence differs from Harvey's developmental theory of a crisis-driven history. But this is negotiable, given Harvey's acceptance of the 'Nietzschian image of creative destruction and destructive creation' as useful for analysing capitalism (*Condition*, p. 16).

So Harvey's image of 'Lyotard' is produced and sustained in a double operation. On the one hand, denying the difference between Lyotard and Jencks helps to create a monolithic postmodernism centred on 'the [visual] image': Lyotard's contempt for 'TV games' disappears in Harvey's quotation, just as his theory of *narrative* knowledge disappears in Harvey's book; here, difference is represented as sameness. On the other hand, Harvey ignores the similarities between Lyotard's work and his own: the philosopher in Harvey's *musée imaginaire* of postmodernism who most shares his own fears and loathings about 'contemporary general culture' is discredited in a routine way for 'relativism and defeatism' (*Condition*, p. 52); difference is reduced to opposition. Similarity is not identity: Lyotard's pragmatics of discourse is incompatible with Harvey's reflection theory, his definition of economics as a 'genre' is at odds with Harvey's foundationalism,[23] and Lyotard envisages a war against 'totality', not 'the image'.[24] But Harvey cannot debate his *differences* with Lyotard or defend his values against him, because his reading strictly does not see what Lyotard's text is saying.

I shan't begin that debate by echoing Lyotard's arguments: as readers of the myth of Narcissus know, an echo is a gendered mode of repetition that can, in certain circumstances, fail to make a difference. Instead, I want to ask how Harvey's reading of Lyotard can make a sense that is *not* 'mistaken'. As my own reading so far suggests, I do take *The Condition of Postmodernity* to be mistaken in its account of much of the work that it subsumes as postmodern: confusing some discourses (Sherman, Lyotard) with their objects of criticism, it conscripts others to a cause to which they are indifferent (Foucault) or hostile (Guattari);[25] its inattention to the distinct forms of feminist and postcolonial debate entails a serious misunderstanding of what it calls 'oppositional' movements. However, I also take it to be fully engaged in constructing *imaginary* objects. On this reading, *The Condition of Postmodernity* is not only a narrative but, in a strong sense, a fiction. It is reasonable, then, to suspend disbelief, and to ask what makes its 'mistakes' make sense.

For example, there is a difference between Lyotard and Harvey at stake in the word 'eclecticism'. Eclecticism for Lyotard involves an *absence* of 'aesthetic criteria', whereby the realism of money ('anything goes') flourishes in complicity with both a 'slackening' of judgement, and popular consumerism.[26] For Harvey, in contrast, eclecticism implies a *dominance* of aesthetics over ethical and 'narrative' perception. So while both mistrust mass media images and the 'pot-pourri' of global culture (*Condition*, p. 87), each accords a different value to aesthetics. In Lyotard's sense of the term, a philosopher 'does' aesthetics: it is a *practice* of the critique of judgement and hence entails a rigorous rereading of Kant. Harvey's usage is more eclectic. He talks 'about' aesthetics in vaguely Kantian terms: it is a discursive *object* which he construes in massive ways (as cultural production, as artistic practice, as semiosis, as mass mediation, as sensibility), and which he maintains in an ambivalent relationship to Marxist social theory.

I want to give a strong sense to 'ambivalence' here, taking it as a process, not an attitude. Ambivalence is a way of struggling with the problem posed by an impossible object, at once benevolent and hostile, by splitting it in two. Harvey's discourse involves a splitting of this kind: 'the' aesthetic domain is monolithic, but also constructed in opposing ways; the 'overpowering' aesthetic *consciousness* of postmodernity is a regime of illusion, while the aesthetic *theory* specific to modernity (exemplified for Harvey by Baudelaire; *Condition*, p. 10) is a mediating force that can generate knowledge of the real. I want briefly to examine each of these to see how their relationship shapes Harvey's fiction of postmodernism.

The mirror of aesthetics

In one line of argument in the book, aesthetics is effectively the object of a critique of *ideology* understood as false consciousness, and of *myth* as the 'aestheticization' of politics. In this capacity, it is closely associated with the dangerous but appealing figure of Heidegger (*Condition*, pp. 207–210) and its emblem is 'the image'. Aesthetics in this sense is a reservoir of powerful affective forces. It appears on the side of the 'flexible postmodernity' that Harvey opposes to 'Fordist modernity' (*Condition*, p. 340) in his table of 'interpenetrating' tendencies in capitalism, and its value is constructed within an extensive series of binary oppositions. The oppositions most pertinent here give a definition of postmodernity as a dominance of aesthetics over ethics, image over narrative, surface over depth, 'Being' over 'Becoming', place over 'relative space', space over time, language games over 'meta-theory', social movements over class politics – and of 'pluralistic *otherness*' [*sic*] over 'technical-scientific *rationality*'.

Without going any further, it is apparent that this remarkable web of assumptions can act as a reading grid whereby 'language games' will have ontological status (Being), and so will be taken as affirming an 'otherness' opposed to 'rationality' – and may thus be described as 'opaque' (*Condition*, p. 117). The grid also makes it reasonable to assume that a theorist of language games will celebrate 'image' and 'place', and thus approve of Jencks' eclecticism. Within this system, it is not receivable that 'language games' for Lyotard have *methodological* status, and that they affirm the necessity for a theory of social practice to confront changing 'technical-scientific' conditions for the production and status of knowledge under capitalism.[27] Nor is it receivable that this entails a theory of struggle and thus of *linkage* ('genre'), not opacity, and of *conflict* ('the differend'), not impenetrability, in conditions where there is no universal genre, and certainly no 'pristine' justice. In Harvey's terms, the problems posed to Marxism by this theory, and thus the possibility of criticizing it seriously, cannot arise.

Harvey describes his table as a collage compiled in a spirit of fun (*Condition*, p. 338). But this is serious fun: it derives its authority from the rest of the book, and its coherence from a proliferating series of mistaken identities resembling a hall of mirrors. Deleuze and Guattari, for example, appear as a 'Foucault' who 'instructs us' to 'believe that what is productive is not sedentary but nomadic' (*Condition*, p. 44). Foucault does so summarize (in the laudatory genre of a preface) not his own views, but what he calls the 'principles' of Deleuze and Guattari's *Anti-Oedipus*; he means *ethical* principles, and on the same page he calls *Anti-Oedipus* 'the first book of ethics to be written in France in quite a long time'.[28] In Harvey's fiction, however, there is no significant difference between Deleuze and Guattari and 'Foucault'; the latter's 'spatial metaphors' align all three with Being and *aesthetics* (*Condition*, p. 304). Harvey's Foucault even confesses to being 'obsessed' with spatial metaphors, but, Harvey tells us, 'even Foucault' has to ask, 'when pressed', a historical question about the privileging of time over space in modern social theory (*Condition*, p. 205). Historically, of course, a reluctant Foucault was in fact being pressed by a group of geographers to admit that his 'obsessions' and 'metaphors' could usefully be *described* as 'spatial'.[29]

A hall of mirrors can be an obsessional place, every image referring us to another. One way out of this one is to notice that all the paradigmatic sliding between terms on each side of the dichotomy between Fordism and flexible accumulation, modernity and postmodernity, simply serves to restate the modern 'dialectic' of Tradition and Modernity. This is why 'otherness' can be opposed to 'rationality'. Postmodernism is then a new traditionalism – a good description of the *self-presentation* of much architecture, painting and advertising in the 1980s. Yuppies, post-structuralism, feminism and blood-and-fatherland nationalism can all come into equivalence as opposed to the project of Enlightenment. It follows, then, that aesthetics can be to ethics as Reaction is to Progress, and that any discourse questioning the pertinence of the dialectic itself can be subsumed within it as 'aesthetic'.

This is a relentlessly effective way of erasing the possibility of a non-'Heideggerian' criticism that might not be centred by the European history of 'exclusively masculine modernism'.[30] It thus erases the actuality of many projects that share Harvey's suspicion of *irrationalist* discourse on otherness; the work of Michèle Le Doeuff and Michele Wallace comes to mind.[31] Yet it is easy to see why Harvey takes this tack. One of his main concerns is the relation between globally circulating images of commodified ethnicity and *place* ('a plethora of little Italies, Havanas, Tokyos ...') and a global economy that in its hegemony over *space* is generating 'strong migration streams (not only of labour but of capital)' (*Condition*, p. 87). These streams entail the inter-locational competition that divides and conquers working class movements. So Harvey wants to examine the role played in this process by localizing myths of place, and the role that the geography of 'differentiated tastes and cultures' may play in fostering new forms of politics, many of them reactionary. This is one reason why Harvey is interested in postmodernism in the first place, and also ambivalent about it (*Condition*, pp. viii–ix).

These are crucial questions for feminism as well as for Harvey. But describing presentation is not the same as analysing practice. What is said about texts is not the same as, though it may be part of, what they do, and what people do with them; self-promotion does not exhaust social meaning. A great deal of work in cultural studies has addressed these issues; postmodernism is not the only reason why the attempt to read culture as 'aesthetic', aesthetics as ideology, and ideology as false consciousness has long been largely abandoned in cultural analysis.[32] Never asking *how* to connect political economy to a theory of cultural practice, Harvey short-circuits his own enquiry by, first, consigning images to a simple 'masking' role (costume dramas and staged ethnic festivals 'draw a veil over real geography'; *Condition*, p. 87) and, second, by reading the culture/economy relation as somehow isomorphic with his own place/space, local/global, tradition/modernity distinctions.

Taken together, these assumptions have several consequences. First, since 'images' cannot be theorized as practice, it is not really significant that the meaning and function of a 'staged ethnic festival' may be changed by community action. Second, the meaning and function of images are not construed as *conflictual*. Therefore images, in this formulation, are effectively outside politics. Third, since their general mode of action is already known (they 'veil', 'mask') , there is little point in studying particular instances of images in action except to confirm what Marxism already knows. Fourth, to do so extensively would risk 'the Heideggerian trap', and the 'reactionary politics of an aestheticized spatiality' (*Condition*, p. 305). To push this logic to its absurd extreme, only 'global economy' and 'real geography' then remain as proper objects of Marxist enquiry.

Convention tempts me to write, 'of course, Harvey never goes to that extreme' – and of course, he doesn't. *The Condition of Postmodernity* is a vivid as well as erudite cultural history. However, I am interested in asking *why* he doesn't, since in one sense Harvey's history relies in practice on treating aesthetics as an *im*proper object of Marxist enquiry.

Harvey's second line of argument counters his first by giving 'aesthetic and cultural practices' the capacity to 'broker between Being and Becoming' (*Condition*, p. 327); more precisely, they mediate between an aesthetic consciousness aligned with Being (the spatialization of time) and the ethical projects of Becoming (the annihilation of space by time). Harvey adapts this idea from Kant (*Condition*, p. 19, 207), but he does not try to theorize the *material* modalities of aesthetic mediation. Its function for his text is purely formal: he uses it to articulate sympathy for Being, and aesthetics in the first sense, *in* his text: 'there is much to be learned from aesthetic theory about how different forms of spatialization inhibit or facilitate processes of social change' (*Condition*, p. 207). This means, however, that aesthetic forms are thought of as strictly external ('inhibit', 'facilitate') to the processes of social change.

'Spatialization' is a complex term for Harvey, invested as it is in his work with at least three struggles: *for* geography against a vulgar historicism in Marxism; *for* Marxism against a crude empiricism in geography; and *for* a political economy of 'relative space' (global) against an aesthetics of place (local) (*Condition*, p. 257).[33] Here, I am only concerned with the function of 'spatialization' for his theory of representation. There is much to be said about the conviction adopted by Harvey that 'aesthetic judgement prioritizes space over time' (*Condition*, p. 207) and that aesthetic practices involve 'the construction of spatial representations and artefacts out of the flow of human experience' (*Condition*, p. 327); as Ian Hunter has argued, this conviction belongs to a theory of culture binding Marxism tightly to Romanticism.[34] While Harvey is well aware of its historical character in terms of its links with Enlightenment 'mapping', he does not question its general validity as a model of representation, subsuming challenges as a 'crisis' internal to it (*Condition*, pp. 252–259), and he never doubts that aesthetics is 'spatial'. On the contrary: this is what definitively opposes 'aesthetic *and* cultural' concerns from those proper to the history-minded disciplines: 'there is much to be learned from social theory concerning the flux and change with which aesthetic theory has to cope' (*Condition*, p. 207).

'Flux and change' involve the creative destruction intrinsic to capitalism; aesthetic consciousness is one way that people can hold on to their memories and social values, and it is thus immensely important. Harvey is a far from dogmatic Marxist aesthetician. Indeed, from assuming that art is more to do with space than time – coping with, rather than constituted in, flux and change – Harvey goes on to accept that art ('not-time') can have more to do with *eternity* than with ordinary social history. Aesthetic *theory* then 'seeks out the rules that allow eternal and immutable truths to be conveyed in the midst of the maelstrom of flux and change' (*Condition*, p. 205). Again, Harvey notes the historical character of what he calls the 'disjunction' underpinning this discourse. But instead of asking how its tensions are constituted (and for whom), Harvey allows them to constitute his own discourse on a generally 'ephemeral', 'fragmented', 'chaotic' *cultural* condition of postmodernity. On this point he opts out of materialism altogether to affirm with Baudelaire that modern art *is* the 'conjoining of the ephemeral and the fleeting with the eternal and immutable' (*Condition*, p. 10).

This has grave consequences for his thesis. First, it locks in a theory of representation as reductive, not *productive*, of social experience. To say that representation 'converts the fluid, confused but none the less objective spaces and time of work and social reproduction into a fixed schema' (*Condition*, p. 253) denies that representation is always already caught up in social processes of 'work and reproduction'. It is difficult to base a materialist theory of culture on such a premise,[35] and it is impossible thereby to theorize the role of images in service economies, media societies. Second, the idea that representation 'fixes' while experience 'flows' gives the former a magical exemption from historicity; once 'done', it is relatively immutable. This is why Harvey's discourse cannot read a materialist art like Sherman's: it cannot tell the difference between critical strategies of transformation, and eclecticism or 'nostalgia'. This is also why Harvey's discourse cannot tell the difference (which need not be an opposition) between an essentialist cultural politics *dependent* on inherited traditions of identity and community (*Condition*, p. 303), and a 'differential' or 'diasporic' identity politics understood as an historical, as well as cultural, *production* carried out in the midst of, precisely, flux and change.[36]

Harvey's second argument, then, displaces and compounds the problems of the first. Aesthetics as broker between Being and Becoming promises to redeem the reactionary tendencies of aesthetic consciousness; the relation could wishfully be called dialectical. In fact, it gives a positive value to what ends up in both cases as the same operation: an ejection of culture from 'real geography' and (in Jameson's infamous phrase) 'real history'.[37] The relationship between the positive (brokering) and negative ('masking') poles may be described as ambivalent because, in splitting its massified aesthetic domain into good and bad objects, Harvey's discourse sets up 'a non-dialectical opposition which the subject, saying "yes" and "no" at the same time, is incapable of transcending'.[38] Harvey says 'no' to mystification, and to the crushing effects of the time–space compression on which postmodernism thrives. However, the strength with which he says 'yes' to 'the tenets of mainstream idealist aesthetics'[39] is apparent when he presumes that a critical discourse saying 'no' to eternal truths in culture – 'deconstructionism' – must *therefore* be saying 'yes' to ephemerality: 'if it is impossible to say anything of solidity and permanence in the midst of this ephemeral and fragmented world' he writes sardonically, 'then why not join in the [language] game?' (*Condition*, p. 291).

There is nothing unusual in Harvey's refusal here to distinguish deconstruction from pragmatics, or to read the former as asking how 'solidity and permanence' are, none the less, secured and truth constructed;[40] many critics share his views. Nor is it exceptional for a Marxist discourse on culture to promote idealist aesthetics; as Tony Bennett argues, Marxism 'is now virtually the only avenue through which the idealist concerns of bourgeois aesthetics retain a contemporary currency'.[41] What is remarkable here is that 'deconstructionism' is condemned as complicit with capitalism's destructiveness *because* it fails to perpetuate nineteenth century European bourgeois aesthetics. But then, Harvey's fiction is a product of those aesthetics: the one feature common to most of the elements composing the whole fantastic collage that he calls postmodernism – its unifying principle – is, in fact, an abandonment of Platonic theories of the sign and, concomitantly, a forgetting of aesthetic idealism.

The real question, then, is what is at stake for Harvey's Marxism in this ambivalence. McRobbie notes that for Harvey as for Jameson, the critique of postmodernism functions in a peculiar way. There is a 'postmodern *warranty*' that allows them 'a breathing space' from the rigours of Marxist analysis, while bringing them back to that simpler, more direct determination.[42] In Harvey's case, the projection of an 'other space' of aesthetics exempt from materialist analysis is all the more striking in contrast to the subtlety with which he has elsewhere studied the historical production of architectural space.[43] Here, only the *refusal* of materiality to signifying practices makes it possible for Harvey to read cultural 'postmodernism' as a reflection of his own economic narrative ('from Fordism to flexible accumulation') – and then to call that reflection, 'postmodernity'. But why do this in defence of a *Marxist* analysis of culture?

Narrative theory teaches us to look for the 'point' of a story in those self-situating moments when a text inscribes the projected conditions of its own readability.[44] There is a figure of ambivalence inscribed in Harvey's text: the mirror. *The Condition of Postmodernity* unequivocally asserts a reflection model of culture: ignoring all the criticism of this model written by Marxists,[45] Harvey unifies challenges to it as typically postmodern (*Condition*, pp. 331, 336). What I have earlier called the sub-plot of his text is then a duel, with mirrors: the truth of coherent reflection (Marxism) grapples with a formidable force for dispersal ('postmodern' thinking) created in the (negative) image of its own categories.

This duelling story is not a thriller: that reflection must prevail is made clear at the beginning by the prefatory 'argument' and by the early fusion of diverse figures (Foucault, Lyotard, Fish, Aronowitz, Huyssens and feminist Carol

Gilligan) in one coherent representation of 'postmodern thought' (*Condition*, pp. 46–48). But it is none the less a *story* of intellectual struggle. It begins, classically, with reminiscence; 'I cannot remember exactly when I first encountered the term postmodernism' (*Condition*, p. xviii). As a kind of victory approaches after hundreds of pages of conflict ("We feel that postmodernism is over", a major United States developer told the architect Moshe Safdie [*New York Times*, May 29, 1988]'; *Condition*, p. 356), it ends with the narrator meditatively turning toward a future now more strongly sustained by the past: 'from the standpoint of the [moderns], every age is judged to attain "the fullness of its time, not by being but by becoming". I could not agree more' (*Condition*, p. 359).

The story of this struggle is also a self-reflexive or specular narrative text. Written in the genre of polemic, its function in *The Condition of Postmodernity* is to legitimize both the process that it performs (writing difference as sameness) and the interpretive method of the history (reading cultural change as economic change) in which it is embedded. In specular texts, 'significant differences can be perceived only against a background of sameness, rather than the contrary, and consequently … reading such texts is based essentially on a process of comparison'.[46] It follows that the figure of the mirror works in Harvey's text as a how-to-read instruction – a *mise en abyme* of the narrative code.

Mirrors duly organize economic and aesthetic discourse in the book *as well as* the relation between their objects. 'Economics with mirrors', a chapter on Reagan's 'voodoo' economics (in George Bush's famous phrase) and his 'image-building' politics, leads to 'Postmodernism as the mirror of mirrors', a defence of economic determinism *and* an attack on the cultural shift 'from ethics to aesthetics' (*Condition*, p. 336). The argument here seems clear: postmodernism reflects the aestheticization of politics with which Reagan deflected attention from the devastating results of his economic and social policies. But to read this, we must split the figure of reflection into *two* mirrors – the good mirror of Marxist narration (reflection theory) and the bad mirror of the world narrated (voodoo economics/postmodernism).

The bad mirror belongs to the regime of illusion that Harvey calls 'the image'. It not only deflects our gaze, but hides or 'screens' another reality; the 1987 crash occurred when someone 'peeked behind' the policy mirrors (*Condition*, p. 356), just as Sherman's images 'mask the person' behind (*Condition*, p. 316). In this infinite regress of images, the primitive meets the feminine and even 'we' are seduced: postmodernism 'has us … actually celebrating' masking, cover-up and fetishism (*Condition*, pp. 116–117). The good mirror, transcendent, is not projected in social space: it does not mirror the bad mirror, but breaks it. This is the mirror of mimesis, in the sense that it is a metonym of a *theory* of mimesis able to reveal that bad mirrors are mirrors – and to reflect the reality behind them.

The good mirror belongs to the regime of 'historical and geographical truths' that Harvey calls 'meta-theory' (*Condition*, p. 355); its function is to transcend the 'fetishisms of locality, place or social grouping' to 'grasp the political-economic processes ... that are becoming ever more universalizing in their depth, intensity, reach and power over daily life' (*Condition*, p. 117).

The terms of comparison, and the point of its ambivalence, are quite explicit. One mirror commands the universal, the other is mired in the local; one grasps (or 'penetrates'), the other masks (or 'veils'); one wants to know reality, the other worships the fetish; one quests for truth, the other lives in illusion. We are reading here, unequivocally, the dream of Enlightenment Man. I shall also be unequivocal. I am not 'revealing' that Harvey's rhetoric is sexist or 'Eurocentric' – tearing off its mask, so to speak. That gesture would echo the very discourse I am criticizing. Rather, I am claiming that his discourse is forced to produce othering tropes in response to images because its readability depends on denying its own status – *like theirs* – as representation, as material production, as 'image'. Harvey is frank about the playful aspects of his text, but style is not the issue. The problem is that the irresolvable dichotomy of the good mirror ('social theory') and the bad mirror ('aesthetics'), each necessary to the other, installs his discourse in the endless circuit of its own specularity – oscillating between desire and hostility for that 'other' space, its mirror image.

In this kind of circuit, the break that Harvey expects from the mirror of mimesis is impossible. The way out is not for social theory to become more self-consciously literary. It is to think images materially: that is, to take them seriously as proper objects of Marxist enquiry. Refusing to do so gets Harvey into difficulties that he might have avoided. For example, he wants to acknowledge a 'radical edge' to what he calls postmodernism's stress on 'the multiple forms of otherness', and he also wants to see postmodernism as 'mimetic of the social, economic and political practices in society' (*Condition*, p. 113) – again, putting cultural practice outside social relations. He next wants to say that postmodernism is *not* 'solely mimetic', but 'an aesthetic intervention in politics, economy and social life in its own right' (*Condition*, p. 114). But he now has no way of thinking the *how* of that intervention, no way of differentiating one aesthetic intervention from another, no way of explaining how these interventions relate to other kinds of action, and no way of theorizing the '*conjoining* of mimesis and aesthetic intervention' that he asserts but cannot explain (*Condition*, p. 115; my emphasis).

Mimesis does not have to be represented as 'mirroring': Deleuze and Guattari, for example, define it as camouflage, rejecting formalism while avoiding the problems posed by an image/action opposition.[47] Alternatively, feminist rewritings of Lacan's mirror stage have theorized specular processes as socially active.[48]

Jane Gallop's theory of the *temporality* of the mirror stage even offers a way of thinking the Imaginary in terms of creative jubilation rather than ambivalence.[49] But these solutions cannot operate within the image/narrative, local/universal, 'other'/rational polarities crucial to Harvey's discourse. While each, like Harvey, is committed to progressive political projects, their help, for Enlightenment Man, is unreceivable.

The man in the mirror

Beginning an essay on 'Thresholds of Difference: Structures of Address in Zora Neale Hurston', Barbara Johnson asks what she, as a 'white deconstructor', was doing talking about a black novelist and anthropologist, and whom she was addressing ('white critics, black critics, or myself?'). Her answer is that she 'had a lot to learn from Hurston's way of dealing with multiple agendas and hetero-geneous implied readers'; her own text addresses 'all of the above'.[50]

In 'Who Owns Zora Neale Hurston?', Michele Wallace asks as a black femi-nist what the 'mostly ill-mannered stampede' to talk about Hurston is doing for critics addressing 'the crisis in signification that fuels postmodernism and haunts Western self-esteem – and which, not coincidentally, lies at the core of the Afro-American experience'.[51] She appreciatively develops what Johnson learns from Hurston about representation, difference and sameness into a new point about deconstruction, narrative and history:

> The point here ... is both political and literary: black and white, male and female exist in asymmetrical relation to one another; they are not neat little opposites to be drawn and quartered. We recognize the persistence of such measures in our narratives in order to dismantle them in our lives.[52]

It is easy to say that Harvey, with the neat little symmetries of his opposi-tional grids, suppresses this complexity. But it must be said. One reason why 'dif-ference and "otherness"' in Harvey's sense ('the tradition of Fanon and de Beauvoir') is erased from the beginning of his text is that its metonymic method – 'Fanon' and 'de Beauvoir'/postcolonialism and feminism/blacks and women – classifies other discourses as always already *known*. Caricature is not strong on curiosity ('learning'): one or two salient features do duty for 'the rest'; this is why it is a weapon not only for creating new perceptions of familiar objects (as I think Harvey means to do), but for mobilizing familiar ideologies against new objects (which is what I think he does). Caricature is also unifying or divisive in its mode of address, not heterogeneous and conjunctive: 'women, blacks, etc.' defines the reader as someone whose identity must not be at stake in such a splitting of gender and race; we are asked to read, whoever we are, as not-black-women. Caricature is not strong on multiple agendas.

That said, I have to ask what I am doing by appropriating these American exchanges (brought to me in Sydney courtesy of the global economy) for my own white feminist reflection on a book by a man who ignores them. This is the problem of *my* ambivalence (and its mode of address); why do I focus on Harvey? One reason is certainly a sense of frustration at the immense *waste* attending the persistence of what Hunter calls 'the gigantic pincer of the dialectic' in blockbuster narratives of postmodernity.[53] Global problems are posed with a sense of urgency verging on moral panic, but then existing practical experiments in dealing with these on a plausible scale are dismissed for the usual vices ('relativism', 'defeatism'), reclassified as what they contest ('postmodernism'), or altogether ignored. 'One of the prime conditions of postmodernity', says Harvey, 'is that no one can or should discuss it as a historical-geographical condition' (*Condition*, p. 337). This is simply false. Harvey has not consulted the feminist and postcolonial work that does: had he done so, he would have enriched his own account of modernity and modernism.[54] Postmodernism in this sense works for Marxists as a 'back to square one' machine: at square one (unlike 'zero'), Marxism is not seriously in question, and nothing serious has yet been done by anyone else.

Hunter's argument that the cultural dialectic provides Marxism with a technique for *withdrawing* from the actual discursive and institutional sites of present struggle is then convincing. After all, much of the work dismissed, reclassified or ignored by Harvey for its emphasis on gender, race and ethnicity is *about* the problems of articulation which must be faced for any kind of internationalism in a post-Bretton Woods world to be possible. This work counterposes to its critique of 'exclusion' not a demand for inclusion – an adding of minutely specified differences to attain totality – but a politics of conjunction and disjunction. This is what the *feminist* (not 'postmodern') shift in emphasis from 'exclusion' to 'difference' has been about. This is also why feminist critique has not been restricted to canonical forms of 'white Western heterosexual male' domination, or confined to divisive modes. Sandoval's 'US Third World feminist' rewriting of feminism's own hegemonic histories is exemplary of this: discussing the exclusion by white feminists of thirty years' work by women of colour, she argues that an analysis of the latters' alliance-enabling practice can 'produce a *more general* theory and method of oppositional consciousness' in the United States.[55] The non-sectarian implications of this should be clear.

It is more than irritating, then, to see this difficult dialogue between countries as well as cultures condemned as place-*bound*, just as it is more than bemusing to see gender, race and 'ecology' considered local, while class is global. It is utterly unrealistic in the global economic conditions that Harvey so well describes and crippling for the internationalism that he recommends. This, for me, makes a counter-narrative (addressed to social theorists) worthwhile. The flip side of this, however, is that I have to agree with Harvey that of course it *is* dangerous to avoid 'confronting the realities of political economy and the circumstances of global power' (*Condition*, p. 117). I also agree that much work in cultural studies (more significantly than postmodernism) has done so.[56]

At this point, ambivalence encourages me to split its object into the good Harvey (the Marxist geographer) and the bad Harvey (the cultural critic). This is a non-dialectical or 'turf' opposition which I want to dismantle by rejecting Harvey's premise that confronting those realities means accepting that 'meta-theory cannot be dispensed with' (*Condition*, p. 117) – as if geographically global space requires a philosophically *transcendent* space of analysis. I agree that *political economy* must not be dispensed with by cultural theory, but this is not the same as installing it as queen of the disciplines. More abstractly, but more crucially for understanding what is at stake in a feminist discourse on difference, it is also not the same as construing the practice of 'meta-theory' as an *available* option. For if feminist enquiry is not reducible to a demand for inclusion in existing fields, it also does not accept the possibility of a transcendent space from which to subordinate different projects to a unifying logic that would derive its authority from *one* of these (political economy) – nor the foreclosure of conflict such unification entails. It is not, however, 'pluralist' or anarchic: it requires, as Deutsche insists in relation to 'mergers' of critical urban and cultural studies, 'a rearticulation of the terms of urban political struggle and, concomitantly, new conceptions of interdisciplinarity'.[57]

But what does Harvey mean by 'meta-theory'? A large volume could be written about the weird and wonderful mythology flourishing in English around the prefix 'meta-'. One of its features is that 'meta-language', 'meta-discourse', 'meta-narrative' and 'meta-theory' may be used interchangeably to designate a crucial value under fierce attack from precisely those post-structuralist discourses in which the first three terms have quite distinct meanings and the fourth, whether as tautology or positivist dream, is barely intelligible. This 'value' can then be invested with any content that suits the mythologist: thus for Christopher Norris, there are people out there who mistrust 'explanatory systems, "meta-narrative" schemas or any attempt to arrive at a position outside or above the register of bodily experience'[58] (an amazing thought). This *content* is then made the object of an impassioned defence in the name of defending 'meta-(whatever)'. So while it is clear that Harvey often uses 'meta-theory' as a synonym for political economy (*Condition*, p. 117), it is still necessary to ask what value he is defending.

Harvey's four-point plan for the future is explicit but puzzling about the meaning of meta-theory. The latter is 'not a statement of total truth but an attempt to come to terms with the historical and geographical truths that characterize capitalism both in general as well as in its present phase' (*Condition*, p. 355). It is hard to know what is meant to be left over here. If capitalism in general is taken to subsume racism and patriarchy, 'etc.', as characterizing truths, then meta-theoretical statements must be totalizing, if not 'total', in portent. But if we reject this subsumption, then a theory taking, say, patriarchy as its object is excluded from the *meta*-theoretical attempt, thus becoming itself a characterizing truth of capitalism in its present phase, and an object of meta-theory; in which case, meta-theory is a theory of theories that must, by definition, be totalizing.

Part of the problem here, I think, is that Harvey formulates his definition of meta-theory against a critique of 'total truth' that he takes to be fairly trivial. He is not alone in reading any critique of meta-(whatever) as a rejection of those rash claims to exhaustive analysis which are easily forsworn by a serious scholar. 'Total truth' in this sense works, in fact, as a code phrase for 'the other': by invoking resentment from feminists, postmodernists, post-structuralists, 'etc.', of big syntheses, grand narratives, dominant perspectives and loud voices (*Condition*, pp. 48, 253), the mythology of meta-(whatever) works magically to resolve a number of problems. For example, to suggest, as Lyotard does, that postmodern science is defined by an 'incredulity toward meta-*narratives*' is not to say that they have ceased to exist, or to urge us to abandon them for democratic reasons.[59] It is to claim that they are not believed, and that this has consequences for action. To assert that 'meta-theory cannot be dispensed with' (Condition, p. 117) is a non sequitur that merely substitutes faith for argument. It further ignores the institutional context not only of Lyotard's thesis (a report written for a university administration about university-based knowledges) but of its own profession of faith – substituting for 'materialist' analysis a universalizing (university) discourse of moral choice.

The feminist and psychoanalytic critique of totalization raises another issue again. This is a claim that 'meta-theory' is a *fantasy* projected by a subject who imagines that his own discursive position can be external to those 'historical and geographical truths' with which meta-theory, for Harvey, would attempt to 'come to terms'. Thus Deutsche argues that 'the subject of Harvey's discourse generates the illusion that he stands outside, not in, the world. His identity then owes nothing either to his real situation or to the objects he studies'.[60] To qualify as 'open-ended' and 'dialectical' the attempt to come to terms with those objects (*Condition*, p. 355), she continues, can only displace, not solve, this problem: 'in the act of denying the discursive character of those objects, such depictions also disavow the condition of subjectivity as a partial and situated *position*, positing instead an autonomous subject who observes social conflict from a privileged and unconflicted place'. This 'place' can be converted from fantasy into reality only by 'denying the relational character of subjectivity' – that is, by entering the specular circuit of mistaken identity.

From this point of view, the costs of pretending to 'deploy' meta-theory (*Condition*, p. 337) are high. The question then is why some versions of Marxism are still prepared to pay them. Noting that 'in its fear' of postmodernism and post-structuralism '[Marxism] has been unable to distinguish between its friends and its adversaries', Montag suggests that it fears 'its own practice, whose image it cannot bear to contemplate'; postmodernism functions for Marxism as a way of displacing 'what is in reality a crisis of its own theory'.[61] Hence the complicity between Jameson and Baudrillard (and Harvey) in affirming a theory of postmodern culture ('simulation') which is, as Montag says, Platonic in the most traditional sense of the term; in refusing material reality to art and culture, Marxist theory denies its own materiality and hence its inadequacy to its practice. The myth of meta-theory secures the space – transcendent, 'other' – of this denial.

Perhaps this mythic space of meta-theory is really, in Harvey's terms, a place – nostalgic, traditional, local. This locale is 'proper' to a totalizing Marxism mesmerized by aesthetic idealism. It is the place from which it articulates its belongingness to the nineteenth century European society of its origins, while securing its intellectual traditions against the flux and change to which all, under capitalism, are subject. Harvey's fiction of postmodernism is as much about this place and its present dilemmas as it is about flexible accumulation. To say this is not to declare it invalid. It is to say that we can also read it in terms other than his, noting that the postmodern 'crisis of meaning is not everybody's crisis (even in the West)',[62] and asking what Harvey's discourse says about its own sense of crisis. It may be time to ask why the critique of postmodernism has long outlasted the flurry of promotion for the Bull Market art and architecture of the mid-1980s, and why the major narratives of postmodernity have in fact been produced by Marxists – Jameson's work is exemplary – and further developed by social theorists examining the conditions, including Marxism, of their own practice.[63] In other words, perhaps 'postmodernism' is now a privileged space for Marxist self-reflection.

Foucault has a term for an 'other space': heterotopia. Harvey, thinking of an 'impossible space', relates this to the postmodern sense of 'incongruous worlds' that he finds in the film *Blue Velvet* (*Condition*, p. 48). For Foucault, 'other' does not mean 'impossible'. Utopia is a placeless place; heterotopias are *real* places, social counter-sites (like rest homes, cemeteries, prisons in our society) which may, but need not, juxtapose *incompatible* spaces: an example is the traditional Persian garden.[64] Between utopia and heterotopia there exists 'a sort of mixed, joint experience' – the mirror. The mirror is utopian since 'I see myself there where I am not, in an unreal virtual space that opens up behind the surface'. But the mirror does exist in reality, where it exerts 'a sort of counteraction' on my own position; gazing back at myself, I 'reconstitute myself there where I am'.[65]

The relationship of Marxism to postmodernism may now well be of this order. The relationship of feminism to Marxism and postmodernism cannot, or should not, be the same; there are already at least two other terms to contend with. Yet in criticizing postmodernism as a feminist, I have found myself arguing in the past that the critique of 'meta-theory' could be dispensed with; I was mistaken, and in that respect my critique of *The Condition of Postmodernity* is also self-reflexive.

NOTES

1 Barbara Johnson, *A World of Difference* (Baltimore: Johns Hopkins University Press, 1987), p. 178.

2 Michel Foucault, *The Order of Things* (London: Tavistock Press, 1970), p. xv.

3 Ibid.

4 Meaghan Morris, *Too Soon Too Late: History in Popular Culture* (Bloomington and Indianapolis: Indiana University Press, 1998), Chs 1 and 4. On the complexities of cultural studies as an international formation, see John Frow and Meaghan Morris, 'Cultural Studies' in *The Handbook of Qualitative Research,* 2nd edn Norman K. Denzin and Yvonna S. Lincoln, eds (Thousand Oaks, London and Delhi: Sage, 2000), pp. 315–346.

5 David Harvey, *The Condition of Postmodernity* (Oxford: Blackwell, 1989), p. 337. Henceforth '*Condition*'; further references are given in parentheses in the text.

6 David Harvey, *Consciousness and the Urban Experience* (Oxford: Blackwell, 1985); *The Urbanization of Capital* (Oxford: Blackwell, 1985).

7 Graeme Turner, 'Return to Oz: Populism, the Academy and the Future of Australian Studies', *Meanjin* 50:1 (1991): 22.

8 Doreen Massey, 'Flexible Sexism', *Environment and Planning D: Society and Space* 9 (1991): 31–57.

9 Angela McRobbie, 'New Times in Cultural Studies', *New Formations* 13 (1991): 6.

10 Classic sites of this argument are Fredric Jameson, 'Postmodernism, or the Cultural Logic of Late Capitalism', *New Left Review* 146 (1984): 53–92; and Jochen Schulte-Sasse, 'Electronic Media and Cultural Politics in the Reagan Era: the Attack on Libya and *Hands Across America* as Postmodern Events', *Cultural Critique* 8 (1987–8): 123–152.

11 See Mary Ann Doane, *The Desire to Desire: The Woman's Film of the 1940s* (Bloomington: Indiana University Press, 1987).

12 Massey, 'Flexible Sexism'; see also Doreen Massey, 'The Political Place Of Locality Studies', *Environment and Planning A* 23 (1991): 267–281.

13 Rosalyn Deutsche, 'Men in Space', *Strategies* 3 (1990): 130–137; 'Boys town', *Environment and Planning D: Society and Space* 9 (1991): 5–30.

14 McRobbie, 'New Times in Cultural Studies'.

15 Roland Barthes, *Writing Degree Zero* (London: Jonathan Cape, 1967), p. 11.

16 Jean-François Lyotard, *The Postmodern Condition: A Report on Knowledge* (Manchester: University of Manchester Press, 1984), p. 76; my emphasis.

17 See Richard Rorty, 'Habermas and Lyotard on Postmodernity' in *Habermas and Modernity*, ed. R. Bernstein (Cambridge: Polity Press, 1985); and W. van Reijen and

D. Veerman, 'An Interview with Jean-François Lyotard', *Theory, Culture & Society* 5:2–3 (1988): 277–309.

18 Deutsche, 'Boys Town', p, 7.

19 Ibid., p. 6; see Giuliana Bruno 'Ramble City: Postmodernism and *Blade Runner*', *October* 41 (1987): 61–74.

20 *Condition*, pp. 52, 117, 1, respectively; see Jean-François Lyotard and Jean-Loup Thébaud, *Just Gaming* (Manchester: Manchester University Press, 1985); and Jean-François Lyotard, *The Differend* (Minneapolis: University of Minnesota Press, 1988).

21 Jean-François Lyotard, 'The Sublime and the Avant-Garde', *Artforum* XXII: 8 (1984): 36–43.

22 Lyotard, *The Postmodern Condition*, p. 79

23 See Lyotard, *The Differend*.

24 Lyotard, *The Postmodern Condition*, p. 82.

25 Félix Guattari, 'The Postmodern Dead End', *Flash Art* 128 (1986): 40–41.

26 Lyotard, *The Postmodern Condition*, p. 76.

27 Ibid., p. 9.

28 Michel Foucault in Gilles Deleuze and Félix Guattari, *Anti-Oedipus*: *Capitalism and Schizophrenia*, trans. Robert Hurley, Mark Seem and Helen R. Lane (Minneapolis: University of Minnesota Press, 1983), p. xiii.

29 Michel Foucault, *Power/Knowledge,* ed. Colin Gordon (Brighton: Harvester, 1980), pp. 68–70.

30 See Massey, 'The Political Place of Locality Studies'.

31 Michèle Le Doeuff, *The Philosophical Imaginary* (Palo Alto, CA: Stanford University Press, 1989); Michele Wallace, *Invisibility Blues: From Pop to Theory* (London: Verso, 1990).

32 See Tony Bennett, *Outside Literature* (London: Routledge, 1990); John Frow, *Marxism and Literary History* (Cambridge, MA: Harvard University Press, 1986).

33 See also David Harvey, 'Between Space and Time: Reflections on the Geographical Imagination', *Annals of the Association of American Geographers*, 80:3 (1990): 418–434.

34 Ian Hunter, 'Setting Limits to Culture', *New Formations* 4 (1988): 103–123; and 'Aesthetics and Cultural Studies' in *Cultural Studies,* eds Lawrence Grossberg, Cary Nelson and Paula Treichler (London and New York: Routledge, 1991).

35 See John Frow, 'Accounting for Tastes: Some Problems in Bourdieu's Sociology of Culture', *Cultural Studies* 1:1 (1987): 59–73.

36 Significant texts include: Homi K. Bhabha (ed.), *Nation and Narration* (London: Routledge, 1990); Erica Carter, 'Radical Difference', *New Formations* 10 (1990): iii–vii; Dai Jinhua, *Cinema and Desire: Feminist Marxism and Cultural Politics in the Work of Dai Jinhua,* ed. Jing Wang and Tani E. Barlow (London: Verso, 2002); Paul Gilroy, 'It Ain't Where You're From, It's Where You're At … The Dialectics of Diasporic Identification', *Third Text* 13 (1991): 3–16; Chela Sandoval, 'U.S. Third World Feminism: The Theory and Method of Oppositional Consciousness in the Postmodern World', *Genders* 10 (1991): 1–24.

37 See Jameson, 'Postmodernism, or the Cultural Logic of Late Capitalism'.

38 J. Laplanche, and J.-B. Pontalis, *The Language of Psycho-Analysis* (London: Hogarth Press, 1980), p. 28.

39 Deutsche, 'Boys Town', p. 17.

40 See Gayatri Chakravorty Spivak, *The Post-Colonial Critic* (London: Routledge, 1990), pp. 133–137.

41 Bennett, *Outside Literature*, p. 33.

42 McRobbie, 'New Times in Cultural Studies', p. 6.

43 For example, in Harvey, *Consciousness and the Urban Experience*.

44 Ross Chambers, *Story and Situation* (Manchester: Manchester University Press, 1984).

45 On this literature see Frow, *Marxism and Literary History*; Pierre Macherey, *Pour une théorie de la production littéraire* (Paris: Maspero, 1971); Warren Montag, 'What Is at Stake in the Debate on Postmodernism' in *Postmodernism and Its Discontents*, ed. E. Ann Kaplan (London: Verso, 1988).

46 Chambers, *Story and Situation*, p. 29; see also p. 33.

47 Gilles Deleuze and Félix Guattari, *A Thousand Plateaus: Capitalism and Schizophrenia*, trans. Brian Massumi (Minneapolis: University of Minnesota Press, 1987).

48 Doane, *The Desire to Desire*; Jacqueline Rose, *Sexuality in the Field of Vision* (London: Verso, 1986).

49 Jane Gallop, *Reading Lacan* (Ithaca, NY: Cornell University Press).

50 The citations in this paragraph are from Johnson, *A World of Difference*, p. 172.

51 In Wallace, *Invisibility Blues*, p. 174.

52 Ibid., p. 181.

53 Hunter, 'Setting Limits to Culture', p. 110.

54 Along with work already mentioned, see Griselda Pollock, *Vision and Difference: Femininity, Feminism and Histories of Art* (London: Routledge, 1988); and Janet Wolff, 'The Invisible Flaneuse: Women and the Literature of Modernity', *Theory, Culture & Society* 2:3 (1985): 37–46.

55 Sandoval, 'U.S. Third World Feminism', p. 3; my emphasis.

56 Meaghan Morris, 'Banality in Cultural Studies' in *Logics of Television*, ed. Patricia Mellencamp (Bloomington: Indiana University Press, 1990), pp. 14–43.

57 Deutsche, 'Boys Town', p. 7.

58 Christoper Norris, *Spinoza and the Origins of Modern Critical Theory* (Oxford: Blackwell, 1991), p. 50.

59 Lyotard, *The Postmodern Condition*, p. xiv.

60 Deutsche, 'Boys Town', p. 7.

61 The citations in this paragraph are from Montag, 'What Is at Stake ...?', pp. 98–101.

62 Kum-kum Sangari, 'The Politics of the Possible', *Cultural Critique* 7 (1987) 184.

63 Zygmunt Bauman, 'Is There a Postmodern Sociology?', *Theory, Culture & Society* 5:23 (1988): 217–237; Scott Lash, *Sociology of Postmodernism* (London: Routledge, 1990).

64 Michel Foucault, 'Of Other Spaces', *Diacritics* 16:1 (1986): 25.

65 Foucault, 'Of Other Spaces', p. 24.

A Way of Inhabiting a Culture: Paul Willemen's Looks and Frictions

These three film-makers [Nelson Pereira dos Santos, Ousmane Sembene and Ritwik Ghatak] exemplify a way of inhabiting one's culture which is neither myopically nationalist nor evasively cosmopolitan. Their way of inhabiting their cultures ... founded the search for a cinematic discourse able to convey their sense of a diagnostic understanding (to borrow a happy phrase from Raymond Williams) of the situation in which they worked and to which their work is primarily addressed.

Paul Willemen, 'The Third Cinema Question'[1]

What I feel energised enough to try to theorise, the issues I feel compelled to address and the terms in which I address them, are significantly determined by the situation in which I live and work. In my case, that is contemporary Britain. While this is a readily acknowledged truism for most intellectuals, it is also something rarely taken into account in the actual formulation of our work.

Paul Willemen, 'Bangkok–Bahrain–Berlin–Jerusalem: Amos Gitai's Editing'.[2]

Paul Willemen is probably most familiar to film students in Britain and the United States today for his work on 'Third Cinema', a project that emerged, or re-emerged, in the 1980s with an aim of rearticulating the radical internationalist traditions of Latin American, Soviet and European cinemas to contemporary concerns with neo-colonialism, multiculturalism and national-historical experience. The *Questions of Third Cinema* anthology (1989) which Willemen co-edited with Jim Pines helped to shape a revival of interest in comparative cinema studies, and to encourage new film scholarship devoted to 'expelling the Euro-American conceptions of cinema from the centre of both film history and critical theory'.[3]

In an international frame, however, the scope and significance of Willemen's work far exceeds that influential anthology. Willemen is not an orthodox academic.

He is a well-known scholar and critic of Indian cinema, and his essays in film history and critical theory have contributed to the development of cinema studies for over twenty years.[4] So has his work as an editorial board member (1972–1980) of the innovative British film theory journal *Screen*, and as an editor (1981–88) of the comparative cinema journal *Framework*. Employed by the British Film Institute from 1976 to 1995 (as an Education Officer, Funding & Development Officer, Planning Officer and Commissioning Editor), he has worked in many countries across every aspect of film culture: funding, production, festival politics and promotion, archival work, critical discussion, teaching, writing and publishing. Above all, he has acted as a travelling interlocutor for filmmakers, theorists, critics, historians, cultural activists and policy workers involved in diverse Asian, European, African and Australian cinemas.

I have benefited personally from the acuity and brilliance of his criticism, and I owe a major intellectual debt to his work. It is not simply that a dialogue with Willemen's writing inflected my own theoretical priorities as an Australian cultural critic, and that a sometimes 'frictive', but always productive, engagement with his politics helped me define, on many occasions, my own commitments and views. The debt I have in mind is even more fundamental, and it bears on my sense of what it can mean to 'live and work' *as* an intellectual 'inhabiting' a culture. When I was a film critic supporting independent Australian cinema through a newspaper column in the early 1980s, I learned two things from Paul Willemen that I have never forgotten. Both are practical strategies which mark the arguments and the rhetorics of *Looks and Frictions*, and both are wisdoms which go against the grain of professionalized practice in the metropolitan (broadly, US-based) humanities academy today. One is that it is crucial to put 'how?' questions to every theoretical argument and to each political claim: this is a way of developing one's social aims beyond shaping a career in 'critique'. The other is that it is just as important to listen as it is to speak in any comparative exchange: this is a way of making connections with others by learning to recognize what Willemen would call 'the many-layeredness' and even the 'otherness' of one's own cultural-historical formation.

Conditions in the academy today make both these activities difficult. As Willemen points out in his essay on Amos Gitai, 'Bangkok–Bahrain–Berlin–Jerusalem', it is one thing to admit that theory and criticism are practices tied to specific historical moments and geographical locations, but quite another to let this affect 'the *actual formulation* of our work'. Travelling theorists routinely do the former in a prefatory way ('this paper was originally written for an American context') before going on to universalize the value of their work ('but I'm not going to change it for you'). Along with the worsening institutional conditions which most teachers and critics face, 'time pressures' on elite personnel who circulate in global metropolitan space (that is, our involvement in the over-production of intellectual goods by the conference industry) ensure that *listening* to others is an ethic more often invoked than practised. The result is a mode of conduct, and a genre of theory, that Willemen calls 'cosmopolitan'. It is an evasive mode because, in its spatial-historical abstractedness and its miserly use of time, it organizes an academic culture in which 'how?' questions – *political* questions about particular social aims – need never be confronted in realistic and reciprocal ways.

Working as a travelling *interlocutor* involves a contrary form of address that Willemen calls diagnostic understanding (after Raymond Williams), or creative understanding (after Mikhail Bakhtin). It is not a polite and restful process: if Willemen always listens, he often expresses 'other' opinions about one's cherished cultural concerns. This refusal of what he calls *ventriloquism* ('the monopolist-imperialist's guilty conscience'; *LF*, p. 213) has a great potential for friction: there are few things more irritating to a nationally oriented critic than losing an argument to a foreigner (let alone, in my situation, to a 'British film theorist') who follows all the intricacies of multi-layered local debates and still presumes to differ. Yet this is why Willemen's diagnostic is so helpful, his labour of understanding so creative in suggesting what an interactive comparative criticism might be able to achieve. In his essay on 'An Avant-Garde for the 90s', Willemen emphasizes Brecht's 'argument for the things artistic practice should be able *to do*' (*LF*, p. 149); in much the same way, I read *Looks and Frictions* as an argument for developing the positive capacities of criticism.

Story and situation

Following Willemen's example, I would like to discuss the essays reproduced in *Looks and Frictions* by placing them historically in relation to what their author modestly calls 'the situation in which I live and work'. However, it is hard to do this directly from my own situation beyond Britain, not because I live and work elsewhere but because a metropolitan narrative about the history of film theory immediately gets in the way. The essays in *Looks and Frictions* were written between 1971 and 1990. The narrative I have in mind is organized *temporally* by a stark opposition between 'the 1970s' and 'the 1980s', and it supports a fiction of disciplinary development and generational/national succession which could serve as a grid for dividing Willemen's work chronologically – rather than historically – into two distinct periods, respectively typified by *Screen* (Parts 1 and 2 of the book) and *Framework* (Part 3).

In the 1970s, the story goes, Anglophone cinema studies fell under the sway of a hyper-speculative and jargon-ridden discourse, 'British Film Theory', primarily disseminated by *Screen*.[5] While intellectual gains were made, especially for feminism, by the introduction of semiotics, Marxist aesthetics and Lacanian psychoanalysis to film culture in this period, an over-emphasis on 'language' as opposed to 'society' and 'history' combined with an exclusive focus on sexual difference to marginalize issues of race, class and colonialism. At the same time, the difficult style of writing favoured by *Screen* combined with its focus on 'classic Hollywood' (canonical texts) to doom the whole project to an 'academic' elitism.

In the 1980s, things looked up. The productive base of cinema studies moved to the United States. Film scholars reaffirmed the need for empirical work, and staged a return to history. New critical movements began to articulate race, class and nation to gender and sexuality, some through ethnographic and social research based on concepts of cultural identity, some by elaborating 'difference' theories. There was a revival of interest in community-oriented film traditions, and a surge of Anglo-American scholarly research into some non-Western cinemas. Firmly installed in the publishing arms of the global academy, critical writing became less *academic*. At the same time, its objects became more 'popular': work on television, advertising, music video, new media technologies and current commercial films enabled a born-again cinema studies to claim its market share of the boom in 'cultural studies'.

The professional value of such fiction is clear enough: US cultural studies was not the first humanities project to use a little old-historicist triumphalism to legitimate the story of its own miraculous birth. There is also descriptive value in this academic family romance. Willemen himself writes eloquently about the 'insufferably ethnocentric bias' of 1970s film theory (*LF*, p. 207) and the 'abstract, ahistorical notion of subjectivity' that secured its failure to realize a theory of the articulation of text and history (*LF*, p. 151). And while the essays in *Looks and Frictions* are not presented in the order of their first publication (the oldest material is in the third chapter, 'The Sirkian System', while the first chapter dates in its final form from 1981), there is also a difference in style between Part 3 and the rest of the book. *Looks and Frictions* is a text of decreasing surface difficulty, and readers new to the dense polemics of Willemen's contributions to *Screen* may find it more rewarding to begin at the end and work backwards.

It is vital, however, to arrive at the beginning and those taxing, innovative essays that make the later writing on Third Cinema both possible and theoretically rich for political work in cinema. If period-myth has its uses, the chronology that sustains it has no analytical value; brought to bear on *Looks and Frictions*, its first consequence would be to marginalize as archival half the argument of the book – in my view, the very half that has most to contribute to 'contemporary' cultural studies. For example, 'Cinematic Discourse: The Problem of Inner Speech' (written in 1975, revised in 1981) is a theory of *translation* that takes as its premise the constitutive heterogeneity of all psychic *and* cultural activity, and works towards an account of the ways in which the subjective and the social articulate in complex historical experience. The famous 'Notes on Subjectivity' (1978) extends this study of the 'carrying over' of meaning to a theory of ideology as an institutional practice.

A critique of the conditions of ethnocentrism is fundamental to *Looks and Frictions* from the first to the last essay in the book.[6] So is one of that critique's immediate corollaries: the refusal of any model of an abstract subjectivity putatively 'constructed' by 'the text' or by a monolithic 'language'. This is why 'Notes on Subjectivity', a brilliant essay which now risks dismissal for its intricate argumentation as well as its publishing period, is able to derive a critique of what Willemen elsewhere calls the 'projective appropriation' (*LF*, p. 212) of Japanese films to Western modernism from an extended, unequivocal demonstration that 'real readers are subjects in history, living in given social formations, rather than mere subjects of a single text' (*LF*, p. 63). This is now an orthodox claim in cultural studies, but its implications for film analysis have rarely been so rigorously drawn out.

If Willemen's essays from the 1970s offered only a prescient glimpse of a problematic to come, then metropolitan chronicles might be justified in leaving them aside. In fact, they were arguments put forward in a many-sided debate about history and subjectivity that linked work in film theory throughout the decade to feminist and socialist thinking as well as to British cultural studies; serious accounts now place the project of *Screen* (and Willemen's highly critical position within it) historically in that context of debate.[7] My concern, however, is that the useful originality of Willemen's theoretical work is rendered unreadable by the populist professionalism that now dominates large swathes of academic cultural studies.

I have two reasons for this concern. One is that Willemen's analysis of the unbridgeable gap between 'real' readers and authors and 'inscribed' ones never gave rise, as it has at times in cultural studies, to a reductive equation of real readers with *consumers* and of their 'pleasure' with purchasing power. He maintains an intensely critical distance from 'celebrants of shopping and devotees of the short-term, rapid turnover (cultural) investment strategy characteristic of contemporary finance capitalism' (*LF*, p. 164), and he argues for a *fighting*, rather than a market, notion of popularity ('The Third Cinema Question'). In other words, reading Willemen requires us strongly to imagine a difference between the popular and the corporate – and the future and the present – at a time when academics are heavily pressured to accept that critical activity is always already *contained* by market forces. In this context, the fighting element of Willemen's work is easily dismissed as *not*-popular, and thus as other to the marketing self-image of academic cultural studies – that is, as 'academic'.

Second, *Looks and Frictions* does not simply offer a negative account of ethnocentrism and the realities of finance capitalism. On the contrary: from the first essay, the book provides a positive framework for comparative cultural analysis that transforms many assumptions about 'language', 'society' and 'history' sustaining cultural studies. As a theory of thinking, 'Cinematic Discourse: The Problem of Inner Speech' is unique in recent film theory, and it was certainly eccentric to the prevailing concerns of *Screen*. It can be difficult, even strange, on first reading, because its frame of reference is unorthodox, drawing on little-read work by Eikhenbaum, Vygotsky and Luria, and its guiding questions are tough: for example, exactly *how* are 'the psychoanalytic subject' and 'the subject in history' bound in the hybridizing process of inner (or unenunciated) speech?; what *kind* of 'speech' is this, and are there really any grounds for attributing separate 'specificities' to 'language' and 'the image'?; can any cultural politics dispense with thinking about what actually happens as people 'think', and is psychoanalysis entirely sufficient to that task?

Professionalism is a corporatist ethos, unresponsive, on the whole, to destabilizing bursts of originality; it prefers to regulate change consensually through the rise and fall of reputations and seasonally adjusted shifts of emphasis of the kind advertised by the '1970s vs. 1980s' story: *this* is the historical context in which I would like to place *Looks and Frictions*. Since I believe that the conceptual difficulty of some of its chapters derives as much from Willemen's steadfast disrespect for professionalism as from their 'style', I want to map the conceptual coherence of the book rather than the shifts between the essays. One way to do this is to tell another story about a way of living and working in the 1970s as a British film theorist.

A way of inhabiting English

Born in Brasschaat, near Antwerp, Paul Willemen emigrated from Belgium to Britain in February, 1968. His wasn't a simple crossing or a cosmopolitan glide. Emigration is a frictional experience; to *inhabit* another language as well as a different culture is not only to encounter barriers, resistances and gaps, but to live and work, every day, in a chafing proximity, *with* them. For Willemen, landing in London as a Flemish-speaking, French-reading cinephile, one such abrasion was a stimulus to thought. On his own account, the immediate context of his early theoretical work in a language he was learning as he wrote was 'the shock of discovering a culture – English – which did not have a trace of surrealism in it'.[8]

Before emigrating, Willemen spent two years working for the Belgian Cinematheque. In 1967 he organized the first women's film programme ever screened (showing ninety films by women directors), and he worked on the Knokke Le Zoute Experimental Film Festival which took place at the turn of that year. For a Belgian coming out of the vital film culture and the turbulent political climate of Europe in the late 1960s, part of the shock of the un-surreal was encountering an alien formation (capitalized in Willemen's usage), the Literary – 'the ruling English ideology described so vividly in all its suffocating decrepitude in Tom Nairn's classic essay on "The English Literary Intelligentsia"' – that was powerful enough to shape the practices of 'dissident' as well as 'compliant' intellectuals (*LF*, p. 177).[9] An energy derived from this discovery lends zest to Willemen's acerbic analyses of English intellectual life. One feature of this ideology was particularly disconcerting to someone who grew up on the border between Belgium and Holland just after the Second World War. With its history of both imperial *and* populist pretensions to common-sense universality, the confidently boundless insularity of the Literary was (and in Willemen's view, still is) that of a country (England rather than 'Britain') unoccupied in living memory by foreign forces.

Two explicit and entangled consequences of Willemen's discovery of English can be traced in *Looks and Frictions*. One has to do with the insistence of 'borders', montage and the problem of translation in his writing, to which I will return. The other is a method of working in between particular fields of cultural activity and, since this method informs his themes and arguments as well as his concept of cultural politics, I do want to situate it briefly in the wider context of his 1970s work.

As a self-taught intellectual with a cinephile background, Willemen began to collaborate on *Screen* with literary academics. The composite text of any significant journal is defined as much by the conflicts developing within it as it is by its differences from other publications; some of Willemen's major pieces ('Cinematic Discourse', 'Notes on Subjectivity', 'Letter to John') were embedded critiques of other contributors or of the journal's general direction. At the same time, he continued to work for independent film culture in Britain: 'The Fourth Look' (1976), a dialogue with Laura Mulvey's work on visual pleasure, and '*Photogénie* and Epstein' (1981), an argument with David Bordwell, were published in the London magazine *Afterimage*. With the feminist critic Claire Johnston, he also organized a series of special events at the Edinburgh Film Festival throughout the decade, including influential retrospectives and publications on Roger Corman (1970), Douglas Sirk (1972), Frank Tashlin (1973), Raoul Walsh (1974), Jacques Tourneur (1975), Brecht and Cinema (1975) and Max Ophuls (1978).

These public events formed critical spaces of the kind that professionalism now projects as 'outside' the academy, and then wonders wistfully where they went. For Willemen and Johnston, the point was not to situate criticism either inside or outside a single institutional space but to develop a triangular practice oriented towards *film* institutions rather than literary institutions, and capable of linking work in film theory to festival culture on the one hand and independent cinema on the other. The idea was to ensure that film theory could engage with work ongoing in film exhibition, distribution and production contexts as well as with secondary and tertiary education. In this spirit, Willemen organized National Film Theatre seasons on Hammer films (focusing on Terence Fisher) in 1971, and on the films of Frank Borzage in 1975.[10]

Willemen's Edinburgh Festival publications can also be read as critiques of the 'literary' tendencies of *Screen*, primarily because most of them were resolutely focused on single films and directors at a time when the journal was intent on destabilizing both of these figures.[11] In an essay later published elsewhere ('Remarks on *Screen*'), he notes that while 'this dissolving of the industrially and ideologically imposed boundaries of the text as it is circulated by the industry and journalism' was important for theorizing cinema as 'signifying practice', it seriously impeded *Screen*'s ability to stay in touch with the dominant institutions of cinema and film studies, in which single films and directors still held sway; *Screen*'s theoretical 'advances' were bought at the price of a tendency towards institutional isolation.[12]

This remark is of more than archival interest, since it suggests that the tendency of any theoretical project to veer off into what Willemen poetically calls 'the deep space of academia' may be accelerated less by a particular intellectual style or 'difficulty' than by the delinking of academic research and pedagogy from other *institutional* practices. If this assumes that 'theory' is not a self-sufficient activity, it also suggests that a rhetorically populist cultural studies can equally find itself in deep space if it has gestural but no practical links to organized institutional forces other than its own. It follows that a cultural politics needs something that a radical rhetoric does not, namely, a realistic way of negotiating differences between *overlapping* social spaces, combined with a willingness to work in contact (however chafing) with 'the main institutions and forces shaping film culture' at any given time.

In Australia, Britain and Canada, a comparable approach to cultural studies has since taken the form of a turn to cultural *policy* rather than populism. The strength and resilience of Willemen's version, however, is suggested by the speed with which some proponents of this turn have hurtled off into *administrative* and *corporate* deep space by disconnecting cultural policy from 'critique'.[13] Theirs might be called a romantic pragmatist argument. While accepting the professionalist move to institutional isolation (a condition often confused with the limited, local authority ascribed by Foucault to 'specific' intellectuals), it rediscovers the universalizing power of the Literary academic, whether in the common-sense corporate popular or in the specialized discourse of the bureaucrat, or some combination of the two.

Willemen's way of working differs from this. He is a thoroughly pragmatic utopian. By asking '*how?*' to move particular forces in a socialist direction ('An Avant-Garde for the 90s'), he values what Foucault called the 'lateral connections across different forms of knowledge and from one focus of politicization to another' that make it possible, Foucault claimed, 'to rearticulate categories which were previously kept separate'.[14] As much through his work as an interlocutor as in his theoretical divergence from *Screen* and his Third Cinema projects, Willemen has argued for over twenty years that cultural politics is a *relational* 'profession'. For professional critics, this means taking into account 'in the actual formulation of our work' the ways in which a practice carried over or *translated* from one area of culture to another will change its value and its direction in the process of lateral connection; a practice *becomes* oppositional only when it is mobilized in relation to something else, and made intelligible as an alternative to others available at any particular 'focus'.

Unlike cosmo-travel, this montage-method of 'responsible intervention'[15] assumes that the borders between spaces are real and that they make a difference, and it affirms (against defensive nationalism) that borders can be crossed in both directions and that the spaces between borders are open and diverse. The border is a dense and busy place in Willemen's writing; he uses it to organize various linguistic, institutional, social, cultural and national orders of reality, and again to map the comings and goings between them. In a sense, what allows him intellectually to inhabit, even to occupy the insular terrain of English – at home as he is in the culturally mixed 'Britain' described in his essay on Gitai – is the conviction he shares with Bakhtin that (as the latter put it) 'the most intense and productive life of culture takes place on the boundaries of its individual areas and not in places where these areas have become enclosed in their own specificity' (cited in *LF*, p. 199).

Looks and Frictions is a book about this border-life in cinema. From the first chapter, refusing the rigid division between verbal and visual 'language' that sustains cinematic modernism, to the closing section on radical cinema in an economy of globalization, Willemen's work affirms the historical reality of boundaries and limits, while contesting their political power. His passion for a translative practice is shared by many activists and writers ('how many people today', Deleuze and Guattari asked in 1975, 'live in a language that is not their own?'[16]) and so is his belief that 'a sense of non-belonging, non-identity with the culture one inhabits' is indispensable to those intense and productive aspects of cultural life. The special force of his book, however, is to frame its exposition of a politics of becoming with a substantial revision of the models of subjectivity, looking and cinematic specificity which have dominated work in film theory for over twenty years. In the process, *Looks and Frictions* makes central to film history and critical theory the concerns of cultural struggles too often called 'marginal' by transforming the 'major' Euro-American theories of film spectatorship.

Notes on specificity

Some of the argumentation of *Looks and Frictions* uses a slightly unfamiliar syntax. Willemen follows Bakhtin in conjoining a concern for the 'inter-connection and interdependence' of diverse areas of culture with a strong mistrust for what Bakhtin in 1970 called 'our enthusiasm for specification'.[17] Work in cultural studies more usually assumes that 'diversity' and 'specificity' go together; we can even predicate an infinite diversity of plural specificities, and then declare a need for coalition.

There is a complication here. Bakhtin's term 'specification' refers both to a formal method seeking to establish 'the specific features of literature' *and* to historicist techniques for encapsulating works in particular epochs or periods ('in their own contemporaneity'). Willemen's usage more widely embraces both a modernist aesthetic ideology *and* 'attempts to enclose cultural practices within class or ethnic or gender specificities' (*LF*, p. 199). Cultural critics now engaged in the latter activity do not always see themselves as committed to the former. Perhaps very few would do so; given the burden of the Literary in the United States as in England, a rejection of 'formalism' is often taken to be basic to the development of an identity politics on the one hand, and to historical research on the other.

The deep ungrammaticality of *Looks and Frictions* is to argue that all these enthusiasms are, in work on cinema, historically interconnected and interdependent; 'specificity as fetish' (*LF*, p. 149) is one of the chief critical targets of the book. Of course, Willemen does not deny particularity or reject individuation, and he is himself meticulous in making distinctions – demonstrating in 'The National', for example, how the governmental, industrial and financial frames of film production make cultural specificity in cinema primarily a national issue. Nor does he accept that formalism (or any other aesthetic) is *intrinsically* undesirable: he stresses its practical value for charting trajectories in a social formation ('Cinematic Discourse') and even its political value for some institutional occasions ('Notes on Subjectivity'). His polemic is against a *notion* of specificity that mimics, in writing about the cinema, the fetishistic regime of split belief ('I know ... but nevertheless') in which cinematic looking is said to be caught, and against the consequences of this mimicry in the history of film theory.

For example, in his discussion of the 1920s French impressionist ideal of *photogénie* – 'that mysterious, indefinable something present in the image which differentiated cinema from all other arts' (*LF*, p. 124) – he notes that these first theoretical writings on cinema put in place a *viewer's aesthetic* that works to distinguish viewers 'sensitive' to *photogénie* from those who are not. Sensitive viewers recognize that something fundamental to cinema is at stake in their fantasies of a 'purely' visual plenitude, but they also want it to remain unspoken; 'the price of this theoretical insight is that it must be relegated to the unspeakable' (*LF*, p. 129). Paradoxically, this something-indefinable relentlessly attracts attempts at definition which spiral around the 'forever unreachable focal point' that they designate and contain. Willemen traces the spiral of this 'wished-for refusal of the fall into language' through to some aspects of the semiotics of Christian Metz, and in the 'audio-visual fantasy' (shared with Metz by many filmmakers, critics and theorists) of two rigorously distinct homogeneous blocks that may be juxtaposed or combined in a 'psychodramatic confrontation of the figure and the word', but never *merged* 'in hybrid forms of signification, interpenetrating each other' (*LF*, p. 28f.).

For Willemen, several problems follow from this splitting of the cinematic operation in the viewer's aesthetic. Since a desire to repress language is a desire to repress difference, any attempt to differentiate cinema on the basis of an 'indefinable something' is doomed theoretically to fail. But it does succeed institutionally in producing the repetitive spirals of discourse that sustain the profession of the 'sensitive viewer' as critic. Film studies divides into two distinct fields, one organized by the text as a self-enclosed object separated from the viewer, the other by the psychology of the spectator; locked into opposition, 'text' and 'viewer' become the poles of an irresolvable, and thus interminable, 'debate'. As a traditional idealist machine for endlessly generating discourse, this 'debate' is carried over in cultural studies as a confrontation between textual analysis and ethnographic research.[18]

'An Avant-Garde for the 90s' examines the slippage that the term 'specificity' allows between its descriptive and evaluative uses. A descriptive definition of cinematic specificity is indiscriminate; it must be able to cover all films without exception, from blockbusters to 'industrial training loops'. An evaluative usage singles out particular films for drawing attention to the *features* of that specificity. These features are, however, the products of a reading practice and also, in most cases, of a particular professional training; they are made available by a viewer's learned ability to distinguish them. So when critics find that texts are 'ever so cinematically specific … chock-a-block with contradictions directing attention to processes of enunciation and requiring active readers', we simply transmute the value of our own theoretical competence into the value of a film (another exercise repeatable across an infinite number of texts). This is one reason why formalist and populist approaches to film have so much in common for Willemen; in practice, both require cultural practices to repeat the terms of a specificity which is rendered a-historical. A formalist reading for signs inscribing cinematic specificity *and* a populist reading for signs soliciting viewer activity are equally engaged in valuing texts on classic modernist terms: that is, 'according to their high art value, which is no more than the value of the consumer's social and educational status delegated to the object' (*LF*, p. 150).

Most of Willemen's disagreements in the 1970s with positions dominant in *Screen* can be related to his mistrust for 'specificity'. 'Notes on Subjectivity' makes some of these explicit. He rejected the prescriptive aesthetics that attacked realist strategies wherever they appeared, and he contested the 'discourse theory' that precluded any mixing of Marxism with psychoanalysis by enclosing each in the immanent specificity of its field. In his powerful analysis of the rhetoric of subject construction, he argues for a theory of discursive practice that can engage with ideology and with the role of institutions; with the historical variability of the enunciative processes and the traditions of representation enabling different modes of cinematic discourse, as well as of the aesthetic techniques which any cinema may usefully explore; and thus with the 'cumbersome extra-textual' created and excluded by the process of specification. This argument lays the basis for his later critique of Stephen Heath's more complex account of cinema as a specific signifying practice, insofar as this account *postpones* history for 'a still to be theorized articulation with an elsewhere of the cinema' (*LF*, p. 150).

'Notes on Subjectivity' is an intense and illuminating argument linking the institutional practices of literary modernism to the problem of ethnocentrism in film studies. Written in response to a well-known essay by Edward Branigan on Oshima's *The Man Who Left His Will on Film* and Fellini's *8 ½*, it shows how the categories of 'point of view' [POV] and 'character'(terms deriving from the study of the nineteenth century novel) carry with them into film studies the 'ahistorical persons' put in place by the communication model that a psychoanalytic theory of the subject was supposed to displace. For Willemen, only a universalizing use of European concepts of personhood and perspective makes it possible for Branigan, first, to pull *The Man who Left his Will on Film* and *8 ½* into the same space of analysis, and, second, to *contrast* them in terms of their formal structures of subjectivity. The result of Branigan's formalism is that Oshima's film emerges as 'the negation, the reverse side of Fellini's film' (and as a break-through to modernism) rather than as opening up a 'radically different approach to signifying practices' in which the literary concept of character 'is not redefined, it is made irrelevant' (*LF*, pp. 57, 60).

Two related lines of argument follow. One examines the complicity between information theory and the viewer's aesthetic in splitting the cinematic operation.

A formal 'twinning' of the author/sender and the reader/receiver confirms the division of the object of film study by, on the one hand, ignoring the cultural history of authorship, and, on the other, by enabling 'the reader' to figure as the locus of truth, 'the point at which the productivity of the text stops' (*LF*, p. 62). The other argument bears on the ethnocentric pull exerted by the literary practice of close reading that informs cinematic studies of POV. As a professional protocol, close reading insists that evidence be drawn from the phenomenal aspects of a text (or, from our own theoretical competence delegated to the text). In the process, it evacuates from the field of pertinent evidence such historical resources as, in this instance, the differences between 'European monocular perspective, Japanese systems of perspective and Byzantine lack of perspective' (*LF*, p. 64), and the cultural histories of different framing procedures, modes of spatial layering and so on.

Close reading creates an 'outside' of the text consisting of precisely the discourses in struggle to which, for Willemen, the concept of subjectivity should be referred. His method is neither to mirror the formalist move by taking the part of the reader, nor to prolong the paranoid game of inside/outside by deconstructing its terms, but to conceptualize enunciation as a *discursive* process, not a textual 'feature', that occurs in historical time; it involves 'a multiplicity of I's and You's' pulled provisionally into coherence as much by institutional strategies and conventions as by a reader's production of subjectivity via the text. On this account, any text is 'a profoundly unstable economy of discourses' while 'readers, like texts (and for that matter characters within texts) are always sites where pluralities intersect' (*LF*, p. 78). This solution to the problem of articulating texts to history is not unique to Willemen; it simply derives directly from the linguistic theory of enunciation as a *temporal* production of rhetorical coherence and referential power, rather than reducing 'enunciation' (as Anglo-American literary theory is wont to do) to a way of reading the personal pronouns, and thence a 'point of view', marked in a text. However, it is a solution always ignored by re-formulations of a text/context, form/history debate for cultural theory – on the interminability of which the critical industry thrives.

Activist concepts

Willemen's theoretical framework emphasizes *looking*, rather than 'the gaze', and *frictions*, not subject 'positions'. Instead of a viewer's or consumer's aesthetic, he proposes a politics of production (filmmaking, viewing, reading) that refers for its theory of consumption to Bakhtin's model of reading as a profoundly social practice. Willemen does not discard semiotics and the study of film language, or psychoanalytic work on viewing pleasure. Instead, he involves them both in asking *how* the experience of the subject in language and cinema is '*transformed into an analysis of the experience of the subject in history*' (*LF*, p. 151).

Willemen develops his ideas casually, almost anecdotally, as a particular argument proceeds. His concepts gather force irregularly in the movement of a reading; *Looks and Frictions* is not a thesis, but a book of notes and reflections by an essayist committed to an activist model of research and experimentation. Nevertheless, several organizing concepts do carry over from essay to essay and from one context of argument to another, and of these the most important are *inner speech* and *the fourth look*, theoretical concepts dealing with the relations between heterogeneous orders of experience; and *double outsidedness* and *the in-between*, methodological concepts addressing the 'how?' of cultural politics.

'Inner speech' and 'the fourth look' are two processes that explain *how* the interweaving of the textual and the social may be traced in relation to the viewer ('Letter to John'). Each participates simultaneously in the textual, and in the social situations within which the textual arises 'as production or as reading'. Inner speech is the discourse of thought or 'attention': it works with heterogeneous signifiers (images, phonemes, fragments of images, fragments or blocks of writing, schemata, mathematical symbols) to bind the subject of psychoanalysis and the subject living in history; it functions 'as a locus of condensation, a site where the two overlap' (*LF*, p. 51). The fourth look is described by Lacan as a gaze that is not seen but *imagined* by me in the field of the Other. In the filmic process, it is a look that can constitute the viewer as a *visible* subject, raising the possibility of being 'over-looked' in one's voyeuristic pleasure. Directly implicated in both the psychic and the social aspects of censorship and the law, the fourth look 'introduces the social into the very act of looking, while remaining an integral part of the textual relations' (*LF*, p. 115).

Both inner speech and the fourth look are border operations involving mechanisms of translation. Citing C.S. Peirce's description of inner speech as 'a dialogue between different phases of the ego', Willemen notes that the subject of inner speech is both split and *sustained* in the force field of this split '*as the tension between "I" and "other"*', thus enabling social discourse to cohere: inner speech is a 'frontier creature' mediating pressures exerted by conscious, unconscious and preconscious psychic systems, and 'lining' any process of meaning production (*LF*, pp. 40–41). 'The Fourth Look' foregrounds the *interactions* of looks at play in the filmic process. These are excluded from most definitions of cinematic specificity, just as the fourth look is suppressed by aesthetic strategies allowing viewers to imagine ourselves invisible. In fact, we are caught in a complex interaction of different looks from different places, rather than having '*a*' point of view; Amos Gitai's films show that we are mobilized not through point-of-view shots, but through the 'differences between one point of view and another, even within the one shot' (*LF*, p. 171).

Again, the conditions of social discourse are at issue in Willemen's stress on an *interdependent* multiplicity. In the cinema, Eikhenbaum claimed, film metaphor is lined by verbal metaphor for which we must find correspondences (usually without translating again from inner to enunciated speech) in order to understand the film. For Willemen it is the lining function of inner speech, rather than an Edenic fantasy of an unsullied visuality, which explains the *excess* of images over verbal language. From this he derives a principle that follows through to the project of Third Cinema: if the 'infinite polysemy' of images always produces untranslated or unanalysed material, there can be no *unanalysable* material; no *photogénie*, no ineffable Difference; all languages have their unspoken, but languages do overlap. On the side of the fourth look, our textual mobilization is always regulated by institutional constraints and incitements. Public concern about pornography, for example, involves 'the institutionalization of the fourth look within a social formation', while games of taste and cultural distinction entail hierarchical valuations: if shame is attached to those caught looking at porn, 'some would even go so far as to want to be seen looking at an Altman film' (*LF*, p. 115). To these examples, we could add political conflicts about ethnic and sexual representations whose public circulation is 'overlooked' by the people to whom they claim, or presume, to refer.

Inner speech and the fourth look are frictional processes for Willemen, and they also overlap in his thinking; together, they map something like a theory of cinematic experience. Inner speech acts as a cement between text, subject and the social, while the textual and social regulation of the fourth look participates in the ideological process whereby bundles of discourses in struggle are pulled into coherence through institutions. Ideology (understood as a discursive formation's *mode* of coherence) is never treated in *Looks and Frictions* as a purely imaginary play of relations, still less as a message or structure smoothly transmitted from 'texts' to 'subjects'. Ideologies are the everyday product of the mundane, grating labour of institutions. In cinema, inner speech and the fourth look enable this endless unifying labour, this production of cohesion, to continue. At the same time, their translative force ensures that coherence is an unstable process, not a static condition, and that unities take a fragile and provisional form. This is why social formations are dynamic and contestable, and why an effective cultural politics must engage with institutions.

This is also why Willemen's theory of experience is not a theory of cinematic specificity, but a theory of historical *particularity*; it is a theory not of the consumption of cultural goods but of the production of social change. Just as inner speech is a 'locus of condensation' where different modes of subjectivity overlap, so group as well as individual identities for Willemen are 'riven as well as constituted' by the processes-in-tension that ceaselessly challenge or consolidate social formations: 'identities are the names we give to the more or less stable figures of condensation located at the intersection of psycho-social processes' (*LF*, p. 217). In the logic of *Looks and Frictions*, it is impossible to oppose 'language' to 'society and history' or to displace one term by the other; there is no such thing as a transcultural or transhistorical 'gaze' to which a twist of difference theory and identity politics must somehow then be applied.

In Willemen's theory of looking, any 'subject production' effected by a film must pass through inner speech to interact with the social and psychoanalytic histories combining to produce that particular 'individual' in that place and at that time. On this foundation, he examines different social and aesthetic strategies used by filmmakers (Douglas Sirk, Steve Dwoskin, Max Ophuls) who formally explore identities by soliciting a complex interaction with a particular *culture* of 'looking', which they work to inflect or modify in different directions. In a third movement, Willemen uses Bakhtin's concept of the chronotope ('time–space articulations characteristic of particular, historically determined ways of conceptualizing social existence'; *LF*, p. 189) to develop a comparative analysis of the ways that nationally as well as aesthetically diverse cinemas use particular cultural spaces (as representation) to make histories intelligible *for* particular cultural spaces (as a mode of address).

'Complex seeing', a phrase taken from Raymond Williams, is one name for this process of diagnostic understanding that binds filmmaking to film viewing in an interactive mode; as a way of inhabiting a culture, it is irreducible to either pole, 'text' or 'subject', of the viewer's aesthetic (*LF*, p. 141). Exploring film's ability to make us recognize spaces in which history can be seen at work, Willemen represents cinema not primarily as staging a drama of the subject in process, as Stephen Heath has suggested, but as engaging people's experience of *history* in process. In this space of analysis, an avant-garde cinema is not involved in reproducing the routine shock of the new, but in working to direct and to intensify cinema's power to connect: it is 'a cinema that doesn't just ask the question of cinema historically, but the questions of history cinematically' (*LF*, p. 159). It follows that formal research and experimentation are – like careful critical analysis – vital aspects of production. Released from the spiral of modernism's search for a redundant specificity, experiment and criticism are basic to a cinema that seeks to render a particular social situation intelligible *for* a particular culture; that is, they are fundamental to a responsive and realistic cultural politics.

'In-between' is a term Willemen uses to describe a double movement of translation between aesthetic and social strategies, and cinematic and historical modes of understanding. First sketched in his study of the 'peculiar in-between strategies' of the films of Max Ophuls (in which 'the look is simultaneously subjected to two forces pulling it in different directions'; *LF*, p. 138), the idea of an 'in-between' *mode of address* is most explicitly developed in his essay on Amos Gitai's editing. Editing, he notes, is traditionally used and discussed as a way of limiting ambiguity, whereas in cinema it might more accurately be called 'the *orchestration* of meaning' (*LF*, p. 165). Like the work of Sembene, Ghatak, Chantal Akerman and David and Judith McDougall, Gitai's films work with, as well as upon, the viewer's knowledges and skills, in a register that is 'in-between intellectual and mood manipulation'; in orchestrating meanings as an argument, not an order, addressed to the viewer, Gitai's is a 'nudging, essentially friendly kind of discourse' in which the authorial voice is neither authoritarian, as in 'social concern' documentaries, nor effaced, as it is in 'community' video (*LF*, pp. 166–167).

Willemen comments that this method is hard to describe, and he often presents it initially as a 'neither/nor' proposition: Gitai's cinema is neither realist nor modernist, neither populist nor formalist, and neither assumes a 'bogus neutrality' nor resorts to the 'flashy enunciation strategies' of stylistic innovation (*LF*, p. 167). The descriptive struggle in these passages testifies to the immediacy with which this cinema mobilizes Willemen's own sense of the need for film theory to disengage from the dualisms that dominate its history; *Looks and Frictions* is at least partly a book about the inadequacy of current critical rhetorics for engaging with creative contemporary cinema. At the same time, his own rejection of 'neutral' and 'flashy' enunciative modes carries his conviction that a cultural politics must work positively as well as polemically with the culture it presumes to address. Willemen's authorial voice is never neutral, and he does not engage in the critic's equivalent of the routine pursuit of the new. He uses the conceptual stock-in-trade of metropolitan critical culture (including our interest in borders and translation) in order to nudge his analyses through the moment of neither/nor to find another way of thinking about familiar issues.

His work on 'the national' is exemplary of this. Arguing in-between the poles of the debate traditionally opposing internationalism to nationalism, he frames the issue of national cinema as 'primarily a question of address' (*LF*, p. 212). On the one hand, he reminds us that the fiscal, legal and educational systems put in place by national governments have consequences both for social power relations and the kind of cinema they enable; people's lives are shaped by histories made 'nationally specific' by the boundaries that frame the terrain of a particular government's writ. On the other hand, the economic facts of cinematic life dictate that an industrially viable cinema must follow one of two cultural logics: it must either address an international market ('multinational' cinema) or a very large domestic market (a 'national film industry' attuned to the project of nationalism).[19] Both of these logics are homogenizing. It follows that only a marginal, poor, dependent and *non*-nationalist cinema can critically engage with the 'multidimensional and multidirectional tensions' of actual social life. So Willemen concludes that a marginal cinema is now the only form of national cinema available: 'the only cinema which consciously and directly works with and addresses the materials at work within the national cultural constellation' (*LF*, p. 212).

The internationalism of Third Cinema and avant-garde cultural practice can then be rethought in terms of a shared methodological field, not a unifying aesthetic, and a comparative, rather than a common, politics of culture. *Double-outsidedness* connects the otherness involved in inhabiting one's culture (non-belonging, non-identity) to the 'outsidedness' involved in creatively understanding *another* culture. This again entails a movement across borders in two directions, and in-between the poles of a neither/nor: double-outsidedness is neither an act of identification with an image of 'one's own' People (the invisibility option for intellectuals), nor a projective appropriation of identities elsewhere (ventriloquism); the analyst must 'relate to his or her own situation as an other' on both sides of a given border (*LF*, p. 216).

This is why the project of displacing Euro-American conceptions of cinema from the centre of film history and critical theory does not confront them with a 'globalized other' imagined as *non*-Euro-American: 'third cinema' for Willemen is not an Oshima–Fellini contrast writ large. Nor does it exclude the relations of otherness and the internal histories of political and cultural suppression constituting 'Europe' and 'America' as metropolitan states of mind. The shared methodological field is organized by unequal power relations as well as by cultural difference; for Western critics studying cinemas which are *not* European or American, a doubly-outside position entails a responsibility for the potential effects of their criticism as it circulates back to the national space of those cinemas. Willemen's essay on melodrama and industrialization, 'The Sirkian System', links up with 'The National' in discussing the example of Western readings of Indian cinema.

Along with these organizing concepts, *Looks and Frictions* also offers practical ways of organizing comparative cinema studies as a project of transformation. One is to investigate 'the mode of *attention*' proposed by particular films, or scenes in films, in interaction with the actual social constraints, the institutional demands and the personal as well as cultural practices of looking that any text may encounter. This is a way of displacing 'the subject', 'the gaze' and 'the text' as privileged terms of analysis by asking a different question about historical experience in cinema. When Willemen argues that films are read unpredictably and can be pulled into more or less any ideological space, he does not do so in the name of the abstract liberty of the consumer. A mode of attention is always negotiated *in-between* a film and the inner speech of subjects looking (not always only at film) in a real, densely layered social space. An emphasis on inner speech requires film theory to take account of attention (thought) itself as a mobile process that 'allows for various degrees of intensity, from day-dreaming to focussed concentration' (*LF*, p. 39).

To do this is to conceptualize cinema in terms of energy, time and mobilizing power; in Willemen's vocabulary, filmic utterances are *corridors*, rather than arte-facts or vehicles of a singular personal expression. His studies of Sirk, Dwoskin, Ophuls, Gitai and films such as *Maeve* and *So That You Can Live* draw out the descriptive implications for film analysis. Unlike many theorists of consumption, Willemen does not erase the labour and desires of filmmakers from his account of cultural practice. On the contrary, he elaborates their efforts to affect the social contexts and historical moments that their work will unpredictably encounter. Correspondingly, an evaluative way of examining cinema's capacity for transfor-mation is provided by the notion of trajectories in meaning production. This is what Willemen calls 'the question of directionality', as distinguished from the question of specificity, in cinema, and it comes down in practice to asking: in which direction do these discourses seek to *move* their viewers and readers?

The same question can be put to the project in which it arises. *Looks and Frictions* seeks to move readers away from the search for specificity in part because of the incapacity this search induces (even in the sophisticated form of a theory of disartic-ulated subjectivity) to formulate social and political directions; it supports a move-ment away from the question 'how to speak?' and towards a critical practice that begins by asking 'how to understand social existence?'. Taken seriously, this question seeks to move academic film studies towards an engagement with the open histori-cal conflicts taking place on the boundaries of culture and in-between institutions. However, the choice of a direction in these conflicts is never a matter of an *aesthet-ics* of transformation for transformation's sake: 'the social can change in a number of different directions, many of which are not especially desirable' (*LF*, p. 151).

Politics now

To map the coherence of *Looks and Frictions* is difficult only in the sense that it means tracing the logic of a project that pushes as far as possible our understand-ing of cinema as a dynamic and creative cultural force. Cinema for Willemen is a mode of action as complex and as varied as the lives of all the people who make films and all the people whom films address. To acknowledge this energy and complexity is readily done; to take it into account in the actual formulation of our work is a much more difficult task. *Looks and Frictions* makes intense demands on academic readers, in that it asks us to question the formulation, as well as the direction, of our own practice.

In this respect, *Looks and Frictions* may well be an untimely publication. Willemen has the same passionate commitment to the value of criticism, to the ethic of social responsibility, and to the pleasure of intellectual work, that he treasures in the Third Cinema manifestos of the 1960s. This commitment is not always shared today by professional students of culture. As Willemen notes, the constant reference to pleasure in British and American discussions of popular culture today has a restrictive force: the pleasures of *understanding* 'are nearly always outlawed or stigmatised' (*LF*, p. 215). At the same time, any suggestion that intellectuals have a responsibility to exercise our knowledges and skills in the analysis of the social formations we inhabit can be dismissed as 'elitist' (*LF*, p. 164). Australian critics are in a slightly different situation. We are encouraged to accept responsibility as long as our work has a clear and constructive 'nation-building' purpose; in this context, the value of critique ('unconstructive') is itself called into question by professional critics.

I think that Willemen is right to see in these developments a movement of deskilling, and I am persuaded by his rage against the class self-hatred that makes it easy for intellectuals to acquiesce in the denial of our knowledges and even to seek virtue in acquiescence. Among the many things I love about *Looks and Frictions* is Willemen's own love of 'critical lucidity': his struggle, not least between languages, to achieve it by responding with care, with pleasure, to a difficult problem or an intricate phase of someone else's thinking; his humour as well as his anger about the frailties of 'compliant' intellectual conduct; his refusal to accept that the only way out of academic deep space is a 'malevolently para-noid anti-intellectualism' (*LF*, p. 164); his devotion to cinemas that strain our powers of translation and intensify our understanding of social life; his irre-pressibly active internationalism; and his practical intelligence in finding ways for the lucidity he values to survive an everyday, grating involvement with cul-tural institutions.

Untimely or not, *Looks and Frictions* has a practical as well as a lucid contri-bution to make to film studies now. As the 1970s–1980s story circulates as dom-inant professional myth, another spiral of discourse takes shape: there are whispers of a formalist revival, fond memories of 'the signifier'; a restless impa-tience with literary celebrations of 'the self' parading as political interventions, and a yearning for textual analysis that 'makes the film read like a film'.[20] Willemen's work does not give support to this (or any other) 'back to ...' move-ment of redoubling in the disciplinary saga. It does offer a lucid account of the pressures shaping the saga itself, and a set of practical alternatives for thinking cinematic discourse, society and history together.

Instead of adopting a comfortless cynicism about the cycles of academic fashion, Willemen reminds us that 'specificity as fetish' *institutionally* imposes an endless pursuit of lost objects: when Text is the privileged object of analysis, we discover that subjectivity has been lost; once the Subject becomes the favourite term, we find that its history has been lost; with History enshrined as the hottest thing, we complain that textuality has been lost. Deleuze and Guattari call this kind of spiral a *tragic regime of infinite debt*: 'nothing is ever over and done with in a regime of this kind. It's made for that'.[21] Like their work in philosophy, however (with which *Looks and Frictions* shares a careful reading of Bakhtin), Willemen's revision of film theory challenges that regime's practical capacity to petrify thought in cinema. His effort to think heterogeneity as constitutive at every level of cinematic activity is also an effort to show how a direct engagement with questions of cultural difference and social identity can accompany, and also sustain, a rigorous as well as a distinctive theoretical project. Willemen's way of inhabiting a culture is unrepentently critical as well as irreducibly political. I think we need that right now.

NOTES

1 In Paul Willemen, *Looks and Frictions: Essays in Cultural Studies and Film Theory* (London, Bloomington and Indianapolis: British Film Institute and Indiana University Press, 1994), pp. 177–178.

2 Willemen, *Looks and Frictions*, henceforth *LF*, p. 162. Further references are in parentheses in the text.

3 Jim Pines and Paul Willemen, eds, *Questions of Third Cinema* (London: British Film Institute, 1989). This publication followed a conference held in Edinburgh in 1986. The citation here is from Willemen, *LF*, p. 190.

4 See *Indian Cinema,* ed. Behroze Ghandy and Paul Willemen (London: British Film Institute, 1980) and *Encyclopaedia of Indian Cinema,* eds Ashish Rajadhyaksha and Paul Willemen (London and Delhi: Oxford University Press and British Film Institute, 1994).

5 See, for example, Jane Gaines, 'White Privilege and Looking Relations: Race and Gender in Feminist Film Theory', *Cultural Critique* 4 (Fall 1986): 59–79; and Judith Mayne, *Cinema and Spectatorship* (London: Routledge, 1993). Critical accounts of this story are given in Patrice Petro, 'Feminism and Film History', *Camera Obscura* 22 (1990): 9–26, and Lesley Stern, 'Remembering Claire Johnston', *Framework* 35 (1988): 114–122.

6 See also Paul Willemen, 'The Films of Akira Kurosawa', *Screen Education Notes* 1:1 (1971): 34–35; and 'Haile Gerima Interview', *Framework* 7:8 (1978): 31–35.

7 See Anthony Easthope, *British Post-Structuralism* (London and New York: Routledge, 1998), and Nicholas Garnham, 'Subjectivity, Ideology, Class and Historical Materialism', *Screen* 20:1 (1979): 121–133.

8 Personal correspondence.

9 See Tom Nairn, 'The English Literary Intelligentsia' in *Bananas,* ed. Emma Tennant (London: Blond & Briggs, 1977), pp. 57–83.

10 See Tom Milne and Paul Willemen, *The Aurum Encyclopaedia of Horror* (London: Aurum Press, 1986).

11 Mike Wallington, David Will and Paul Willemen, eds, *Roger Corman: The Millenic Vision* (Edinburgh: EIFF, 1970); Claire Johnston and Paul Willemen, eds, *Tashlin* (Edinburgh: EIFF, 1973); Paul Willemen, 'The Fugitive Subject' in *Raoul Walsh,* ed. Phil Hardy (Edinburgh: EIFF, 1974); Claire Johnston and Paul Willemen, eds, *Jacques Tourneur* (Edinburgh: EIFF, 1975); Paul Willemen, ed., *Pasolini* (London, British Film Institute, 1977); Paul Willemen, ed., *Ophuls* (London: British Film Institute, 1978).

12 Paul Willemen, 'Remarks on *Screen*', *Southern Review* [Adelaide] 16:2 (July 1983): 292–311.

13 See Tony Bennett, 'Putting Policy into Cultural Studies' in *Cultural Studies,* eds Lawrence Grossberg, Cary Nelson and Paula Treichler (New York and London: Routledge, 1992); Stuart Cunningham, 'TV Violence: the Challenge of Public Policy for Cultural Studies', *Cultural Studies* 6:1 (1992), 97–115; and the critical overview provided by Tom O'Regan, '(Mis)taking Policy: Notes on the Cultural Policy Debate', *Cultural Studies* 6:3 (1992), 409–423.

14 Michel Foucault, *Power/Knowledge: Selected Interviews and Other Writings, 1972–1977,* ed. Colin Gordon (London: The Harvester Press, 1980), p. 127.

15 Willemen, 'Remarks on *Screen*', p. 298.

16 Gilles Deleuze and Félix Guattari, *Kafka: Toward a Minor Literature,* trans. Dana Polan (Minneapolis: University of Minnesota Press, 1986 [1975]), p. 19.

17 Mikhail Bakhtin, *Speech Genres and Other Late Essays,* trans. Vern W. McGee (Austin: University of Texas Press, 1986), p. 2.

18 See Virginia Nightingale, 'What's "Ethnographic" about Ethnographic Audience Research?' in *Australian Cultural Studies: A Reader,* ed. John Frow and Meaghan Morris (Sydney, Urbana and Chicago: Allen & Unwin and University of Illinois Press, 1993), pp. 149–161.

19 See Paul Willemen, 'The Making of an African Cinema', *Transition* 58 (1992): 138–150.

20 Toby Miller, '(How) Does Film Theory Work?', *Continuum* 6:1 (1992): 186–211. See also Geoff Mayer, 'A Return to Form – Russian Formalism and Contemporary Film Practice', *Metro* 93 (1993): 18–29.

21 Gilles Deleuze and Félix Guattari, *A Thousand Plateaus,* trans. Brian Massumi (Minneapolis: University of Minnesota Press, 1987 [1980]), p. 113.

7

An Ethics of Uncertainty: Naoki Sakai's Translation and Subjectivity

In Naoki Sakai's first book, *Voices of the Past: The Status of Language in Eighteenth Century Japanese Discourse*, there is a wonderful passage about a subject with which I am entirely unacquainted, the ethics of Ito Jinsai (a seventeenth century Confucian scholar and critic of Song rationalism), which disconcerts and delights me with a sense of partial familiarity. Expounding the conception of sociality in the Song philosophy of mind, Sakai notes that the primordial agreement of Zhu Xi's ideal community assumed 'a transparency of communication comparable to the face of a clear mirror' secured by subduing the 'dust' of materiality, the 'trace', in Ito's terms, of all the accidents, surprises, blockages and sheer bodily energy of actual social encounters: 'as though incommensurability ought not to have been there, as though it were somewhat outrageous and morbid to admit that one cannot actually know another's mind'.[1]

More than the structuring contrast between idealist and materialist philosophies that guides me through the passage (as I learn that Ito situated virtue outside the mind, in social relationships with others and in the 'actual execution of social action'), the phrase 'somewhat outrageous and morbid' jolts my imagination. By-passing any timidity about extrapolating from a comparison of two modes of Confucianism equally new to me, it irresistibly sets me thinking about the prim dust-busters of the Anglo-American academy today – those so outraged by any sort of 'opacity' in a text, any 'obscurity' clouding (from them) the point of an argument, any 'dense' talk of textuality in relation to practical activities, that they can bear no serious discussion of the social grit of incomprehension as an intrinsic rather than incidental factor in communication.

Certainly, few of today's advocates of 'unruffled empathetic transference'[2] might agree with Zhu Xi that the mind's interior is equivalent to the totality of the universe in its rationality; these days, achieving conformity with corporate formats of thought is ambition enough. They simply prefer not to make a fuss about such stuff as 'incommensurability'; to get on with things *as though* contingency and otherness can be rendered immaterial to the conduct of social life, and *as though* transparency and reciprocity were possible between people of good will. So what strikes them as morbid about the discursively reflexive work called 'theory' in the Humanities is its habit of emphasizing the aporia of 'another's mind' as the problem arises in diverse forms – often trailing clouds of discomfiting social and historical dust – in the everyday life of scholarship.

From this perspective, there is more to the famous opacity of theory than a convoluted syntax or a taste for tainting plain English prose with dense dollops of Latin. Theory's opacity is more incorrigibly a matter of foregrounding whatever smudges *in practice* transparency of communication and ruffles the smoothness of professional exchanges. Complicating activity with paralysing talk of ambivalence and undecidability, querulously finding differences rumpling every situation, endlessly wondering 'what are we doing?' and worrying 'who is "we"?', theory itself is a 'dusty' practice: an irritant or, worse, a divisive agent in an academy streamlined for speedy information flow and efficient knowledge production. By making people think too much about the conditions of their practical agency – about the subject as *shutai*, in Sakai's philosophical vocabulary – theory obscures the clear objects of study required by responsible scholarly work.

Returning to *Voices of the Past*, I find that this detour has taken me no great distance from Sakai's account of how Song rationalism pathologized the very possibility of admitting heterogeneity and contingency as material facts of life; it may in fact bring me closer to appreciating the otherness of Song rationalism. Zhu Xi's argument gained rhetorical force, Sakai says, by proceeding as though incommensurability 'ought not to have been there' in its perfectly ordered world: 'it persuaded readers to accept the image of what would happen if communality were not there and convinced them that such a situation would never ensue'. Now, I well know the device of hinting that the stability of the world as we know it depends on sustaining in communities a *communal* sense of cohesion. However, no argument in the world known to me could carry conviction by rendering harmony primordial and cataclysm impossible. The hints I hear gain their force as threats from an already accepted image of chaos as cosmic in scale, and disaster as ever-ready to ensue from the ordinary disorders of modernity.

Yet this is how jeremiads against theory are able to sound convincing when they pathologize the activity of taking seriously a heterogeneity and a power of contingency widely agreed to be 'there'; volatile forces in an inherently dangerous world, they are best observed by an uninvolved epistemic subject (*shukan*) operating at immense distance, 'as though' from another planet. In this mode of containment, otherness and incommensurability may be 'there' but not in 'this' enunciative practice, 'this' discipline, 'this' community. Hence the resonance of the hint, its threat: what might happen if communality were not *here*?

This is the sort of question that has prompted apparently sober scholars in recent years to credit assorted theoretical practices with nation-wrecking powers beyond the wildest dreams of theory's most unworldly proponents. Given the excesses of such polemics, it is easier now to ridicule the fear impelling this question than to begin to answer it, as Sakai does in his volume of essays, *Translation and Subjectivity: On 'Japan' and Cultural Nationalism*. Ridiculing the fears of others, of course, can be a way of avoiding one's own. Anxiety about 'what might happen' immediately seems less absurd if the question is rephrased as a demand for a practical image of a non-'communal' sociality, for example: how is it possible to create a transnational space of debate that crosses linguistic as well as racial, ethnic, gender, sexual and religious boundaries?

Such a space certainly seems desirable, as existing national modes of regulating community are reshaped by the very forces of economic and technological change that are rendering so uncertain traditional ideals of distance and separation between a scholar and 'his' objects of study, once there to be talked about, now here and talking back. Yet is it *possible*?: a space, say, where people could confront from different contexts the legacy of the imperialisms that have given all the categories of 'culture' so much of their diversely lived rigidity? while also engaging with the new geographies of capitalism transforming the very concept of 'global' power along with the maps and material forms of its distribution? a space in which people who *really* share no sense of communality could articulate their differences – without ignoring the new questions of class interest posed by the emergence of the space itself in the dreams of intellectuals dispersed around the world?

If this scenario, or something like it, seems desirable, it can also seem hopelessly utopian. Formidable problems face any experiment in creating such a space, on however small a scale. Produced in actual places, intellectually transnational spaces are often exhausting, even dire – sizzling with acrimony, accusation, power plays less than candidly pursued, self-servingly tactical essentialisms, and an endless looping of the process of disclosing the ethnocentrism of others that Sakai calls (recognizing its necessity) 'retaliatory debunking'. At the other extreme, such spaces may be transnational in name only, and dull: a product of the locally powerful metropolitan academy in which scholars from different university systems give papers formatted perfectly for international publication in a coherent volume and a single language, understanding each other fluently as they discourse about incommensurability and disjunction.

In between, where the real productivity of the pressures exerted from these extremes is negotiated with hope, patience and a spirit of improvisation, people often talk about the exhausting nature of trying to work across several borders at once without many useful working models of how to go about it. A working model for dealing with a problem is not the same thing as a technical vocabulary describing it or a conceptual framework establishing its significance. Both are plentifully available in cultural theory, but in forms tending to multiply purely rhetorical prescriptions that are stirring as they build a peroration yet have an elusive pertinence to other kinds of activity: what other sort of social action, really, could blast out of the continuum of the history after Walter Benjamin, wage war on totality with Lyotard, or help Habermas to reconcile a modernity at odds with itself – for example?

A working model requires a less apocalyptic concept of historical practice. *Impurely* rhetorical, it should be able to connect with things that people do, or could conceivably do, in the ordinary course of their lives. A working model might be called 'exemplary' in the sense that instead of presenting people with a heroic but unrealized project over which they must puzzle to find practical examples (unless, in a more sophisticated response, they quell all desire for examples), it is itself a 'singular' practice out of which a project might be invented or devised.[3] This does not mean abandoning theoretical or cultural work for other sorts of activity. Poetry is often exemplary in just this inviting, challenging way, and so are essays written as singular experiments in learning, thinking and communicating.

For me, the most exhilarating achievement of *Translation and Subjectivity* as an essay in this sense is that it does offer a working model of transnational cultural theory and history while also setting out a rigorous and, I find, powerfully convincing historical argument in defence of its method. As with any good essay, this method is immediately engaging but not especially easy to describe. Sakai has a formidable range of learning, and *Translation and Subjectivity* is a multi-layered work in which different lines of inquiry cross over each other, densely woven at one point, diverging at another; each chapter has its own coherence, while connecting with all the others. As I found to my cost when I tried to begin writing un-obliquely with a few paragraphs sketching the curve of the main line of Sakai's argument (and drafted several articles on Australian topics I had never thought about before), this book has a way of generating ideas that is immensely productive for a reader.

This urge to extrapolate from Sakai's work is not, I think, a matter of free association on my part but an outcome of the *involving* mode of composition – in Deleuze and Guattari's sense of 'composition' as a way in which multiplicities dynamically hold together[4] – achieved in the fine detail of his writing as well as formulated as a social practice by his book. There is no dodging the issue: it is this propensity of the text to send readings off in many directions unanticipated 'in' the text – and, following Sakai's translation in *Voices of the Past* of a phrase used by Ito Jinsai, the propensity of this text to 'extend and propagate' its principles 'toward the outside'[5] – that gives *Translation and Subjectivity* a clear, practical force as a working model for transnational studies in culture. Making an eloquent case for a 'practice of theory' across national and linguistic borders, tracing the terrible historical complicity of the logics of universalism and particularism as they have deemed such a practice impossible, Sakai's is a thoroughly plausible account of why and how it might be possible to work across boundaries of culture in a productive and sustainable way.

It achieves this by thinking through translation in a rigorously practical manner. In this respect, Sakai clearly shares with other theorists a conception of translation as a practice producing difference out of incommensurability (rather than equivalence out of difference) and of the 'matter' of translation as heterogeneous all the way down; here, the 'body of enunciation' (*shutai*) is as irreducible to '*the* subject', split or whole, of most discourse grammars as it is to the immaterial 'sender' of communication theories. This approach is practical in the sense that it asks what actually happens in an effort of translation, rather than beginning with a presupposed ideal or an already accepted story of what a world without need of translation – that is, without the 'dust' created by linguistic difference and textual materiality, without folds of incommensurability and the grit of incomprehension, in short, a world without language – would or should be like.

Clearly, too, *Translation and Subjectivity* shares with much postcolonial research a commitment to rethinking translation in its worldly uses for the exercise and legitimation of imperial power, the manufacture of national community, and as a site of survival and resistance for people dispossessed by empires and by nations. Beginning with a multilingual text by Theresa Hak Kyung Cha (a Korean American immigrant whose mother was displaced from Korea to Manchuria by Japanese colonialism) and ending with a study of death in the language of the 'Arechi' poets, survivors of the 'Fifteen Year' War (1930–45), these essays on 'the subject of "Japan"' are concerned with what Sakai calls the *unexpected* legacy of imperialism, present effects of past manoeuvres that never failed to generate more than they were designed to achieve. Thus the two extraordinary central chapters on Watsuji Tetsurô's anthropology, ethics and theories of national character trace in sobering detail a trajectory along which the thought of an anti-imperialist critic of the West and a critical admirer of Heidegger became involved in shaping a culturalism that not only helped justify more imperialism (and racism) in midtwentieth century Japan, but continues to inflect debates about 'East' and 'West' today – debates that circulate in complex spirals of translation and theory examined by all four chapters in the middle of the book.

Given these commitments, the distinctive practicality of Sakai's approach derives from the way it brings them together in a wonderfully supple analysis of translation as a *social* relation, a practice always in some way carried out in the company of others and structuring the situation in which it is performed.

Moving intricately between linguistic, philosophical and historical modes of inquiry, drawing materials from television and the history of modern intellectual tourism persuasively together with studies of poetry and social theory, this analysis of translation's sociality seems particularly useful to me for at least three distinct levels or aspects of practice – broadly, rhetorical, institutional and political – significant to most cultural 'studies', projects and activities.

Fundamental to all three aspects is the way Sakai conceives of translation as a mode of address, and of address as preceding communication. Drawing on his own experience of writing these essays 'in' translation simultaneously for English and Japanese-speaking audiences – an approach remarkably different (if one stops to think) from positioning one as the primary audience of the 'original' text, and the other as a secondary receiver of translation – he carefully distinguishes a 'heterolingual' mode of address, one seeking to engage with *mixed* as well as differing audiences, from the 'homolingual' address assumed to mediate two separate language-communities modelled as 'national' in identity ('a' collective subject) and treated as homogeneous.

Now, the difficulty of talking to an irreducibly or 'wildly' mixed audience, and of participating as a member of one, is basic to any effort at transnational intellectual work. Yet this same difficulty is also familiar to a great many people, scholars included, who do not necessarily think of themselves as knowing foreign languages but routinely negotiate 'multiple tongues' in everyday social life, and in conditions that make attempting a homolingual address impossibly arrogant or useless. Of course, for some people 'multiple tongues' has to mean discrete national languages, from which it would follow that the problem of addressing in Japanese a 'mixed' audience of Japanese-speakers has nothing significant in common with transnationalism. However, Sakai shows clearly why this idea is not sustainable outside the homolingual mode, and how a heterolingual address works to produce community precisely by never assuming communality or taking comprehension for granted – across or within the borders of a nation-state.

Sakai's own way of doing this is not only to avoid the posture of a representative national speaker addressing other nationally representative speakers, but also to forgo using the 'we' of cultural or civilizational communality; he writes for what he calls a 'nonaggregate' community of foreigners. I think this protocol as it works through the text is largely responsible for what I called the 'involving' quality of the composition of *Translation and Subjectivity*. It has an openness that has nothing to do with intellectual casualness or whimsy; the book makes serious demands on its readers. However, it is not insiderly in making its demands; the text does not nationally or culturally *characterize* its readers in moments of puzzlement or surprise. Instead of inviting readers 'in' to a discussion from which some would immediately find themselves excluded by, say, 'not knowing' Japanese or 'not doing' Asian Studies, it draws readers 'out', soliciting an engagement that can take place as much in the reader's work of connecting to the text from fields outside Sakai's as in the ordinary activity of reading to understand.

At a second level of Sakai's analysis of translation as a mode of sociality, this questioning of what people actually do, and could conceivably do, in translation is extended to academic disciplines or fields that have specialized in inscribing cultural difference: the formation of 'Japanese Thought' as the object of a discipline in Japan is discussed in Chapter Two, while 'Asian Studies' is the framework for Sakai's second study of Watsuji in Chapter Four. Linked by a back-and-forth movement of translation and commentary, both of these disciplined academic practices have a history of producing 'the subject of "Japan"' as a nexus of theories, debates and desires about 'East'/'West' relations: both have a capacity to shape *by* their practice 'knowing' subjects of desire for cultural otherness or uniqueness in a matrix of comparative identities; both can produce expert enunciators of 'characteristics' who may interpret for other audiences the flow of theories and debates about 'Japan', 'the East' and 'the West'.

Here, too, questions of address and reception are put to practices of cultural distinction. After asking what people actually *do* by studying 'Japanese Thought' or training in 'Asian' Studies, Sakai goes on in each case to consider what they *could* do in a practice of theory that would question historically the operative categories ('Japanese'/'non-Japanese', 'Western'/'non-Western', for example) enabling and structuring each practice; and what might happen if the civilizational others posited by the very idea of a subject called '"Japanese" thought', and positioned as objects of another called '"Asian" Studies', were openly *included in the community potentially addressed* by practitioners of each.

In this way, the question of how to speak to an essentially mixed audience and how to listen as a foreigner in a community of foreigners is transposed from the level of a social protocol as it informs rhetorical conduct (homolingual or heterolingual), to the level of a politics of theory as it transforms disciplinary practices. The continuity of this movement is doubly secured historically: on the one hand, by an account of the relatively recent development of the idea of 'Japan' as a homogeneously 'Japanese'-speaking nation that ought to have its own distinctive thought; on the other hand, by a reading of Watsuji's *Climate and Culture* (1928–34) that frames as Asian Studies his theories of Indian, Chinese and Jewish 'character' – subtly drawing out the supremacist as well as separatist implications of the way that Watsuji excluded the colonized 'natives' and the diasporic 'stateless' he describes from his projected field of address.

Coming to the text (as I do) from a background more or less equally distant from Japanese Thought and Asian Studies, it can be helpful for a while to read these chapters as a pair, making connections that significantly alter one's maps of modern intellectual history. I do cultural studies with a strong Australian inflection, and while there is no formal discipline of 'Australian Thought' (and many jokes about its absence), I might have studied it if there were; reading *Translation and Subjectivity*, I become curious about its non-formation (and the jokes) in a new and more serious way. I also find this book as illuminating about the history of all the anxious punditry on 'Japan' traversing Australian media space – the breathless diagnoses of Japanese responses to American views of Japanese attitudes to trade and regional diplomacy, the ominous forecasts of a culture-scripted disaster lying in wait for 'them' or (more commonly in Australia) for 'us', the exoticizing, often comic pop ethnographies of Japanese 'ways' – as it is invaluable to me as a history of the racist theories of national/ethnic character that were 'common sense' to most Australians from the 1890s to the 1960s, and are still recycled in journalism, political commentary and popular legend today.

At a certain point, however, it becomes more important to ask why this 'pair' of chapters on academic practices is interrupted by a third, 'Return to the West/Return to the East', on Watsuji's revision of Heidegger, on sentimentality in cultural restorationist movements, and on the post-war Emperor System. Tracing *how* Watsuji's mimetic impulse toward European philosophy became, in reaction to the latter's obsessions in the 1930s with recovering the distinctiveness of 'the West', a desire for symmetry that produced in Watsuji's thought an equally ethnocentric 'return to the East', Chapter Three is in fact a powerful critique of the very impulse symmetrically to 'pair' or polarize equivalent terms in a comparative cultural analysis. Showing how this logic of 'co-figuration' can unfold towards corporatism and state assimilationism as well as cultural nationalism, it is also a practical demonstration of how and why a recognition that *asymmetrical* relations hold between *different* terms does not, as some critics suppose, foster an atomistic celebration of so-called 'opaque' particulars,[6] but enables those terms to be articulated by a transnational history.

As a study in the sentimental economy of modern patriotic fury, the third chapter shows unequivocally why this politics of theory matters. It explains *en abyme* why the rhetorical and disciplinary aspects of Sakai's theory of translation fold out of a third, political dimension of his analysis – a critique of the discourse of the modern nation-state and the idea of 'national language' as these have, more or less violently, suppressed heterogeneity and pathologized otherness inside and outside the borders they enable. However, in connecting homolingualism's worldliness to the most aggressive and passionate outbursts of 'communalism' orchestrated by modern imperial nationalism, Sakai does not slide by analogy from the denial of linguistic mixity to the oppression of minorities and migrants. Rather, *Translation and Subjectivity* builds directly on Sakai's historical work in *Voices of the Past* to show how the emergence in the eighteenth century of a new regime of translation made it possible, in actual conditions of linguistic and social diversity, to conceive of a single 'Japanese' language and ethnos capable of claiming a continuous history, and possible to *represent* translation as occurring between two autonomous entities susceptible to nationalization.

Sakai is the author of a well-known critique of co-figuration (a rivalrous mode of comparison organized by symmetry and equivalence) as it shapes the ubiquitous 'West/non-West', 'modern/pre-modern' and 'universal/particular' pairs that pervade social theory through to recent debates about the political uncertainties of postmodernity.[7] Developed in Chapter Five of *Translation and Subjectivity*, this superb demonstration of the underlying complicity or *alliance* binding these virulently opposed terms in a 'projective mutual accusation' (to borrow a phrase from Eve Sedgwick),[8] is all the more persuasive when read in close conjunction with Sakai's critique of the 'national languages and literatures' problematic that so much avowedly postmodern cultural studies would like to have left behind.

Media culture studies, in particular, are often projected immediately into a time-zone already 'after' the nation and 'beyond' modernism's ambivalent preoccupation with so-called natural language. However, the ease with which the concept of 'natural' language is then casually referred to *national* language – 'Japanese, French, English ...', a quick explanation goes – suggests the pertinence of Sakai's claim that we are still very much confined by the latter model, and in fact have difficulty understanding our own practices of translation without recourse to the schema of co-figuration.

Consider how translation crops up today in a variety of public debates in the United States as in Australia. It has a warm, fuzzy use as a metaphor of mutually enriching social relations in a cosmopolitan future (Robert Hughes' vision of multiculturalism, for example).[9] It is sharply contested in institutions as a model for a more just and realistic approach to cultural difference in the unequal, divided societies that now exist (by, say, making multilingualism a premise as well as an aim of pedagogy in state schools). And it is demanded or denounced in disparate battles waged through the media about the impact of anything stigmatized as foreign from immigrants and tourists to political correctness and the internet on the cohesiveness of nations, the integrity of languages and the quality of cultures. The *concept* of translation is not the sole province of linguists and literary scholars, but one of the resources on which people commonly draw to respond to the effects of economic, social and cultural change in their lives.

Yet in all these debates, translation is also commonly understood to be a form of diplomacy carried out by special agents between discrete, homosocial and potentially rivalrous 'cultures' acting like nations – a tool of what Sakai calls 'bilateral internationalism'. This is what Hughes has in mind when, despite his own criticism of the transfiguration of social differences as national, he awards potential elite status to people 'who can think and act with informed grace across ethnic, cultural, linguistic lines'.[10] This is why the claim that more than one language is spoken in the name of 'English' can be heard by *opponents* of 'informed' line-crossing as necessarily a declaration of separatism; and this is how any number of diverse issues and problems intrinsic to the societies in which debates about them arise are paranoiacally unified as a foreign body that can and should be expelled from 'our' communal space.

However, to ascribe these responses simply to someone else's brand of politics would miss the point of Sakai's critique of co-figuration: namely, that it really is hard for anyone now to imagine translation outside it. Consider those experimental intellectual spaces in which 'trans-', 'multi-', 'cross-' and 'inter-' ways of thinking connectedness are heatedly debated, and borders are not conflated with national boundaries or treated as sacred. I think they are most exhausting not when riven by conflicts, which tend to be intelligible *as* 'conflict' to participants to a greater or lesser degree, but in moments of relative calm when people wonder what to do next, how to communicate differently in future – and the scary mirage of an exhaustive knowledge of the world reappears.

The ideal of total 'pluralistic' internationalism is not plausible in today's academy, either for individuals or collectives. Working conditions alone preclude most people from pursuing it past the odd dream of learning several languages and reading dozens of histories in one's spare time, although it does flash by in those long lists of differences that tail off in 'etc. ...'; in global-systems analyses where the overwhelming spread of data deflects attention from the complexity of the world to the awesome athleticism of an author; and in the glazed eyes of people confronting a talk about an overly foreign place, as though the act of listening symmetrically imposes on the hearer an obligation equal to the speaker's to 'know about' that place. It is easy to mock such impulses (personally, I am never free of them), but in this context pluralistic internationalism acts as a model *in default* – a 'default' model that doesn't work – of other ways of coming to terms with the infinity of what one does not or cannot know of others, and with incomprehension as a factor intrinsic to the effort of communication.

Addressing these problems subtly and directly, *Translation and Subjectivity* makes it possible to imagine ways out of the logic of co-figuration. If translation loses in the process its special-agent status, the position of a formal translator is not effaced (as though, once again, there were no linguistic difference and no problem of intelligibility); rendered liminal rather than mediating, it brings out the *ordinary* instability, strenuously concealed by communalism, of the 'we' produced in any communicative effort that is never sure of succeeding. Liminality as a threshold or in-between 'place' is diversely interpreted now by cultural theorists; reading Sakai's book, I came to think of the translator's liminality not only in terms of the inside/outside paradox of the frame or boundary, but also as a movement oscillating between familiar and unfamiliar, actual and potential *exteriors*; in a heterolingual mode of address the translator's position, I would guess, is that of one who accepts to have no choice but to 'extend and propagate toward the outside' in a condition of chronic uncertainty about the outcome.

At the same time, Sakai's careful tracing of historical practices specific to different experiences of liminality is a reframing of 'the subject of "Japan"' that radically alters at least this reader's sense of what that phrase is open to meaning. Most immediately, the idea of a nation in its interiority is displaced in an outsiderly essay on the history of that idea: here is a 'nonaggregate' Japan produced by reading from the oppressed or unliveable edges of national space (in the multilingual unworking of 'literature' by a Korean American, as in the refusal of returned Japanese soldiers to write as 'living' in a new Japan continuous with the old) while also reading *for* the liminality enunciated but disavowed in the texts of a canonical national thinker such as Watsuji – reframed here as the writings of a foreigner and a tourist abroad.

Another movement, however, traces the outside circulation of certain European ideas of interiorized nationality, opening them up to theoretical and historical criticism. Watsuji is also a translator whose philosophical studies and solutions in Japanese of the problem of translating the senses that 'subject' can have in European languages become, in Sakai's revision, the basis for a theory of subjectivity *as* an otherness, a foreignness, and an exteriority 'in' any language or community. Most marvellous to me in this movement is the way it begins from a reading of Watsuji's interpretation of the very distinction between practical and epistemic agency (respectively, *shutai* and *shukan*) that is active now in so much controversy about theory, then expands and transforms the distinction to organize in English a practical understanding of the project of 'theory'; a plausible, limited and very exact definition of that problematic term, 'the West'; and a succinct way of naming and explaining one of theory's most elusive and useful concepts, the *practice* of enunciation.

It is always easier to sense what shutai means than to 'put it into words', not least because it 'means' what occurs as, and vanishes in, any process of putting into words; it is something we know about intimately by doing. Yet an exposition can take pages to draw together ideas of the fleeting and the material, the open and the historical, the involved and the productive in practice, and, after all that effort, there is still no word – just a series of words, like 'practice' and 'body', carrying baggage or traces of hybrid histories, that never quite resonate effectively. Perhaps we are dealing with a 'nonaggregate' concept, or with the core of the concept of the nonaggregate. However, insofar as the opacity of theoretical discourse sometimes is a matter of overdoing the Latin in English, defining one's audience too exclusively as a closed society of experts bound by access to a special language, I suggest that 'shutai' in Sakai's sense is capable of translating those pages of exposition in a way that not only makes the concept more accessible but opens it up to new uses.

At stake here is the serious problem of how a transnational scholarly practice directly essaying heterolingualism might actually work, and the status for such a practice of 'examples'; in his study of Cha's *Dictée*, Sakai draws on an old working model of language-learning and subject-formation (*bungaku*, today translatable as 'literature') used before the birth of Japanese as a national language. Academic theorists today, however, have their own specific reasons for facing this problem; increasingly, scholarly discourse can never be sure of circulating within one linguistic community, however unevenly circulation takes place. Yet this does not mean 'we are all' constrained or incited equally to write for different audiences, any more than 'we all' have the same relationship to nationalism.

If Sakai's is for me an exemplary response to these issues, it is so in its singularity. *Translation and Subjectivity* is no more a general model of what a heterolingual cultural studies should henceforth do than it is an instance of an exceptional or personal bilingualism. Sakai does not propose a universally applicable norm of conduct, a strategy of repetition as return; to write for different audiences is necessarily to care about context, to respond to contingency, to admit limitation: in short, to be willing repeatedly to differ. This 'will', however, is not a property of individuals with a 'talent for translation' but a complex and *variable* condition of sociality; for many people, learning multiple languages is not a gift, a pleasure or a tool of trade but a forced process scored by painful legacies of history – as Sakai emphasizes in his discussion of Cha's desire in *Dictée* for her dead mother's mother tongue.

What I would borrow from Sakai's reading of that text is his defence of the value of making connections 'anachronically' as well as transnationally to other practices, other singularities. On first reading *Voices of the Past*, I puzzled for a long time over my desire to relate what I read appreciatively there about Ito Jinsai's critique of Song rationalism to controversies today: what does it mean to link two ways of stigmatizing talk about heterogeneity and contingency when those ways are so remote from each other, culturally and historically? It can simply mean, of course, that one is reading ('actively', as convention adds). However, to read is not necessarily to read well, and in moving outside one's own patch of expertise there are always questions and doubts, not only about what happens when one's capacity for misunderstanding becomes excessive, but also at the point where my 'adventure' becomes 'appropriation' for someone else.

After reading *Translation and Subjectivity*, however, I came to see the earlier book as itself a powerful work of translation that challenged my sense of cultural and historical propriety, leaving me far less sure of the intellectual remoteness from 'my' concerns of a thinker living in 'Japan' 300 years ago. In Ito's world, incommensurability is very much 'here' as well as 'there', and difficulty in communication has to be accepted as an ordinary condition of social life. If sociality is produced by the participation of many different minds, among the unintended outcomes likely to follow any action there will be unanticipated, perhaps unwelcome or even (in Robert Hughes' phrase) 'fraying' criticisms.

This can be frightening; when there is no communality or when borders are crossed, sometimes unknowingly, one is indeed never sure of 'what will happen'. Sakai explains that 'the core of Ito's ethics is the moment we are forced to face through this fear', since 'one is capable of being ethical precisely because one is uncertain of the consequences of an intended ethical action'.[11] However, because sociality is relational one is not alone in this uncertainty; others have a say in determining an action's value. In Ito's world, 'the virtuous is ... always a collective work'.

A transnational practice of theory could not be grounded now in any agreement about ethics or the value of discussing virtue (for some people, an outrageous and morbid topic). What I learn from this anachronic reading is rather a way to think about non-communal communication as a *project* requiring both practical involvement – one attempts it without knowing what will happen – and 'trust', defined in *Translation and Subjectivity* as an adventurous, unsentimental approach to sociality that accepts the aleatory nature of the latter. The academic community that can evaluate efforts in this spirit may be more potential than actual (a 'coming community' as Giorgio Agamben puts it), but with this book Sakai has given us a history, a theory and a language that will richly contribute to the process of its formation.

NOTES

1 Naoki Sakai, *Voices of the Past: The Status of Language in Eighteenth Century Japanese Discourse* (Ithaca and London: Cornell University Press, 1991), pp. 104–105.

2 Naoki Sakai, *Translation and Subjectivity: On 'Japan' and Cultural Nationalism* (Minneapolis: University of Minnesota Press, 1997), p. 4.

3 I am adapting here from Ann Curthoys and Stephen Muecke, 'Australia, for Example', in *The Republicanism Debate*, eds Wayne Hudson and David Carter (Kensington: New South Wales University Press, 1993), pp. 177–200. Curthoys and Muecke are adapting in turn from Giorgio Agamben, *The Coming Community*, trans. Michael Hardt (Minneapolis: University of Minnesota Press, 1993), pp. 9–11.

4 Gilles Deleuze and Félix Guattari, *A Thousand Plateaus* trans. Brian Massumi (Minneapolis: University of Minnesota Press, 1987), 327–350.

5 Sakai, *Voices of the Past*, p. 101.

6 David Harvey writes in this way of opacity throughout *The Condition of Postmodernity: An Inquiry into the Origins of Cultural Change* (Oxford: Blackwell, 1989). See Chapter 5 above.

7 Naoki Sakai, 'Modernity and Its Critique: the Problem of Universalism and Particularism', in *Postmodernism and Japan (Post-Contemporary Interventions)*, eds Masao Miyoshi and H.D. Harootunian (Durham, NC: Duke University Press, 1989), pp. 93–122.

8 Eve Kosofsky Sedgwick, *Epistemology of the Closet* (Berkeley and Los Angeles: University of California Press, 1990), p. 100.

9 Robert Hughes, *Culture of Complaint: The Fraying of America* (New York and Oxford: Oxford University Press, 1993).

10 Hughes, *Culture of Complaint*, p. 96.

11 Sakai, *Voices of the Past*, p. 106.

Crazy Talk Is Not Enough: Deleuze and Guattari at Muriel's Wedding

1.   A child in the dark, gripped with fear, comforts himself by singing under his breath. He walks and talks to his song. Lost, he takes shelter, or orients himself with his little song as best he can. The song is like a rough sketch of a calming and stabilizing, calm and stable, center in the heart of chaos. Perhaps the child skips as he sings, hastens or slows his pace. But the song itself is already a skip: it jumps from chaos to the beginnings of order in chaos and is in danger of breaking apart at any moment. There is always sonority in Ariadne's thread. Or the song of Orpheus.

Deleuze and Guattari, *A Thousand Plateaus*[1]

In the mythology of cultural theory (the kind that jumps between disciplines as an incantatory recitation of famous proper names), Gilles Deleuze is not often invoked as a *home-making* philosopher, least of all when his writings with Félix Guattari are in play. Much more commonly sounded are those passages of their work that can be jarring to sensibilities attuned to feminism; the very words 'Deleuze and Guattari' carry echoes of wild talk about wolves, weeds, rats, vampires, war machines, 'nomads' (that blokey old romantic tune of 'on the road again'?), warriors becoming-woman, Bodies without Organs – a howling chaos of ugly ideas, repellent jargon, not to be taken seriously.

There is no point simply in saying that this is an impression of a philosophy more talked about than read, or read selectively and at a single speed (very hastily). If much of the English-language reception of Deleuze and Guattari's work has stressed the harsh tone of the polemical parts of *Anti-Oedipus* (1972), and privileged the more obviously bellicose motifs of '1227: Treatise on Nomadology: – The War Machine' from *A Thousand Plateaus* (1980), a narrow emphasis on that work's aggressive qualities has been favoured by admirers as well as detractors.

However, this is not, as gentler readers sometimes suggest, merely a matter of a 'male' delight in the abrasive vulgarity of the rude bits about Freud and Lacan in the first book, or in the action-adventure landscapes of the second. Those jarring notes are, like the wolves and the rats, powerfully real: there is a good deal about chaos and horror in both of the books about capitalism, as there is in *Kafka* (1975), their more historically situated study of a writing in which fascism, communism and Fordism are always 'knocking on the door'.

If there is also a turbulence, at times a ferocity in the substance of their work, I am in no position to ascribe a taste for this to gender. An abrasive use of Deleuze and Guattari served my own purposes when, as a young feminist enraged by what I saw as a blocking of the worldly, exteriorizing force of Women's Liberation by an academic feminist return to Freud, I first picked up from those parts of their work that I was able to understand a few threads that took my work in other directions.[2] To this day – speaking always, no doubt, as a film critic – I find the action-adventure of *A Thousand Plateaus* and its philosophy of the multiple quite as congenial for thinking about women's socially diverse lives as the domestic melodrama, or the family romance.[3] While it is vital to appropriate the latter wherever they are culturally pressing, feminist theory need not be *confined to* those high Fordist gen-res whereby racializing, class-enforcing, patriarchal stories of family, sexuality, domestic labour, emotional service, consumerism and 'national brands' (in Lauren Berlant's phrase) were historically designated 'women's stories'.[4]

None the less, a relentlessly mono-generic rendering of 'Deleuze and Guattari' as 'bad seeds', or the theoretical equivalent of a Nick Cave murder ballad, does a great disservice to a body of work that is immensely varied in its humours and tones and mostly formidable for the gaiety with which it launches into adven-tures of reading, writing and thinking.[5] So does another persisting figure of hearsay, deemed 'Spinozan' as the former is thought to be Nietzschean, of the *silly* philosophers: a couple of wide-eyed, fey affirmers given to un-cool citing of Carlos Castaneda and the lyrics of 'Old Man River' (*ATP*, p. 25; in fact, an echo of the deeply political voice, honoured as such in France, of Paul Robeson). Measured against the accomplishments of Deleuze's long and learned life in philosophy and Guattari's creative work in psychotherapy, the absurdity of both stereotypes, gothic and hippy respectively, is painfully clear.

Yet their force is extraordinary, repeated as they have been for more than thirty years in otherwise critical circles. Like all rumours (and songs), they are creatively defensive; they help to keep something at bay. In time, it may be use-ful for a study of academic politics in the decades after 1968 to ask how the work of Deleuze and Guattari came to function for so much progressive thought as anomalous, that is, as a 'phenomenon of bordering' that *defines* a particular multiplicity by providing 'the enveloping line or farthest dimension, as a function of which it is possible to count the others' (*ATP*, p. 245). Such a study could tell us something about the corporate achievements and sacrifices of a broadly left intellectual culture that struggled, in dauntingly hostile political and economic conditions, to secure itself as 'at home' in the everyday workplaces of the academy.

Now so diverse in its provenances, alliances and self-descriptions that it cannot be named by proponents in a single phrase (but designated from the outside with lethal ease as 'politically correct'), this particular culture or multiplicity encompasses lines and dimensions that are, most of the time, distinctively not 'deleuzian'; not *that* silly, *that* extreme. Insofar as it developed in tension with post-structuralist thinking, and during a period of industrial avidity in the Anglophone academy for products of 'French theory', this particularity is also a peculiarity. One wonders why Deleuze and Guattari's work was so long kept circulating out on the edge; for the anomalous is not abnormal, not 'outside rules or ... against the rules' (*ATP*, p. 244), but *exceptional* in relation to the lines and dimensions constituting a 'band' or a 'pack'. It can't be because of the difficulty of the texts. True, the effects of reading Deleuze and Guattari can be shattering in ways that Brian Massumi vividly describes; yet anyone who has read Lacan or Derrida knows what it means to take masochistic pleasure, like Massumi, in impingement.[6] It can't be the violence *in* the texts. Mild-mannered academics have been 'blasting' things 'out of the continuum of history' with Walter Benjamin for years.[7]

There is another question here. In the process of defining the anomalous position of Deleuze and Guattari's philosophy, haven't I just reiterated all those classic oppositions that feminists have worked to deconstruct (action/sentiment, adventure/domesticity, masculine eventfulness/feminine space)? Well, yes, temporarily: it is difficult not to when they organize socially enforced alternatives or act as grids generating choices that people have to make – and forms of feminist polemic in which good women will have nothing to do with weeds or vampires. Just as 'crazy talk is not enough' (*ATP*, p. 138) to guarantee translation from one semiotic regime to another, let alone the destruction of 'a dominant atmospheric semiotic', so a dismantling and displacement of binaries is not enough to do away with contextually prevailing gender divisions; this point is familiar to any feminism that is materialist as well as deconstructive. Nevertheless, playing variations on the Ulysses (on the road) and Penelope (home-making) theme is not helpful for long when following Deleuze and Guattari's work, and it is useless if that theme's terms are taken unpragmatically as constant, trans-contextually stable points of reference, their value held to be the same wherever and however they occur. It is better to displace the questions they provoke by skipping over to another approach to the texts.

'In the dark, at home, toward the world'

Where to begin? '1.   A child in the dark, gripped with fear, comforts himself by singing under his breath ...'; the passage I have quoted above is the opening paragraph of '1837: Of the Refrain', the plateau immediately before the one about nomad space and the war machine. The paragraph itself can be read as a little song, a nocturnal creation myth or 'sketch' in the middle of the book; it is not a genesis story of the logos and light, but a song of *germination* in darkness.

At the same time, it is the first of three numbered paragraphs opening 'Of the Refrain', each of which develops a thematic phrase sketched in the Contents pages of the book: 'in the dark, at home, toward the world' (*ATP*, p. vii). Only in the second paragraph are we at home, for 'home does not pre-exist': like the lost child's shelter, home is made of mixed components and, while homeliness *follows* the drawing of a circle round an 'uncertain and fragile center', it is a new activity of 'organizing a space' in which deeds and tasks may be performed. In a third phase, 'one opens the circle' and lets the world in or 'launches forth', not on the side of the chaos still pressing on the circle and filtering in to the home, but towards a new region created by the circle itself; 'one ventures from home on the thread of a tune' (*ATP*, p. 311). So home is in the middle of things, like 'place' in the work of Doreen Massey;[8] neither origin nor destination, home is produced in an effort to *organize* a 'limited space' that is never sealed in, and so it is not an enclosure but a way of going outside.

This sequence opens a text about the abode, milieus, territoriality, 'the Natal', the earth and the cosmos (the thematic movement swells like a kookaburra chorus, unfolds like a child's home address) conceptualized in terms of *sonic* spaces, boundary-markings, forces, passages and 'the cosmic refrain of a *sound* machine' (*ATP*, p. 349; my emphasis). This 'movement' is also one of the threads that can be followed through the texture of 'Of the Refrain'. It leads back, for example, to passages about multiplicities, anomalies and 'modes of expansion, propagation, occupation, contagion, peopling' (*ATP*, p. 239) in the previous plateau, '1730: Becoming-Intense, Becoming-Animal, Becoming-Imperceptible', and further back again to those about landscape in 'Year Zero: Faciality' (*ATP*, p. 172). It also runs forward to the differentiation of spatial practices, territorial principles and rhythms of deterritorialization – nomadic, sedentary, migratory, itinerant – in the 'Treatise on Nomadology' (*ATP*, pp. 380–382).

'Of the Refrain' does not have to be read before 'Nomadology', although the resonances between them in a book 'composed ... of plateaus that communicate with one another across microfissures, as in a brain' (*ATP*, p. 22) are very clear. *Both* texts are about home-making, if we allow variability as well as ambiguity to this term's potentials of capture and escape, danger and security, subjection and empowerment, work and song. Both establish a correlation between dwelling as a temporal practice and the space of what Marcus Doel calls 'a motionless trip' (famously, the nomad 'does not move' but has 'absolute movement, ... speed'; *ATP*, p. 381),[9] and both expand on the concept of the interval (the in-between in 'Of the Refrain', the intermezzo in 'Nomadology') in ways that are useful for analysing practical situations. For example, writing in the middle of old and new suburban backyards, contemporary and colonial city streets, traditional White and modern Aboriginal ways of mapping the Australian outback, Stephen Muecke essays a smooth trajectory precisely between the refrain of 'home' and nomadological space, in the process finding (as such a line must in a not-yet postcolonial society) points of loss and impediment, periods of disorientation, folds of incommensurability.[10]

Yet few commentators explicitly make much of the connections between these two plateaus, and few readings of 'Deleuze and Guattari' begin with a lost child in the dark or with the figures that people the space opened up by his song – a schoolchild humming up the strength to do her homework, a housewife singing or playing the radio 'as she marshalls the antichaos forces of her work' (*ATP*, p. 311). I often do begin here when I have to face teaching *A Thousand Plateaus*: I am happy with these figures, familiar with what they do and, unlike gazing at a portrait of Deleuze and Guattari as grim super-virilists obsessed with 'unimpeded flow' and 'leaving the body behind',[11] listening to their songs and gestures can open our reading to that rhythmic sense of the frailty, vulnerability, erratic power and resourceful joy in every living experiment that makes *A Thousand Plateaus* so positive and encouraging an ethics. The child's humming and the housewife's singing also draw out the importance of thinking limits and limitation (that is, *impeded* flow) in Deleuze and Guattari's philosophy, and the importance for it of tracing moments when things stop, energies falter, measures fail, or lines are blocked or arrested. 'One ventures from home on the thread of a tune' that is always in danger of breaking.

Limitation, in its rhythmic or 'folding' relation to becomings, trajectories and continuous variation (to which 'rhythm is critical; it ties together critical moments, or ties itself together in passing from one milieu to another'; *ATP*, p. 313), is also critical in the 'Treatise on Nomadology'. Yet when I am just beginning to read, trying to get involved in the book all over again, I am deeply bored by chariots, weapons and metallurgy; a metrical noise warps my reading, as a restless schoolchild within me drones, 'The Assyrian came down like a wolf on the fold and his cohorts were gleaming in purple and gold'[12] – and, since boredom is catching, I prefer to work with other plateaus first. There is nothing irresponsible, cute or dippy about this procedure. *A Thousand Plateaus* really can be read rigorously from the middle, and 'each plateau can be read starting anywhere and can be related to any other plateau' (*ATP*, p. 22). However, this is not a matter of fragmented thinking, 'crazy talk', or an aesthetic maximization of random effects of semiosis. As Massumi and Doel both demonstrate, Deleuze and Guattari's writing is highly ordered and strongly cohesive – intensively 'composed' in Massumi's terms, 'superglutinous' in Doel's[13] – and it makes sense (in all senses of the word) in every direction: *du sens, dans tous les sens*.[14]

There is no special analytical virtue in emphasizing 'Of the Refrain'. However, beginning there is a good way of orienting a feminist approach to the more heavily frequented parts of Deleuze and Guattari's work. It makes it easier to see, for example, how important the themes of family, home and dwelling are in *Kafka*: the anxious, noise-tormented animal struggling with fear of the outside in Kafka's story 'The Burrow' is an inspired and demented home-maker, whose dwelling is a map for one version of the concept of rhizome and offers one way into the concepts of multiplicity and assemblage.[15] *Kafka* itself transforms the family-romantic genre of literary biography by effecting a becoming-musical of the 'portrait of the artist'.

Reading 'Of the Refrain' with care can also make it harder to misread the 'Treatise on Nomadology' as a road romance that valorizes homelessness, or to construe the relationship between the two plateaus fixedly in terms of a gendered dualism of stasis and movement, home and travel, domesticity and war, creativity and destruction. For example, 'Of the Refrain' helps us to *notice*, when we are reading 'Nomadology', that Ulysses himself is not a nomad like the warrior-figures Achilles and Penthisilea the Amazon, but rather 'a man of the nascent modern State, the first man of the modern State' (*ATP*, p. 355), whose odyssey orders a *sedentary* space striated by 'walls, enclosures, and roads between enclosures' (*ATP*, p. 381).

On the more domestic side of dwelling, this observation about Ulysses leads us to consider – extrapolating, now, from Deleuze and Guattari's text – that their nomads are in fact *like Penelope*, 'the one who does not depart, does not want to depart', and who 'knows how to wait' with 'infinite patience' (*ATP*, p. 381). The nomad is an *occupant* and *inhabitant* who 'clings to the smooth space left by the receding forest, where the steppe or the desert advances, and who invents nomadism as a response to this challenge' (*ATP*, p. 381) – as Penelope inventively holds, in response to the comings and goings of importunate men, to the smooth space and sonority of her un- and anti-weaving (see *ATP*, pp. 474–476). Consider the story again. When Ulysses fails to return home after the fall of Troy, his wife Penelope is pestered by suitors. She promises to choose one as soon as she has finished weaving a shroud for her father-in-law. At night, however, she unravels what she has accomplished during the day and continually defers the ending of her labours. Ulysses travels from place to place, but Penelope, 'model of all the domestic virtues'[16] is the quick one; her gestures of 'continuous variation, continuous development of form' (*ATP*, p. 478) unravel a smooth trajectory, and her traits are exactly those of 'immobility and speed, catatonia and rush, a "stationary process", station as process' (*ATP*, p. 381).

As a temporary measure, this role reversal of the social and spatial values customarily attributed to one of the West's recurring legendary couples helps to highlight Deleuze and Guattari's insistence that *'the war machine has an extremely variable relation to war itself'* (*ATP*, p. 422: emphasis in original). Penelope's web is itself a war machine, one that functions in connection with war in the story (the siege of Troy, the besieging of Penelope herself), but does not have war as its *object*; rather, its rhythmic values effect 'the drawing of a creative line of flight, the composition of a smooth space and of the movement of the people in that space' (*ATP*, p. 422). In this respect, Penelope's web is at one pole of the war machine's variability – for Deleuze and Guattari, the essential pole, at which the machine comprises very low quantities of force. The end of the story suggests what can happen at the other pole when the State appropriates the war machine and subordinates it to political aims (*ATP*, p. 420). On his return, Ulysses kills Penelope's suitors, re-striates domestic and political space in Ithaca, and blocks innumerable lines of flight (including, no doubt, Penelope's).

This role reversal is temporary, however, because it isn't really a *reversal*. In fact, what has happened in my reading is that an abstract couple has 'skipped' from a narrative field *oppositionally organized* by stories about men going off to war, having adventures, or away at work, while women drudge endlessly at home (the narrative field of classical white feminist criticism, and modern-industrial Penelope lore; an Australian *locus classicus* is Henry Lawson's 1892 story 'The Drover's Wife'[17]) – and into another, *rhizomatically composed* field, in which dwelling encompasses both venturing and abiding and in which the extended couple *movement/stasis* becomes an intensive rhythm, *flight/line/blockage*, that is critical on every side of any gender division, whether rigid (two sides) or supple (*n* sides). In this field, differing spatial practices have many variable relations, and enter into combinations with diverse other components – including those abidingly oppressive economic and social divisions and power relations at issue for feminist criticism.

A way of going outside textual exegesis opens up with Deleuze and Guattari's distinction between the nomads as an abstraction, 'real and nonactual', and the equally real but actual 'mixed objects' in which *elements of* nomadism always 'enter into de facto mixes' with other territorial principles and forms of social organization (*ATP*, p. 420; see also p. 474). This distinction between non-actual (abstract) and actual realities is not an opposition between theory and practice, or spatial ideas and social realities. In Stephen Muecke's 'outback', for example, it is impossible to ignore the actual co-presence of different knowledge claims and their inequality in the institutional spacings of white Australian society. Yet this co-presence is precisely why an inevitably partial, self-interested, often comic, sedentary effort to follow 'Aboriginal ways of knowing and behaving in specific places' can sometimes combine with Aboriginal struggles for access to European knowledges and social sites, along with the protection of their own, to create the conditions *for* postcolonialism in Australian society.[18] Non-Aboriginal Australians, Muecke suggests, have yet to learn the extent to which we have already been 'formed by indigenous discourses'[19] – or, mixed from elements of nomadism as well as of settlement and migration.

Mixed objects are also 'combinations of space and composition' (*ATP*, p. 420). Muecke unfolds a series of differing social architectures of dwelling that manage, more or less, to co-exist in what is imperiously composed by one of them as Australian national space. In contrast, Ghassan Hage's work on the spatial imaginary of national practices[20] and Sandra Buckley's study of Japanese 'domestic tales'[21] follow discourses of nation and family that imperatively manage space and social 'composition' (that is, the sticking-together of a bordered multiplicity) precisely by limiting combination, by domesticating elements that drift in from the outside, and by sieving out or destroying inassimilable differences. Their accounts are of a harmony and homeliness violently produced by closure, blockage and exclusion, by sexism, racism, allophobia; obliquely, they offer a critical perspective on the value, for feminist knowledges, of domestic 'melodrama' and family 'romance'. The nationalist songs cited by Hage and the grisly kitchen-stories retold by Buckley equally well remind us that tragedy and horror are also 'women's' genres – and that stories, songs and genres are powerfully active components of social and spatial experience.

'Sometimes, sometimes, sometimes'

In P.J. Hogan's film *Muriel's Wedding* (Australia, 1994) the exuberant heroine spends most of the film compounding a genre confusion. Muriel (Toni Collette) is actually on an adventure, but she sees herself in a fairy-tale romance – complete with wedding, confetti and sporting-hero husband. However, her romantic object is not the man she marries. What Muriel most desires is a white dress, flashing cameras and the admiring looks of friends; she wants to become a wedding *photo* in a glossy magazine. So she robs her family, runs away to Sydney and changes her identity, becoming 'Mariel'. While Mariel might become mainstream, 'Muriel' is an anomaly. Living in a small outpost of the seedy end of Australia's Pacific tourism- and real-estate economy (colloquially known as the 'white shoe' sector, after the footwear affected in the 1980s by prominent property developers), Muriel is just too much for Porpoise Spit. Too fat to be glamorous, too loud in her joy to be cool; too weird in her style and her love of Abba songs to be a useful social accessory for her beautiful beach-blonde friends; too 'slow' for the low-skill, low-paid, casualized jobs that her sleazy booster father nags her to accept: Muriel Heslop is desperate to get married.

For a girl with no prospects, there are few ways out of a home town ringed by billboards shouting, 'You Can't Stop Progress'. In response to this challenge, Muriel reinvents her life to the tune of an Abba song. A line of flight opens up with a blank cheque blindly handed over by Muriel's poor, brow-beaten, down-trodden, sad and infinitely loyal mother. Muriel betrays her mother. She rips off the family bank account, flees to a tourist resort, makes a new friend, Rhonda (Rachel Griffiths) – and ventures forth to win a karaoke contest with a full-dress performance of Abba's 'Waterloo'. From here, threads unravel in all directions. In Sydney, Rhonda gets cancer. To realize her dream of a society wedding, 'Mariel' betrays her friend. Back in Porpoise Spit, the family collapses: bankrupt, Muriel's father is investigated for corruption; blamed, deserted, abused, Muriel's mother kills herself to save the family 'embarrassment' – after burning out the suburban backyard that no-one would willingly mow.

The term 'line of flight' (*une ligne de fuite*) is often read as an escapist slogan, a signature theme of the ratty romanticism that 'Deleuze and Guattari' are held to represent. In the ruined backyard of her family home, Muriel Heslop knows better. Like Mariel's 'wedded bliss' with a man she doesn't love, the scorched clothes-line and blackened weeds 'emanate a strange despair, like an odor of death and immolation' (*ATP*, p. 229); were Muriel a literary creature like F. Scott Fitzgerald (whom Deleuze and Guattari cite on this point) she, too, might have said: 'No problem set – simply a silence with only the sound of my own breathing. … My self-immolation was something sodden-dark.'[22] Romantics may believe that the only risk of practising 'a sort of mutation or creation drawn not only in the imagination but also in the very fabric of social reality' (*ATP*, p. 229) is the risk of re-territorialization, or, in another political vocabulary, 'co-optation'. As veterans of many a leftist attempt to produce that sort of mutation, Deleuze and Guattari stress another danger: 'crossing the wall … but instead of connecting with other lines and each time augmenting its valence, *turning to destruction, abolition pure and simple, the passion of abolition*' (*ATP*, p. 229: emphasis in original).

This is not only a practical wisdom but a conceptual consistency. Flight for Deleuze and Guattari is sometimes a matter of escape, but rarely of running away; flight is intensive rather than extensive, a matter of composition. '*Une fuite*' in French is more commonly a leak from a humble gas or water tap than it is a rattling turn of chariots, and a *line* of flight is the one that runs toward the 'vanishing point' (*point de fuite*) in so-called Renaissance perspective; in other words, it is a compositional aspect of any assemblage, multiplicity or *de facto* mix of elements by means of which its field may be *de*-composed. Sometimes a leak will wear away or infuse its surroundings over many years, imperceptibly transforming their colour, grain, shape and smell; sometimes it blows abruptly to devastate a room, a building, or a city block. When the 'mutant' line of flight becomes a 'pure, cold line of abolition' (*ATP*, p. 230), it is incomparably destructive; Deleuze and Guattari write of fascism, suicide and suicidal States in this respect. In *Muriel's Wedding*, it is the self-sacrificing 'wife and mother' who flees along that path.

Sometimes, if a line retains its mutancy, things come together in a different way. *Muriel's Wedding* settles in the end for a kind of comedy that can do without the restoration of the old domestic order. While nothing can alter what she has done, Muriel stops short of self-destruction; abandoning the maternal melodrama as well as fairy-tale romance, she takes Rhonda 'home' to Sydney, rather than Porpoise Spit, to start a different kind of adventure, one with no set goal. In this, *Muriel's Wedding* does not 'illustrate' *A Thousand Plateaus*. My point is not to 'apply' Deleuze and Guattari to a film, but to sketch a *limited* context – neither Deleuzian nor film-critical, but a mix of elements of both with an inhabitant's knowledge of Australian small town beach culture – for returning to those feminist questions of reading that I earlier set aside.

In my first approach to 'Of the Refrain', I stressed the movement of the opening towards a notion of the outside (*toward* the world). The crazy women in *Muriel's Wedding* are impelled along this line, yet so are those who are frightened, trapped, or destroyed like Muriel's mother, by economic and cultural forces that block their desires and re-direct their energies into keeping chaos out of the home. In twice managing to cross the wall that is the ring of Progress Association billboards surrounding Porpoise Spit, fleeing the entrapment that the town's economy imposes on working class women, Muriel and Rhonda aspire not to a 'life on the road' – for these women, homelessness is all too real a possibility – but to reach the outside that Deleuze and Guattari call 'the unknown homeland' or 'the natal' (*ATP*, pp. 332–326).

There is nothing fey or mystical about this idea. Described less simply as 'a decoding of innateness and a territorialization of learning, one atop the other, one alongside the other' (*ATP*, p. 332), it is familiar to all forms of difference politics that have wrestled with the problem of how to articulate real historical and social experiences of differentiation without resorting either to an essentialism of identity, or to an anti-essentialism that would deny the burden and the wisdom of that experience and thereby block the elaboration of what Cindi Katz calls 'the knowledge claims of those working from nondominant positions'.[23] Left here, however, my exposition risks remaining a comforting allegory that fails to connect to practical dilemmas that feminist academics face. Let me return once again to 'Of the Refrain', this time attending to the word *'sometimes'* mixed in to the formulation of 'the outside'.

In the plateau's fourth paragraph (the first to be unnumbered), the spatial contexts developed in the preceding three – *in* the dark, *at* home, *toward* the world – are described, in a seemingly sudden shift, as *not* 'three successive moments in an evolution', but rather as 'three aspects of a single thing, the Refrain (*ritournelle*)', which 'makes them simultaneous or mixes them: sometimes, sometimes, sometimes' (*ATP*, p. 312). In fact, the first situation is already marked off as an independent case by the second paragraph that so smoothly proceeded from it. From the beginning, it is clear that becoming lost, making a home and going towards the world can be distinct but simultaneously available activities – or, as Massumi puts it, co-present *potentials* – at any given point.[24] However, my first reading privileged the 'outside' over the accompanying 'sometimes' until the end of the home-making sequence, where a distinct but connected passage about continuous variation ('sometimes …') in the painting of Paul Klee begins (*ATP*, p. 312). Massumi calls these moments when a reading varies with the direction it takes 'bifurcation points'. Feminists and film critics are familiar with these: when they loom large, they are those moments such as Muriel confronts in a blank cheque, her mother's trusting face, the scorched earth of a dead backyard, the moments of which we say that anything could happen, or 'things could go either way'; lived microscopically every day, they are a million routine moments in which decisions are taken for us, or we only seek familiar paths.

This recursive (repeat to differ) aspect of composition in Deleuze and Guattari involves a process of continual revision that is itself an aspect of their work on an *open system*, of which a rhizome, or a burrow, is only 'one example'.[25] This mode of composition is not anomalous to feminist politics, well aware as these are of the need for a supple responsiveness to varying contexts and circumstances ('sometimes …'). The notion of a line of flight includes one perspective on this, since it allows for distinguishing a feminist *pragmatics* from any puritanical politics that, in its passion for abolition, fails to '[connect] with other lines' (such as those sketched by a couple of European white male philosophers). When revolutionary parties and programmes predominate, 'romantic anarchism' might be a useful term for such a failure, but it seems to me that in a time of identity politics, 'authoritarian PC' is more apt.

Katz succinctly discusses the literature on such problems as the difficult figure of 'woman' in Deleuze and Guattari's writings. I want to sketch a line of argument that goes in the other direction, asking what kinds of difficulty are *added* to their texts by a mythology (for want of a better word) of critical theory that is not exclusive to feminism. One such difficulty occurs at the bifurcation point that is the word *system* in 'open system'. If concepts of systematicity are closely attended to in disciplinary contexts, I would claim that they are weakly used, or rarely followed up, in those mixed, germinal, commonplace discourses of feminist politics and theory that help to shape disciplinary work. There, we commonly tell each other that (as Deleuze himself insists) 'systems have in fact lost absolutely none of their power'[26] – while treating 'system' as synonymous with binary oppositions and 'closure', and then moralizing binaries and closure as though they were always *bad*.

Whatever genealogies we might like to propose for this casually dogmatic habit (I'd guess a lingering Romanticism mixed with too many bad primers on post-structuralism), its effect is to make the work of Deleuze and Guattari very hard to read. For there, as Massumi points out:

> An open system is not one that sets closure entirely aside as its other, as a closed system purports to do with openness. An open system is open even to closure. A closed system locally integrates openness in order to remain the same, as opposed to its other; an open system integrates closure as one of its local conditions (the condition under which it effectively becomes other).[27]

Closure at the beginning of 'Of the Refrain' enables, without preceding, 'the outside', and closure and openness are two phases of a single process ('*sometimes, sometimes, sometimes ...*'). Furthermore, far from being free of 'binaries' and 'linearity' (as a theory-shorthand often implies that a good text should be), the rhizomatic text is one with, as Massumi puts it, 'linearities that bifurcate infinitely but punctually'.[28]

Many different kinds of relations are possible in this sort of system. If binarization is, for Deleuze and Guattari, 'the most general of functions' (*ATP*, p. 176) binarization, too, has differing aspects: not all binarized terms are *opposed* (the drawing of a distinction is not always oppositional), and oppositions can be alternating, or 'only relative' (*ATP*, p. 351), as well as rigidly divisive; no positioning of a term is final, and non-symmetrical reversals are always possible between terms (*ATP*, p. 14). In a feminist pragmatics of social usages, values and actions, nothing requires us to pre-emptively moralize distinctions and oppositions, as though to define one term were necessarily to condemn another, and as if the potentials co-present at every point were coded *at the outset*, 'good' and 'bad': as Deleuze plainly says, 'we can't assume that lines of flight are necessarily creative, that smooth spaces are always better than segmented or striated ones'.[29]

Does this mean that we hurl ourselves into a chaotic horror of aimless and uncaring amorality? Of course not: it means that good and bad are in the middle of things, in the processes and the conflicts of social life. A perhaps more difficult issue, however, inhabits one of Deleuze's simplest definitions of (his) philosophy:

> Everyone knows that philosophy deals with concepts. A system's a set of concepts. And it's an open system when the concepts relate to circumstances rather than essences.[30]

Relating concepts to circumstances is a task that materialist feminisms share with cultural studies. So how do we understand our own circumstances in the academy, variable and shifting as these are in time as well as space?

From a disciplinary position in geography, Katz argues while 'one of the most sticky binaries in social theory involves feminism and Marxism', usefully altering both, it soon becomes unproductive; both feminist and Marxist work can be dominant or 'major' in some worldly contexts, while utterly marginalized in others.[31] She opens up a discussion that runs in the other direction, asking – how do circumstances affect the concepts that we value? Referring rhizomatic thought back *and* forward to the transformation of profound, reproductive social structures is an operation that Deleuze and Guattari call 'putting the tracing back on the map' (*ATP*, pp. 12–15). For Katz, the task is one of thinking seriously about the institutions that we inhabit, refusing the position of 'outsider' therein, and acting to 'change the nature and meaning of our academic "home"'.[32] The university is not the only institution in which we can be 'in the dark' and 'at home' while moving 'towards the world', but it is certainly a workplace that could use a little more humming and singing.

NOTES

1 Gilles Deleuze and Félix Guattari, *A Thousand Plateaus,* vol. 2 of *Capitalism and Schizophrenia,* trans. Brian Massumi (Minneapolis: University of Minnesota Press, 1987 [1980]), p. 311. Henceforth '*ATP*'; further references are given in parentheses in the text.

2 Paul Foss and Meaghan Morris, eds, *Language, Sexuality and Subversion* (Sydney: Feral Publications, 1978); Meaghan Morris, 'The Pirate's Fiancée' in *Michel Foucault: Power, Truth, Strategy,* ed. Meaghan Morris and Paul Patton (Sydney: Feral Publications, 1979), pp. 148–168.

3 On feminist family romance, see Jane Gallop, *Around 1981: Academic Feminist Literary Theory* (London and New York: Routledge, 1992), p. 239.

4 Lauren Berlant, 'National Brands/National Body: *Imitation of Life*' in *Comparative American Identities: Race, Sex and Nationality in the Modern Text*, ed. Hortense Spillers (London and New York: Routledge, 1991), pp. 110–140.

5 Nick Cave and the Bad Seeds, *Murder Ballads*. Mute Records, UK; Mushroom Records, Australia,1996.

6 Brian Massumi, 'Becoming-deleuzian', *Environment and Planning D: Society and Space* 14:4 (1996): 395–406.

7 See Terry Eagleton, *Walter Benjamin, or, Towards a Revolutionary Criticism* (London, Verso: 1981).

8 Doreen Massey, *Space, Place and Gender* (Cambridge: Polity Press, 1994).

9 Marcus A. Doel, 'A Hundred Thousand Lines of Flight: a Machinic Introduction to the Nomad Thought and Scrumpled Geography of Gilles Deleuze and Félix Guattari', *Environment and Planning D: Society and Space* 14:4 (1996): 430.

10 Stephen Muecke, 'Outback', *Environment and Planning D: Society and Space* 14:4 (1996): 407–420. See also Krim Benterrak, Stephen Muecke and Paddy Roe, *Reading the Country: Introduction to Nomadology*, rev. edn (Fremantle: Fremantle Arts Centre Press, 1996).

11 Lorraine Mortimer, 'Will the New Woman Keep Some of the Old Organs?' *Arena Journal* 4 (1994/5): 122–123.

12 George G.N. (Lord) Byron, 'The Destruction of Sennacherib' (from 'Occasional Pieces', 1807–1824), *Poetical Works* (Oxford University Press, London, 1945), p. 83. This is a poem that Australians of my generation learned by heart at school.

13 See Massumi, 'Becoming-deleuzian', p. 401, and Doel, 'A Hundred Thousand Lines of Flight', pp. 421–423.

14 Jean-Luc Nancy, 'Du sens, dans tous les sens', *Libération* 7 November, 1995, p. 36.

15 Gilles Deleuze and Félix Guattari, *Kafka: Toward a Minor Literature,* trans. by Dana Polan (Minneapolis: University of Minnesota Press, 1986 [1975]), pp. 3, 41, 37; Franz Kafka, 'The Burrow' in *Metamorphosis and Other Stories,* trans. by W. and E. Muir (Harmondsworth: Penguin Books, 1961 [1931]), pp. 129–166.

16 I. Evans, ed., *Brewer's Dictionary of Phrase and Fable* (London, Cassell, 1981), p. 847.

17 Henry Lawson, 'The Drover's Wife' in *The Portable Henry Lawson,* ed. Brian Kiernan (St Lucia: University of Queensland Press, 1976 [1892]), pp. 96–103.

18 For an elaboration see Stephen Muecke, *No Road (Bitumen All the Way),* (Fremantle: Fremantle Arts Centre Press, 1997).

19 Muecke, 'Outback', p. 411.

20 Ghassan Hage, 'The Spatial Imaginary of National Practices: Dwelling–domesticating/being–exterminating', *Environment and Planning D: Society and Space* 14:4 (1996): 463–485.

21 Sandra Buckley, 'A Guided Tour of the Kitchen: Seven Japanese Domestic Tales', *Environment and Planning D: Society and Space* 14:4 (1996): 441–461.

22 F. Scott Fitzgerald, 'The Crack-up' in *The Crack-up: With Other Uncollected Pieces,* ed. Edmund Wilson (New York: New Directions, 1956), pp. 77–78, 81. Cited *ATP*, p. 538.

23 Cindi Katz, 'Towards Minor Theory', *Environment and Planning D: Society and Space* 14:4 (1996), p. 488.

24 Massumi, 'Becoming-deleuzian', p. 397.

25 See Gilles Deleuze, *Negotiations, 1972–1990,* trans. Martin Joughin (New York: Columbia University Press, 1995 [1990]), p. 32.

26 Deleuze, *Negotiations,* p. 31.

27 Massumi, 'Becoming-deleuzian', p. 402.

28 Ibid., p. 400.

29 Deleuze, *Negotiations,* p. 33.

30 Ibid., p. 32.

31 Katz, 'Towards Minor Theory', pp. 496–497.

32 Ibid., p. 497.

PART THREE

Institutionally Speaking

Sticks and Stones and Stereotypes: What Are Speech Codes For?

Every time someone learns to chant that 'sticks and stones may break my bones, but names can never hurt me', a lesson is passed on about language. Several lessons, really. We learn, first of all, to tell a whopping lie about language, and usually also about ourselves. Names can hurt all right, even if they don't break bones; as children, we learn to say that they can't precisely because they just have ('there, there, don't cry: remember, "sticks and stones"'). Names hurt hearts and minds and souls, and a 'me' truly *never* hurt by names would be impervious to other human beings – an angel or a sociopath, perhaps.

Yet the lesson of the chant is not itself a lie, but a magical theory of language: 'saying makes it so'. The chant is an incantation, a spell that we cast at aggressors to keep the power of their words at bay. When someone pelts words at us to try to hurt our feelings, we block them with a ritual formula that vows they will never succeed. So, like all good spells, this formula 'means' something different from what it seems to say: 'names can never hurt me' means '*you* can't hurt me – who cares what you think? your insults are powerless; you don't matter, and I am stronger than you are'.

We may be telling the truth or we may be dying inside. Either way, the chant teaches us an art of self-defence along with some basic facts of social life. We learn that language is powerful, and that we can do things to each other with words; that language is a social bond, as flexible as it as forceful; and that meaning depends on how we *use* language in all the varying situations of life. From its singsong cadence, we also learn something obvious that language-moralists forget when they call some words good and others irredeemably bad: there's a lot more to language than names – or verbs and prepositions, for that matter. The powers of language, written or spoken, include rhythm, tone, accent, pitch and rhyme as well as reason. How something is said affects us as much as who says it and why: we may accept an 'affectionate insult' from a friend more easily than from a stranger, but if the friend says the same thing in a nasty tone in the middle of an argument, affectionate words become stinging. Much more than a way of describing things and trading information, language is a relationship between people. However routine or perfunctory most everyday contact may be, we touch each other with words.

Some verbal gestures pack a wallop no magic spell can contain. I learned this one morning in about 1965 when I walked to school like any other day, past the cow paddock and the shops, under the railway bridge and past the prison farm, then up the road dividing the brick of Maitland Girls' High School from the stone of Maitland Gaol. I did this every day, and hardly ever watched where I was going; sleepy from reading into the night and doing homework before breakfast, I floated, snoozed and chatted myself to school. On that particular morning, from half-way up the hill even I could see through my dreamy haze the white letters on the dull brick wall:

MEAGHAN MORRIS IS A SLUT

They seemed to be enormous, sky-high. And so bright! As the world froze quietly inside me, I wondered if people could see my name from the main street miles away. No doubt at all, every pupil and teacher could; girls were hanging off the fence by their fingernails to see what I would do.

'Stereotypes ... take away a person's individuality', says *Language Matters*, a brochure for staff and students at the University of Technology, Sydney (UTS). They certainly do: with a glancing gesture – 'spastic', 'wog', 'dole-bludger', 'dwarf', 'slant-eyes', 'slut', 'dirty Abo' (there are hundreds of ways to do this) – a human personality is squashed into someone else's idea of its essential shape in less than a second flat. Hurled at people as insults or whispered around them as rumours, stereotypes are also intensely isolating. From a comfortable, warm, hissing little place secured for 'all of *us*', we turf out *them*, the scapegoats – the ones publicly punished for breaking the rules so the rest of us know what they are.[1]

It can be quite a spectacle. Luckily, I knew what a scapegoat should do to survive the next five minutes: keep walking, look at nothing, eyeball anyone who stood in my way; push through, scrape an ankle or two if necessary, go inside, open a book. I'd been bullied by experts as a child in a small rural town; 'four-eyes!', 'commie!' and 'swot!' were the names I feared then, for the pinching and punching that followed. When someone ground my face into a wall as a short-cut to breaking my glasses, my father taught me how to fight back. The effect was astonishing; after months of muttering about sticks and stones, I flattened one of my tormentors once and the bullying stopped. Still, I had been happy to move to Maitland, a cosmopolitan city of 30,000 people, where quite a few kids wore glasses and had politically incorrect parents who didn't like Mister Menzies.[2]

Verbally humiliated in my new home, I should have been shattered but I wasn't. Maybe all that chanting had toughened me up. At any rate, the wall was slinging the wrong name at the wrong fourteen-year-old virgin. Far from being a slut, I was still a swot. The message should have read (in the idiom of those halcyon days of Australian cultural unity), MEAGHAN MORRIS READS DIRTY BOOKS. My downfall was a book by Bertrand Russell, probably *Why I Am Not A Christian*. I found it in the town library and it shocked me to the core: what if people could live good lives without going to church? what if I tried to think for myself what the right way to live might be? what if you could love someone without getting married?

Reading didn't make me a slut. Talking about it did. On the bus, I told a boy I knew slightly about this amazing book I was reading. Not a total fool, I confided in him only because I thought he was like me, 'bookish', and picked on, I'd heard, by the boys at his school. In the solitude of my second five minutes as a scapegoat, I understood that he'd sold me out to buy favour with those boys. I couldn't really blame him. Besides, 'slut' was a step up from 'swot' if both were just rude names for reading; it gave me a warmer, more friendly social identity. I hitched up my uniform, grew my hair, and never looked back.

Because we touch each other with words, language passes on values: yes, no, good, bad, maybe, so-so ... what if? The writing on that wall spelt out the 'codes' of language and my community in mid-1960s Australia. It told me that ideas were dangerous when merely to ask 'what if?' could put you beyond the pale; that thinking freely was a sin and speaking openly a vice; and that conformity was valued more than truth. It also told me, 'it's different for girls': a boy-swot might have been called a 'poof' instead of a slut, but no boy would have been punished by his peers for contemplating sex outside marriage – unless (unthinkably in those days) he declared *himself* a poof. So it told me my egalitarian society had rigid, intolerant rules of speech that assured my inequality.

'PC language': the boot on the other's foot?

Most people can tell a story about facing up to insults, abuse, unpopularity or even persecution at some point in their lives. Whether told as funny anecdotes, painful confessions, or 'life is hard, get used to it' moral fables, whether recounting trivial incidents or one person's experience of mass suffering and oppression, these stories are important to those who tell them. They help us explain who we are and how we feel about others in the present.

They are not much help in understanding the fuss about so-called 'politically correct' language that has broken out over the past few years. They don't explain why 'speech codes' have suddenly appeared in workplaces, public organizations and universities, supposedly bastions of free speech, or what these codes have to do with censorship, anti-vilification laws, defamation and protests about advertisements. Above all, tales of tough times survived in closed, intolerant little communities may have an indirect bearing at best on debates about what counts as civil behaviour in big, diverse social spaces densely populated by strangers and open to the world.

True, after all the hysteria and myth-mongering of recent years about the 'enforcement' of 'PC' language in Australian institutions, it's useful to remember just how strictly speech was policed back in the good old days when minorities weren't noisy, and how effectively name-calling, stereotyping, shunning and moral pressure kept women, wogs and weirdoes in their place. These, the modern methods of imposing orthodoxy without breaking bones, were not invented in the 1980s by academic leftists and their media mates, and they certainly did not vanish with the election of John Howard. There is always orthodoxy in human affairs, and always someone who loves to impose it. For people puzzled by an abrasive new sensitivity to words in social life, or stung by a hostile reaction to their harmless comment as 'sexist' or 'racist', it is comforting to believe there is nothing new in all this – just another rabid bunch of bullies telling ordinary people how to talk. The fuss is blamed on former scapegoats, exacting revenge for real or imagined slights in the past – the boot on the other's foot.

It happens. But it would be wrong to suggest that nothing changes under the sun but the scapegoats in season – sluts and wogs a while ago, rednecks and Anglo-Celts yesterday, 'feminazis' and 'the Aboriginal industry' today. Shifts in language are related to deep social change. Even orthodoxy isn't what it used to be in Christian-dominated societies. Once it was the name of a state to which almost everyone sane aspired. Now, 'orthodoxy' is a term of abuse for *other* people's beliefs, and those who want to influence public opinion routinely pose as heretics, often in the name of 'the silent majority'. It is rare in Australia to hear someone say, 'I am orthodox'. *They* are orthodox, and a minority; *we* are heretical, and mainstream.

All this overblown rhetoric obscures the fact that most of the time in modern democracies we are comparing different orthodoxies and assessing their implications. Faced with rival models of how we ought to act – say, one that relentlessly stomps on every single expression of social prejudice, or one that bellows 'I can call your kid a mongrel if I want to, so you shut up about it!' – the practical issue before us has nothing to do with 'correctness' in the sense of conformity to an orthodoxy. It is which of these codes of behaviour is more likely to shape a tolerant society that cherishes debate, protects dissent, and gives us all a chance to participate.

If I had to choose between these extremes, I'd take my chances with the first one. Po-faced puritanism is usually too busy finding sins and crimes within the ranks ('aha! *more* sexism and racism, and just where you'd least expect it!') to organize social violence against scapegoats or outsiders. However, the main problem with the notion that PC is just a new brand of intolerance is that it fools us into thinking that we do, as a community, face choices of such stark simplicity; that today's battles about language are just like yesterday's wars of ideology, and that the world hasn't changed in thirty years. PC sympathizers indulge this fantasy too when they laugh at people's anxieties that speech matters in strange new ways, or their fears that any casual utterance might expose them to criticism.

It can happen – why deny it? We all see it on television every other week. When the flamboyant Queensland politician Bob Katter once mixed up 'slanty' (which he said) and 'squinty' (which he meant to say) in an unloving ode to 'feminazi' eyes, all hell broke loose in the media. Labor Prime Minister Paul Keating caused an international incident in 1993 when he called the Malaysian Prime Minister, Dr Mahathir Mohamed, 'recalcitrant' instead of 'intransigent'. Watching the feeding frenzy that follows whenever somebody trips on their tongue, it's not surprising if everyone who has ever mixed up a few words wonders when their turn will come.

Language does have a new kind of volatility in Australian social and economic life. I remember when words were used sparsely: men said little when they came home from work, women did family business at morning tea, and no-one talked politics or religion at dinner (for good reason, in a society where 'mixed marriages' were Catholic–Protestant and families were wrecked by sectarianism). PC language is an issue in a different world. Today, words, symbols, images, interpersonal gestures, the relationships they create and the feelings they provoke are the very stuff of the service and culture industries, in which carelessly giving offence is bad business practice and employment is insecure. A working day has no definite end for those who work, and word-machines fill the home; few women can care full-time for families, while political, religious, social and, yes, linguistic disputes stream off the TV over breakfast, lunch and dinner.

At the same time, new communications technologies and the expansion of education and tourism have, quite as powerfully as immigration and multiculturalism, increased our exposure to other people's parochialisms and to ideas of civility that differ from our own. The noise of all this difference can no more be kept out of Australian social spaces than words can be stripped of their social power. In this world, the truly ex-*communicated* are not professional heretics fighting this or that 'correct line', but people left without access to jobs, education and technology; those without word-machines and 'pc' (personal computer) skills are beginning to be excluded from society. If promoters of unpopular ideas do suffer for their faith, they can tell the world about it; new media are giving the most eccentric people ways to find partners in dissent.

Public institutions are changing along with the rest of society. Once, universities were communities of people like-minded enough to stage a few ding-dong battles that made sense to everyone. The Sydney University that I attended in the 1970s was even more homogeneous than a country town with a bit of a woman shortage. It didn't always seem so at the time; coming from Maitland, I spent two years of what I thought was culture shock amongst aliens from North Shore Sydney. However, most students I met were Australian-born, white, Christian or lapsed, studied full-time, had middle class backgrounds or, like me, aspirations, were about the same age, and spoke English as a first or fluent second language.

Today, someone entering a classroom in all but a few elite institutions can take none of these things for granted, not a one – except for, usually, the middle class aspirations. Universities now are not communal *at all*. They are huge networks – or networks of networks, if the truth be told – of communities linked to other communities inside and outside the university, the city, the state, and the nation. They are diverse in composition from the outset, without anyone needing to 'impose' multiculturalism, and they vary greatly from each other.

These changes have practical consequences that are only slowly filtering through to public debate. In the 1970s, it was meaningful to talk of 'academics' and 'students' as social groups with coherent fashion tendencies in ideas as well as clothing: the cartoon image of the typical PC activist as a spiky-haired, be-overalled, jack-booted feminist belongs to that era, along with the tweedy professor. There are people who match both images. However, as tenure declines, short-term contracts become normal, and teachers come in from industry, community groups and foreign countries to perform specific tasks, the academic body is becoming as diverse and fluid as the student body is at any given time.

Universities are not the only institutions discussed in a language or a set of stereotypes that no longer help us deal with reality. There is a reality-lag between the economic and social changes of the past thirty years and how we represent them, which makes it hard to imagine their consequences. Thus some people dream of reviving the family values of the 1950s and 1960s, while embracing the destruction of the protected, unionized, job-for-life, full white male employment, eight-hour day economy which sustained them. In language matters, reality-lag inclines us to go on talking *about* 'language' as though it were a single issue, something part of but detachable from the rest of our social lives – a tool to use, but sparely.

The idea that there is a coherent 'politically correct language' movement – a visible group of people who stomp on every expression of what they see as prejudice – is a product of this lag. It is not a myth in the sense of having no basis in reality. It is a stereotype that makes it harder to *deal with* reality. There are many conflicts about language use in societies that are open and diverse (sometimes more so than we are prepared to accept), and different people have varying views about all of them. This student is insulted by racial epithets while believing on religious grounds that homosexuality is evil. That student loathes *white* feminists. This one self-righteously jumps on every second word that other people say, while being tone deaf to the meanings of rural or working class speech. That one couldn't care less about words and wants to find a job.

By the same token, the same person can oppose the passing of laws against vilification (as I do, thinking that it does more harm than good), while supporting a minimal censorship of violence in books and films; attack racist cartoons selling beer or washing-machines, without wanting to have them banned; oppose campaigns waged against gorgeous bodies on billboards; and think it a good idea for workplaces to offer guidelines to polite, fair and realistic ways of talking to a mixed bunch of strangers. These issues have not been created by PC militants. They arise from practical problems of daily life in diverse, democratic societies, and neither mockery nor stereotyping will make them go away.

Courtesy or euphemism: what are speech codes for?

In a very funny film called *Demolition Man*, Sylvester Stallone plays a late twentieth century cop thawed out of cryogenic prison by the wimps who pass for cops in a politically correct future. Meat-eating, hostility and carnal sex are forbidden (the future Los Angeles is ruled by a girlish sort of fascism), and machines spew out fines whenever someone says a bad word. Unable to use the hi-tech toilets, Sly murmurs obscenities at one of these machines to get a good supply of paper.

Contrary to rumour, this is not how things work today in Australian universities with equal opportunity language strategies and iffy plumbing. 'Speech codes' is an American term, much less of a mouthful than Australian bureaucracy's 'guidelines for the use of non-discriminatory language', but it is also a lot less accurate for our conditions. Codes can be compulsory, like road rules. Guidelines are not. Codes may formalize moral philosophies, guidelines make suggestions for how to get things done.

Call them what you will, they are not lists of bad words and they do not turn red-blooded men and women vegetarian. Let me talk about a real one, *Language Matters* – a 32-page brochure available at my time of writing from the Equal Opportunity Unit at UTS. Unlike the 'house style' routinely imposed by newspaper editors and book publishers, it does not spell out an obligatory or enforceable policy. It is not used for fining or in any way punishing people. It does not outlaw hostility, ban prejudice, forbid hatred or censor opinion. It is not about preventing deliberate verbal abuse, or speech inciting others to hatred (that is 'vilification', not 'discrimination').

Language Matters deals with problems that are far more common than overt conflict when a diverse group of strangers gets together for a limited, practical purpose, like taking a class. How do you talk politely to everyone at once when you haven't got a clue who they are? How can you avoid offending people unwittingly, when you don't know about their culture or their personal experience of life? How do you make everyone feel equally included, valued and able to participate – when the class itself is as likely to have tensions and hostilities as any other social group? How do you create enough tolerance in the room to let everyone get on with the job?

These problems may seem precious or trivial to people who don't spend their time working with strangers, or who think of universities as the cosy communities of old. They can actually be very destructive, not least because people falsely accused of intending an insult feel humiliated in turn. They also waste a lot of time. I once casually used the phrase 'calling a spade a spade' (as Australian idiom has it, implying a contrast with 'gardening implement' on the one hand and 'bloody shovel' on the other) ten minutes into a talk in the United States, where I was taken as enthusiastically recommending the use of a derogatory word for a black person. I never did extricate myself or finish the talk, and while I learned an important lesson in public about how meanings vary with contexts, I would much rather have read it in a speech code.

Most of the advice in *Language Matters* is simple, or can seem so from the cosmopolitan, I've-been-around, my-best-friends-are perspective of some of the pundits who send up PC language. The truth is that many people new to university haven't 'been around' much at all, and that some staff spend most of their private lives without being around people like their students. I also had to learn the hard way – a testy public rebuke – that girls from Bankstown who don't look British or Irish tire of being asked where they're 'originally from' (to take one example from the brochure), and it is surprising how often people simply don't know that the Australian habit of 'friendly insult' is not a universally understood custom, or a wise way to bond with a cultural stranger. Of course, if you *want* to insult strangers you are free to go ahead, although these days you are not entitled to expect that the person you insult will obligingly pretend not to be insulted.

The real problem is that we are all parochial to some extent now in relation to the complexity of our own society. Basically, *Language Matters* is an etiquette for dealing with this situation – something social conservatives should approve. As a guide to good manners in the midst of diversity it is more experimental, but much simpler, than the etiquettes of old which tried to produce uniformity. It boils down to four basic principles of politeness: don't harp about people's differences when it isn't necessary; do try to treat everyone equally and fairly; don't use euphemisms for disabilities or make jocular remarks to people you don't know about their race, their looks or their sexuality; do call people whatever they prefer to be called, and if you don't know, ask them.

In what sort of a society are these principles thought sinister or laughable? Not ours, I hope, especially since the last allows anyone who wants to be called a cripple rather than a wheelchair user, Australian without an ethnic prefix, or Mrs rather than Ms, to have their wishes respected. Anti-PC crusaders who do find tolerance a joke have made mileage out of treating examples from workplace codes as though they were absolute rules of life: 'these lunatics want to ban ladies!' *Language Matters* does say, accurately, that 'women' is used more widely now than 'ladies' as a neutral term, but it also suggests that 'men' goes with 'women' and 'ladies' goes with 'gentlemen': to talk about 'men and ladies' may be fine in some contexts, but in a working environment it comes over as trivializing. However, if I want to be called a lady at work, a lady I can ask to be called.

Speech guidelines do not suggest euphemistic ways of talking about people but polite ways of talking *to* them; they do not promote piety behind the back but courtesy face to face. There is a difference. Robert Hughes may be right to say in *Culture of Complaint* that 'the usual American response to inequality is to rename it, in the hope that it will then go away'.[3] Americans do exist who say 'differently abled' with a straight face, though I have rarely seen it done; *Language Matters* gets all stern and finger-waggish about such phrases ('strongly discouraged'). However, the point about sharing a workplace with people is that they do not go away, and they are neither named nor 'renamed' in their absence. Of course all the inequality in the world does not vanish when we encourage respect – it doesn't have to be love – in a classroom. Is that really a reason not to do it?

A more serious criticism, it seems to me, is that too much fuss about phrasing and names can make people feel like victims – frail petals in need of special linguistic delicacy of touch. Being rather partial myself to 'life is hard, get used to it' moral fables, I am always ambivalent about this. How much fuss is too much fuss? There is no simple answer, because people are different. Glorifying toughness is no improvement on sanctified whining.

I do know that unthinking cruelty can devastate people already feeling frail. My education was kinked for years by that early brush with late Menzies-era PC. I became an ardent writer but a furtive scholar, staying out late at night then studying until dawn so no-one would know I did it (sluts don't swot), and by the time I made it to university I was terrified of talking out loud about books. As a silent girl, I was treated as dumb by some of my tutors. One accused me of plagiarism (of what he couldn't say) when he read my first essay; a dumb girl couldn't have written it. Another did something much worse for my confidence about talking out loud. One day, we were reading a scatological poem by Dryden. I was enjoying it, dreamily, when I heard him say: 'What does the lady in the green dress think? *Does* the lady think?'

This is the kind of casual discriminatory gesture – not really meant to hurt, not thought out, not even malicious – that *Language Matters* asks us to imagine from the receiving end. When I looked up, there was a roomful of men (I think no other ladies were present) sniggering at my bright red face, and I knew they thought I was embarrassed by the bad words in the poem. Until then, I'd assumed I was one of the class, a student among students, getting used to the relentless demand of universities for fluency in speech. Suddenly I was an outsider, a lady in a green dress caught reading dirty books.

There is nothing new in the idea of language reform. It is a fundamental tradition of Western civilization; without it, Christianity would not have survived as a major religion, education would still be conducted in Latin, and democracy might have remained a loony radical idea. This does not mean that every reform is good, or that reformers ever get exactly what they want. Language is a collective product, and no-one can control it or prevent it from changing.

PC language sets out to help us represent and, above all, *address* the social world the way it is now, not the way it was thirty years ago when most people in university seminars really were white males, give or take the odd white lady. In the process, it easily becomes coy, pedantic and prissy. But when it gets too absurd or fails to serve any useful purpose, people laugh, quarrel about it, criticize each other and come up with better ideas. Soon, someone will improve on 'person with paraplegia', and someone else will find an alternative to multiculturalism that will seize our imagination.

In the meanwhile, fussing a little bit about phrasing and names can actually help reduce the need for 'special delicacy' in talking together about important things. These are not always social or political issues. Even in universities, no-one wants to turn every class into a workshop in personal tensions and, except in language, literature and media classes (a minuscule part of any university), most people do not want to spend their time poring over words. At UTS, much of the demand for *Language Matters* comes from people working in technical and practical fields who do not centre their lives on language – unlike those of us who fight about PC.[4]

Speech codes have no hope whatsoever of eradicating inequality and intolerance, and they fail dismally as brain-washing programmes. But that is not what they are for. They do help create spaces of temporary equality, working tolerance, in which everyone has a good chance to participate. The price of retreating from this effort is one that almost all of us would have to pay.

NOTES

1 'For "all of us"' was a slogan used by the Liberal party in its victorious 1996 Australian election campaign; the message and its promise were closely associated personally with the party's leader, John Howard.

2 Robert Gordon Menzies was Prime Minister of Australia between 1939 and 1941 (earning the nickname of 'Pig-iron Bob' for forcing waterside workers to load a cargo of pig-iron bound for Japan), and, as leader of the Liberal Party, from 1949 to 1966. Knighted in 1963, he was assiduously referred to as 'Mister' by Labor-voting families.

3 Robert Hughes, *The Culture of Complaint: The Fraying of America* (New York and Oxford; Oxford University Press, 1993), pp. 17–18.

4 My thanks to Lyn Shoemark for explaining this to me.

The Scully Protocol ('The truth is out there ...')

I have made a humiliating discovery. The world is full of people who believe in alien abductions, Satanic conspiracies and the ineffable evil of government; people who believe that Aborigines are privileged in Australian society, and that minorities have too much power; people who believe that deconstruction caused 'Baa Baa Black Sheep' to be banned in English schools, and that Geoffrey Blainey and Leonie Kramer are 'victims' of political correctness.[3] Some people believe all of these things. I believe none of them. It's an X-Files world – and, goddammit, I'm with Agent Scully.

That's the humiliating part. FBI Agent Dana Scully (Gillian Anderson) is the bimbo-figure of *The X-Files*, the 'spooky TV' show that reshaped TV drama in the 1990s as the glitzy 'power TV' of *Dallas* did in the 1980s. Yes, Scully is a highly trained, impeccably professional and immaculately groomed bimbo, but her role throughout most of the series is to be almost infallibly wrong.[4] She begins as the sceptical sidekick of wise, sad, sensitive FBI Agent Fox Mulder (David Duchovny), para-normality expert, who lost his sister to aliens. Scully is a Catholic, and some say that this renders her scepticism ambiguous from the outset. I disagree. Scully's cool, post-Enlightenment acceptance of an incommensurability between reason and faith is always in a tight contrast with Mulder's violently romantic, New Age drive to reconcile the two. However, Mulder is right about what is really going on in the world. 'The truth is out there', but Scully doesn't learn. No matter how many abductees she encounters, how much terror she faces and how clear are the signs of a deep and sinister conspiracy ('government denies knowledge' is the other key slogan of the show), Scully bounces back from the brink, time after time, to whine about logical argument, evidence and a rational explanation. Now that the TV series has ended, she is out there doing it on tape and DVD.

Good for her. Thanks to the wholesome professionalism Scully exudes as a government employee, *The X-Files* (1994–2002) is not the most paranoid of the post-*Twin Peaks*, neo-*Twilight Zone* shows about the evil in the hearts of men and the wickedness of public institutions that accompanied the rise to power in the 1990s of a globalizing neo-liberalism backed by religious zealots.[5] That honour belongs to the brilliant *Nowhere Man*, a 1995–96 update of *The Fugitive* which added an acute cyber-anxiety to the deep social fear in the 1960s model. The hero's life has been erased electronically by dark institutional powers; as they hunt him through the Edward Hopper landscapes of Middle America, we see humanity being erased by the media, computers, virtual reality – and a criminal, all-powerful state. Even the communities of the cyber-disappeared turn out to be bad to the bone; with truth and reality under attack, the only hope lies with lone, a-social, questing individuals (as it happens, white males) who know what they believe – and, by gum, mean to prove it.

'Spooky TV' is a misnomer for this stuff, which in the mid-1990s began to waft through all sorts of cultural genres as a diffuse yet panicky sense of embattlement. A sinister air came to pervade even *Melrose Place* (1992–99), the most successful of the third generation power-glitz shows with their roots in the 1980s; by the end, anyone's neighbour might be a murderer or married to a mobster. Some of the series were spooky, like the relatively liberal *American Gothic* (1995–96), the only one to make the madness of the US citizen militia groups seem less, not more, acceptable.[6] But para-normality is rarely the point in spooky popular culture: leaking through these shows and the wider media world is a deep, deep worry that normality isn't normal any more. Somebody is doing something to normality. Someone is changing things, experimenting on us, doubling our every move. In *Nowhere Man*, something is even killing history.

In short, the body-snatchers are back – with a difference, as there always is in commodity cyclical time. The aliens of McCarthy era films were, like the communists, foreign ('un-American'); once exposed, a pod was clearly a pod. In neo-body-snatcher culture, the evil emanates from Western institutions. The truth is out there, but 'they' are right here, insidiously warping reality. They are scientists, doctors, bureaucrats, teachers and academics. They are vengeful feminists, extremist blacks and irresponsible queers. And they are infinitely cunning; new and ever more fantastic ploys of political correctness are exposed every day. The furore over sexual harassment codes and regulations (ignited in Australia by Helen Garner's *The First Stone*) might have led the innocent to believe that feminist snatchers are anti-erotic puritans.[7] However, Marlene Goldsmith's *Political Incorrectness: Defying the Thought Police* exposed the fanaticism with which these same feminists also defend pornography.[8]

In an X-Files world, the tiniest thing can push a seemingly normal person over the edge. Having watched with bemusement the sprouting of a thicket of screamingly weird propositions around my zone of the academy – 'deconstruction junks truth!'; 'literary theory kills author!'; 'cultural studies smashes canon!'; 'post-structuralists were Nazis!' and (a personal favourite) 'postmoderns deny Holocaust!' – my Agent Scully bullshit-alarm finally went off on April 10, 1996, at the sight of a *Sydney Morning Herald* editorial suggesting that 'the structuralists' might have had a hand in a Sydney Theatre Company production of David Williamson's *Heretic* that greatly displeased the playwright himself.

Heretic is a play about the lifelong struggle of Derek Freeman, a somewhat feral Australian anthropologist influenced in the 1960s by the 'naked ape' school of socio-biology, to discredit Margaret Mead's research in *Coming of Age in Samoa* and, by extension, the presumed social ideas and experimental moral attitudes of modern feminism. Williamson is an immensely popular dramatist specializing in baby-boomer moral dilemmas and urban Australian middle class manners. Declaring himself at this time a convert to the more liberal 'moral animal' school of popular evolutionism,[9] Williamson staged in *Heretic* an encounter between Mead and Freeman in which the latter is vindicated as a truth-seeker, but taught to be more sensitive to women's needs and (marginally) more aware of the racist social uses of biological argumentation.

In late March 1996, the play opened to saturation publicity stirred up by Williamson himself. He attacked Wayne Harrison's production for distorting his intentions by trivializing Mead, who was (in my view) wonderfully 'travestied' on stage as Marilyn Monroe, Jackie Kennedy and Barbra Streisand, all tough, camp, sexy, *popular* women who terrify the obsessive and unlovable Freeman character. Harrison was also accused by Williamson of caricaturing Fa'apua'a Fa'amu (an elderly Samoan woman whose testimony about tricking Mead supports Freeman's case) by substituting for documentary footage 'a giant rubber head'.[10] Media coverage of the dispute ran for weeks, with debate about the legal rights of the author as opposed to those of his 'interpreters' (critics and directors) gaining as much attention as the issues raised by the play.

So, who got the blame from the *Herald* editorialist for Harrison's lapses of taste? The structuralists. That's right, structuralism – the attempt in the 1950s and 1960s in France to develop a unified method for the humanities and social sciences by working out the implications for each discipline of a Saussurean model of language as rule-governed and profoundly social. The great structuralists – Lévi-Strauss, Greimas, Genette, the early Barthes – saw themselves as scientists, just as Freeman did. They believed that society is intelligible, but they wanted to know *how*; they asked how we understand each other and ourselves. Not taken up widely till the 1970s in the English-speaking world, French structuralism overlaps historically with existentialism; it peaked between 1960 and 1962, with a great debate about history between Sartre and Lévi-Strauss. While structuralism was as important for what it enabled as for what its exponents achieved, it has to be said that this particular bird is a very dead parrot. Yet there it was, flapping around in the *Herald*, playing tricks with Margaret Mead (turning earnest anthropologists into blonde bombshells is a classic body-snatcher move), killing the author (again), and – large as life, present tense – promoting a 'gospel' that the work of interpreters is 'more important and creative than the text itself'.[11]

What can an earnest interpreter say to this? The media stew of fantasy and fiction about contemporary criticism has become so thick that lumps of nonsense are now presented to the public, with solemn authority, as fact – and, very often, in the name of truth and reason. It is hard to respond to a false attribution; deny such claims about structuralism, or the strange accounts of post-structuralism promoted by pundits such as (in Australia) Keith Windschuttle and Beatrice Faust,[12] and – well, you would say that, wouldn't you? This used to be called the 'have you stopped beating your wife?' manoeuvre, and there is nothing new about its use in public debate. The X-Files factor is that we, the scholars who spend our time reasoning and testing our claims against the rules of evidence accepted in our disciplines, now find ourselves charged thereby with assaulting truth and reason.

May I propose a brief reality check? For the moment, I leave aside the grossly silly polemics ('post-structuralists read Heidegger, Heidegger was a Nazi, therefore, post-structuralists are Nazis'). More interesting are those polemics penned by Williamson himself, in articles as well as in *Dead White Males* and *Heretic*. His have a serious intent, and they try to engage with what academics are saying. Let me share that sense of engagement. To commit the sin of comparing apples and oranges (a critical activity that often offends Australian artists, including

Williamson): I admire David Williamson's plays as I admire the novels of Eleanor Dark and Sumner Locke Elliott – they imaginatively enhance Australian life. I also enjoy his plays of ideas as I enjoy Michael Crichton's novels about contemporary issues (*Rising Sun, Disclosure*). They bring out people's anxieties about social and cultural change, and encourage us all to talk about them. I even agree with Williamson that the 'recriminations of identity politics' do little to combat poverty and social inequity, and may well do harm.[13] However, many 'post-structuralists' would agree with him about that. There's the rub.

In Williamson's *Dead White Males*, William Shakespeare says of the 'feminist multiculturalist' villain, 'that prattling knave Swain speaks through his fundament'.[14] Shakespeare is not wrong. The play is a farce about literary theory, sexual politics and class tensions in the academy and in suburban family life; Angela Judd, the youthful heroine torn between the tenets of post-structuralism and her natural common sense, takes her Foucault home with her. A commercial hit, the play presents feminist literary theory as little more than the latest means for a preening lecturer, Grant Swain, to seduce his female students; the real debates about life, love and literature are held on stage between the feisty Angela and William Shakespeare's ghost. Swain talks a lot about 'Foucault', but he has Foucault confused with Barthes, Barthes confused with British 'cultural materialism' (the real source of his jargon, as the book of the play makes clear), and Foucault himself back to front.

For example, Swain has Foucault exposing 'the way in which concepts of liberal humanist "ethical responsibility" are used to prevent the expression of "jouissance" in every structured organisation'.[15] On the contrary, insofar as he talked at all about 'jouissance' (that's Barthes on the thrill of reading, not Foucault on libido, as Swain does remember at one point), Foucault asked why we say we are prevented from expressing sexuality when institutions have invited us to talk about sex for centuries. Foucault did not sneer at ethical responsibility. His last two books were on ethics. Foucault did not wage war on 'liberal humanism'; that's largely an Anglo thing. Foucault was sympathetic to the reinvention of liberalism, and he outraged the 'PC' forces of his day by taking seriously the neo-liberal critique of the welfare state. He was 'anti-humanist', but that means that he rejected Descartes as a useful point of departure for thought in the modern world; he did not despise sociality or hold human initiative in contempt. And, unlike Swain, Foucault never ranted against 'patriarchal corporate ideology'. For one thing, he was a happily Eurocentric white male who was uneasy with women and ambivalent about feminism. For another, he did not believe in the existence of ideology.

There is something po-faced about arguing with a fictional character; I feel like Dan Quayle reproving Murphy Brown. I have heard it said that because Swain is a comic creation, clearly intended to come across as a charlatan, we cannot attribute his views to Williamson. Of course, that is so. As a sleazy pedagogue, Swain is very convincing; in my day, Leavisite English lecturers would whisper to students about 'maturity' and 'discrimination' in exactly the same way. The difficulty is that nothing in the play suggests that we cannot attribute Swain's views to Michel Foucault. The vast majority of Williamson's audience do not have Foucault at their fingertips, and I'd be prepared to bet that Swain's is the only version that most will ever encounter.

Does this matter? I think so, if the play is to be taken seriously as part of a wider debate. The problem of its accuracy is compounded by some of Williamson's own claims. In the *Bulletin* article ('Universal Moral Soldier') from which I took my opening quotation, Williamson attributes to Foucault the very determinism ('ideologies ... controlling the unconscious') that Foucault spent his life fighting. In fact, one way of understanding post-structuralism is as a renewed insistence on the role of agency – freedom, responsibility and creativity – in 'structuring' social life. Like Derek Freeman in *Heretic*, post-structuralism assumes from the outset that human beings are not blank slates or endlessly malleable plasticine; this assumption is one of the legacies of Saussure's linguistic theory. Like Margaret Mead, however, post-structuralist thinkers generally care about how sociable human beings can act to better their lives.

Williamson makes his Foucault do a lot of work. In another article, the latter turns up as an exponent of US-style identity politics, not only declaring truth a white male myth (when the truth is that Foucault wrote copiously about what makes truths true) but now insisting that politics can only be small-scale and local (when the truth is that Foucault, angered by exactly this misreading of his *History of Sexuality*, spent years lecturing on the history and the efficacy of modern 'governmentality').[16]

However, in media contexts where using academic evidence – extensive quotations and footnotes – is out of the question, this kind of tit-for-tat, "'tis!/'tisn't!' exchange can go on indefinitely. The trickiest issues arise, therefore, when a polemicist wants to admit the grain of truth in what their opponent says. This is often Williamson's stated desire, and here it is also mine. In his pieces around *Heretic*, Williamson seems to suggest that post-structuralism is a form of social constructivism. He uses the tag 'there is no human nature' to convert the claim that social conventions vary from culture to culture (a mundane idea shared by post-structuralism with a dozen other philosophies) into a claim that biology plays no role in human life.

Some of the innumerable bad cribs on post-structuralism do say something like this, and it is silly on at least three scores. First, from the proposition that many things we take to be natural are in fact historical, it concludes that there is no such thing as nature; this is a non-sequitur. Second, it forgets the crucial role that psychoanalysis plays in post-structuralist thought; the work of Lacan, for example, is all about what happens when the biological is forced to become the social. Third, it ignores the fact that 'post-structuralist' feminism emphasizes sexual difference, not the sameness of the sexes. That is precisely why equality-oriented feminists do not like it very much, and why academic bookshops are bursting with feminist books about the body. Mostly, primers on post-structuralism make none of these mistakes; they simply overwork the word 'construct', along with other Latinisms inherited from the translation-ese of the 1970s. French is a Romance language; *construire* often simply means 'to make'. From this I derive Scully's First Law of Interpretation: saying 'construction' does not make you a constructivist, any more than talking about 'structure' makes you a structuralist.

Why is there so much exaggeration, hyperbole and panic around these once esoteric debates? Some hypotheses in the air remark that much of the extremism comes now from '1960s people', today's fifty and sixty-somethings, who dismissed critical theory twenty-five years ago as a passing fad, and who are finding – more thanks to John Dawkins than to Michel Foucault – that the intellectual world they grew up in has vanished.[17] This seems uncharitable, and it is not an argument. Yet, watching *Heretic*, I did have a sense of generational dislocation. It was educational, but like a trip to a fun museum. The 1960s props did not create this distance; like most people around me, I loved the first act and the wild incarnations of Mead (though not, it is true, the cartoon Samoans). My problem was to share the sense of immediacy the play was trying to give the 'nature or nurture' debate. I saw it with older women, neighbours (not academics), who talked afterwards about the influence that Margaret Mead had in their lives. This was quite new to me. When I began adult life in the early 1970s, my friends were reading Lévi-Strauss and Gregory Bateson. The first big structuralist book I ploughed through myself was Anthony Wilden's now neglected *System and Structure* (1972), a book written under Bateson's influence and including several chapters on evolution and molecular biology.

Nature vs. nurture is not an issue for most of the theories that Williamson wants to criticize, although the role of 'binary oppositions' certainly is an issue. Today, alongside the Bergson revival and a flourishing interest in the work of Gilles Deleuze, feminists, too, are engaging with non-determinist notions of 'creative' evolution.[18] This does not mean that critics who will call themselves post-structuralist if they have to (the word is little more than an English marketing category) do not take sides when a nature/nurture debate, or the pressing issue of the social uses of the Human Genome project, arises. It means that they can take either side, and that they hold conflicting views. Some, like Paul

Rabinow, argue that the damage done by eugenics in the past should not hold us back from using this new knowledge.[19] Others join Noel Pearson in caring more about the harm that the old eugenics is still doing to black people in Australia to this day.[20]

When do we decide to let it matter that people's views really are different? How much can we let it matter, and in which contexts? Summary, paraphrase, narrative, description all depend on ignoring difference to some degree; without doing it, we cannot speak. If we overdo it, however, our discourse can become so far out of whack with other people's perceptions that it acquires, for them, a strangeness to which they can't respond. My hypothesis about the hysteria around 'theory' is that it derives from ignoring intellectual differences to a socially *unrealistic* degree. In one sense, Williamson, Windschuttle and Faust (to name three vocal Australian critics) are much more 'postmodern' than those of us who analyse postmodernism. They often seem to accept the 'count the column inches' theory of discourse as publicity, which holds that to discuss something is to endorse it (if Lyotard writes a book about the historians who deny the Holocaust, he must be complicit with those historians) and that to ignore something is to attack it (post-structuralism focuses on the social, therefore it rejects biology).

These critics are also well enough at ease in the media's permanent present to talk confidently about structuralism, post-structuralism, postmodernism, literary theory and cultural studies as equivalent options in the present, just like all the music in the CD store. That's how you can create post-structuralist Nazis: Paul de Man's name goes under deconstruction, deconstruction goes under Derrida, Derrida goes under post-structuralism, therefore ... Most academics are too paralysed by disciplinary history and our habit of making meticulous distinctions (de Man was not a post-structuralist, but one of the last New Critics) to participate well in this game. Whining 'but that's not true!' ('you don't know that, Mulder!'), we come across as pedants.

In another sense, though, Williamson and Co. are still flogging a very dead parrot, or rather, they are shooting the messengers telling them the parrot is dead. Something is tampering with reality, truth and the relationship between bodies and souls, but it isn't post-war French philosophy. It is probably the same thing that worried Heidegger: new technology. Compared with Heidegger, a figure whom most scholars treat with caution, post-structuralism fosters a positive critical attitude to technology and its uses. This is not surprising. After all, the post-War French philosophers had a far more direct experience than most Australians have these days of what nostalgia and irrationalism unleashed in Nazi Germany. One of the other 'fathers' of their thought – for ideas are promiscuous, and thought has many parents – was Emmanuel Levinas, who wrote *Existence and Existents* in a concentration camp.

In the midst of the *Heretic* furore, clipping out another article on PC and the assault on truth, I came across an item in another part of the paper (now lost) about technical progress towards creating 'vactors', or virtual actors. Soon, it said, thousands of photos of, say, Marilyn Monroe will be digitally scanned to make a sculpture, and the sculpture will be animated; Marilyn will be able to star endlessly in brand new films. What will happen, the writer wondered, if this technology is turned on the visual documents that are part of our 'historical record'? What becomes of ideas of evidence, of reality, of truth? Post-structuralism does not give us the answer to such questions. Its premise is that the truth is not 'out there', transcendent and elsewhere, but here, in the activities and strivings of social life. That is why it can help us to *ask* critical questions about history, and to look for ways to secure a humane, as well as 'human', future for reality and truth.

Patricia Mellencamp says that in the United States there is a National Association for the Advancement of Time dedicated to 'ending the 1960s in your lifetime'.[21] Good luck to them. As for me, I'm founding the Agent Scully League for the Defence of Reasonable Argument. I haven't written a manifesto yet, but I'm working on the following Protocol for the guidance of people who'd like to join:

1. When asked 'have you stopped beating your wife?', on no account reply, 'You mean, "your partner or your spouse"'. The best response for men as well as women to give is: 'Hey! I *am* a wife!'

2. Remember that there are more things in heaven and earth than are dreamt of in your philosophy.

3. It is unfair to compare apples and oranges if the topic of discussion is 'apples' and you attack an orange for failing to be an apple, or an orange-grower for denying the reality of apples. However, it is perfectly reasonable to compare apples and oranges when your topic of discussion is 'fruit'.

NOTES

1 David Williamson, 'Universal Moral Soldier', *Bulletin* April 2, 1996.

2 Cited in Rux Martin, 'Truth, Power, Self: An Interview with Michel Foucault October 25, 1982', *Technologies of the Self: A Seminar with Michel Foucault*, ed. Luther H. Martin, Huck Gutman and Patrick H. Hutton (London: Tavistock, 1982), p. 10.

·3 Among the academic elders of Australian neo-conservatism, Blainey, a historian, was widely attacked in the late 1980s for saying that Asian immigration to Australia was increasing too fast for social peace. Leonie Kramer, a literary critic, long played a public role akin (on a much smaller scale) to that of Lynne Cheney in the United States.

4 That Scully's world view collapses after Mulder's disappearance in the last two seasons of the show is entirely consistent with this. For a perceptive analysis of the detrimental impact of the loss of Mulder as 'passionate quack' on season eight of the X-Files in general and on the Agent Scully character in particular, see Calore Baker, 'Agent Scully in Review', http://collegian.washcoll.edu/dec00/scully.html.

5 A substantial reading of the series as 'an allegory of the ambiguous status of the nation at the end of the twentieth century' is Paul A. Cantor, *Gilligan Unbound: Pop Culture in the Age of Globalization* (Lanham, MD and Oxford: Rowman & Littlefield, 2001), pp. 111–198. On the early seasons, see *'Deny All Knowledge': Reading the X-Files,* ed. David Lavery, Angela Hague and Marla Cartwright (Syracuse, NY: Syracuse University Press, 1996).

6 See http://www.cyberpursuits.com/heckifiknow/ag/ag.asp.

7 Helen Garner, *The First Stone: Some Questions about Sex and Power* (Sydney: Picador, 1995).

8 Marlene Goldsmith, *Political Incorrectness: Defying the Thought Police* (Rydalmere: Hodder & Stoughton, 1996).

9 Robert Wright, *The Moral Animal: Evolutionary Psychology and Everyday Life* (London: Little, Brown and Co., 1994).

10 See Amanda Meade, 'Heretic Director Lost the Plot: Playwright', *Australian* April 1, 1996; Diana Simmonds, 'Humourless Feminist v Drag Queen Fantasies', *Bulletin* April 16, 1996.

11 'Heretic and Players', *Sydney Morning Herald* editorial, April 10, 1996.

12 See Keith Windschuttle, *The Killing of History: How a Discipline Is Being Murdered by Literary Critics and Social Theorists,* (Sydney: Macleay Press, 1994); and Beatrice Faust, 'Beatrice Faust replies', *Australian Rationalist* 39 (1995/6): 33. Both are well-known writers of the '1960s' generation who promote their views widely in the media.

13 David Williamson, 'Truce in the Identity Wars', *Weekend Australian* May 11–12, 1996.

14 David Williamson, *Dead White Males* (Sydney: Currency Press, 1995), p. 81.

15 Ibid., p. 40.

16 Williamson, 'Truce in the Identity Wars'.

17 John Dawkins was a key figure in Australia's Labor government (1983–96). As the federal Minister responsible, he led a reform of higher education which combined an expansion of the system with deep budget cuts and institutional amalgamations. In these conditions, 'low cost' multidisciplinary and theory-oriented programmes thrived. On the importance of cheapness to the spread of such programmes see Carolyn Steedman, 'Culture, Cultural Studies, and the Historians' in *Cultural Studies,* eds Lawrence Grossberg, Cary Nelson and Paula Treichler (New York and London: Routledge, 1992), pp. 613–622.

18 For example, Elizabeth Grosz, ed., *Becomings: Exploration in Time, Memory and Futures* (Ithaca, NY and London: Cornell University Press, 1999).

19 Paul Rabinow, 'Nostalgia for Eugenics', *Contention* 3:1: (1993) 143–152.

20 Noel Pearson, 'Mabo and the Humanities: Shifting Frontiers', *The Humanities and a Creative Nation: Jubilee Essays,* ed. Deryck M. Schreuder (Canberra: Australian Academy of the Humanities, 1995), pp. 43–62.

21 Patricia Mellencamp, *High Anxiety: Catastrophe, Scandal, Age, and Comedy* (Bloomington and Indianapolis: Indiana University Press, 1992), p. 378.

'Please Explain?': Ignorance, Poverty and the Past

Hanson really would have subsided into history's footnotes if the self-righteous, thumbscrew Left had not been so loud in its efforts to shout her down.

Frank Devine, *Australian*, June 29, 1998

I do not agree with this assessment of the popularity of 'Pauline Hanson's One Nation Party' as it exploded through Australian politics after the defeat of the Keating Labor government in November 1996. As a single working mother turned 'amateur' politician, Hanson led a surge of economic-protectionist, anti-immigration, anti-Asian and anti-Aboriginal popular feeling powerful enough to sustain a new political party and shift the mood of the national social debate drastically to the right. In my view, she might have subsided into history's footnotes if the new Liberal Prime Minister, John Howard, had shouted her down from the very day that he won government and she was elected to the House of Representatives on the same wave of popular anger and disaffection after thirteen years of Labor's economic and social reforms.[1]

Better, Howard should simply have *talked* her down. Hanson was alone in Parliament and barely capable of defending her policies. Had he wished to do so, he could have stood on the distinguished human rights record of his own Liberal Party to take a stand against Hanson's xenophobic and often racist positions. He was in a good position for this. Hanson had tried to run for Parliament as a Liberal but lost her endorsement for making racist remarks about Aborigines, whereupon she stood as an independent; emotionally, this freed Labor supporters to vote for her and she went on to win a hitherto 'safe Labor seat'. However, instead of maintaining a stand against her, Howard began his leadership by attacking Hanson's *critics* as cultural terrorists opposed to free speech. Strongly appealing to social reactionaries like Frank Devine – columnist for Rupert Murdoch's *Australian*, our only national newspaper – this strategy was modelled on former US President George Bush's campaign against 'political correctness' in the early 1990s.

Transposed to Australia, the strategy unexpectedly succeeded in amplifying and legitimizing Hanson's voice to a degree unwelcome even to Howard in his first term of office.[2] Driven by a media frenzy of fears, thrills and excitement that Australia, too, was developing a far right wing racist movement, Hanson's popularity peaked at the Queensland state elections of June 13, 1998, when eleven One Nationers were elected with the support of twenty-three per cent of the voters in that state. Within a month, high-profile defections and messy legal problems began to beset the movement, turning the banner-headlines negative ('Fish-'n-chips fascism takes a battering', 'One nation starts to crack').[3] At the subsequent federal election of October 3, 1998, Howard's government retained power with a reduced majority; despite predictions of a sweeping victory for the Hanson forces, One Nation succeeding in electing only one Senator and Hanson herself failed in her bid for re-election in a Queensland lower House seat.

In reality, many of One Nation's policies (in particular, protectionism) were antithetical to Howard's. However, Howard hoped to secure the votes of her admirers, a volatile mix of racists, survivalists, flat-tax utopians and 'gun lobby' extremists along with a much larger constituency of 'losers' from economic globalization; struggling rural communities, residents of country towns enduring bank closures and high youth suicide rates along with deeply entrenched unemployment, the no-longer mobile middle classes in the outer suburban regions of major cities, and working families convinced that immigration causes job insecurity. These melded with a wide range of people *culturally* disaffected by two decades of government-backed multiculturalism. Many were long established Anglo-Australians, often elderly, who saw their heritage as denigrated and their values despised. However, some were recent immigrants who wanted an 'Australian' rather than an ethnically hyphenated identity, or who themselves saw further immigration from Asia as a threat to the Australia they had chosen as their home. By appeasing these people Howard risked losing some of his supporters to a movement which really looked for a while like a popular fascist line of flight; indeed, in 1998 some Liberal voters, disgusted by his handling of Hanson, turned to Labor. By splitting the conservative vote in this way, Hansonism followed the usual pattern of Australian *breakaway* parties; usually short-lived, sometimes lasting two decades or more, they tend to do more electoral damage to their 'natural allies' of the Right or the Left, than to their obvious opponents.

All that said, I believe that Frank Devine had a point about the negative impact of a politics of shouting down. One Nation did much more than *electoral* damage to Australian civic and community life, perhaps most of all in the phase of its decline as the Liberal and Labor parties alike absorbed key aspects of the fear-driven Hansonite platform on race and immigration, rendering One Nation itself redundant and installing a mean-minded, harsh-mouthed *ressentiment* at the core of national policy-making and the heart of 'popular' debate. To understand better how this happened, I look closely here at an instance of the media mobilization of popular support for Hanson in the late 1990s. My topic is not Hansonism as a movement,[4] but rather the role played by national media elites (including those who attack intellectuals as a 'cultural elite') in shaping the *mood* that helps make a movement. I cite that slippery term, 'elite', with purpose.[5] Class is a crucial dimension of culture wars in media-saturated democracies, and while there is a growing literature on this at an analytical level, I suggest that we have not paid enough attention to its *performative* dimension – how it actually gets played out in media spacings of class conflict.[6]

An attention to language in action is crucial for understanding Hansonism's populist appeal, insofar as the struggles over 'proper' English and politeness that marked her political rise and fall are struggles over questions of power, identity and class in the social practice of speech. Hansonism was a local response to the global reconstitution of class structure around the 20/80, wealthy/poor, division that Cho Hae-Joang discusses in a South Korean context of 'compressed development'.[7] While Australia experienced compression only at the level of a highly relative degree of rural and lower middle class impoverishment, those experiences were linked to the rapid socio-economic transformation of Australia's East Asian trading partners in this period – links widely discussed in the media. Hanson is a media creature, if not wholly a media creation, and her movement emerged with a wave of non-metropolitan hostility to the *vocal* power of the 'cultural elites' identified with multiculturalism, 'Asianization', republicanism, feminism and Aboriginal land rights politics. Hanson was loved for her ability to 'talk back' to vocal power, and her popularity for this has outlasted her political career. When Hanson resurfaced (after a brief stint in prison for election fraud in 2003) as a ballroom dancing TV 'personality', winning A$250,000 for charity on *Who Wants to Be a Millionaire?*, a journalist noted that 'as far as her fans are concerned she has had her ups and downs and, like anyone else, has just picked herself up'.[8]

In stressing the class dimension of her popular appeal, I do not deny that Hansonism had powerful racist elements and a fascist drift. However, racism is not new to Australian politics and what helped to convert an initial two to five per cent support for One Nation into potentially twenty to twenty-five per cent support was something also not new to fascism: a surge of anti-cosmopolitanism fuelled by economic despair, political disillusion, and a culturalized resentment of the imagined 'winners' of the 1980s and 1990s – Aborigines (ludicrously), Asians (globally) and immigrant 'ethnic groups' as invoked or performed audio-visually by *privileged representatives of these speaking positions* in the media. I have argued elsewhere that John Howard exploited this resentment by collapsing media discourses with their putative social referents in a flagrantly cynical way.[9]

Why does this matter? Scapegoating movements are occurring in much larger polities than Australia's in response to globalization and the new class order that Cho describes. By 1996, Australians had been hearing for over a decade that 'cultural changes' to diverse Anglo-Celtic attitudes, values and even speech habits would help improve 'the economy' and allow us to handle the 'globalization monster' (as Melani Budianta puts it in her analysis of crisis identity politics in Indonesia).[10] Yet that same decade saw a fifty per cent increase in recognized poverty, which jumped from twenty per cent of the population in 1986 to thirty per cent in 1996. Whole towns were being destroyed by policy, and people were not wrong to feel that some critics of 'culture' were impervious to the grinding despair of many ordinary Australians. It is not surprising that one of Hanson's most successful slogans worked rhythmically as an accusation to academics and the media as well as to politicians: *'You're not listening'*.

In what follows I analyse an example of 'not listening' from the media archive of Hanson's first year of runaway success, her famous 'please explain?' TV moment. 'Please explain?' is now a legendary phrase, lexicalized in Australia to model a hundred headlines, frame a thousand jokes, and sell innumerable products. It was first used by Hanson in an interview with a woman journalist, Tracey Curro, from a special report on 'The Hanson Phenomenon' broadcast by the Australian edition of *60 Minutes* (TCN-9) in October 1997. Running over two of the programme's three 'story' slots, this report interspersed four segments of a formal interview with scenes of Hanson chatting with Curro in varying moods and settings; Hanson relaxing with supporters, family and allies; and Hanson confronting her critics and 'targets', in particular, the Aboriginal leader Charles Perkins and members of the Aboriginal community on Palm Island.

For *60 Minutes*, this was a complex presentation. However, a single moment of the formal interview passed instantly into folklore when Hanson answered a hostile political question from Curro ('Are you xenophobic?') with a meta-linguistic question: 'Please explain?'. If some viewers loved this revelation of Hanson's ignorance (what a joke, a xenophobe who doesn't know the meaning of *xenophobia*), many more rejoiced in her puncturing of educated confidence and authority. Rarely have the limits to popular democratic participation in the nation's official public life more effectively been challenged.

Given the matey as well as male-dominated culture of Australian political reportage, Curro's interview with Hanson had two further extraordinary features. First, it allowed a sharp exchange between two white women to define the terrain of a major national debate; arguably, Hanson's face-off with Curro signalled the real beginning of her popular mobilization. Second, the scene of their encounter was sharply divided by audio-visual markers of class. On the left hand side of the scene, Pauline Hanson: orange hair, a bad haircut, televisually strange make-up, and very ordinary denim clothes. She spoke in her trademark 'nervous', gulping style with the broad, triphthong-rich, consonant-free accent, nasal tones and high pitch used by women across the country but almost never heard on television except in sitcoms and soaps. On the right hand side, Tracey Curro: honey-blonde, well-groomed, wearing a sober, well-cut jacket befitting the solemnity of 'real' current affairs (by no means the regular persona of the generally lightweight Curro). She spoke 'educated' Australian in the deep, soft, clipped, well-modulated tones of good broadcasting style in our quality media: as Shakespeare might have said of Curro in this interview, 'her voice was ever soft, gentle and low, an excellent thing in woman'.

While this contrast was rendered particularly sharp by the formal interview genre (Curro dressed professionally for the occasion, while the 'ordinary' Hanson did not), dress codes worked throughout the programme to style the class contrast between the women. For example, when Hanson in a social setting wore a tailored black outfit set off by sparkly earrings (a working class woman dressed up), Curro wore a chic red polo-neck sweater ('smart casual', a professional woman dressed down). However, before looking at this dynamic in more detail, I must clarify a couple of things about Australian *60 Minutes*. A long-running clone of the famous US show, *60 Minutes* long ago gave away its early pretensions to do serious current affairs. Moderately tabloid in style and range of topics, it has specialized for years in sensationalist, even panic-mongering stories about race and immigrants, single mothers, 'dole bludgers' (welfare cheats), and other demonizable minorities, stories all broadly pitched to a demographic of older, disgruntled, or less well-educated audiences: 'grudge television', you might call it.

Yet as soon as this 'demographic' found a parliamentary heroine in Hanson, *60 Minutes* began to play the bastion of well-informed opinion – taking its distance from the truly 'trash' TV and radio shows that gave Hanson a rapturous welcome. At one point in the programme, this distance was tacitly marked. When Hanson is shown working in the fish and chip shop where she learned that 'no-one else owes me a living', a Curro voice-over frames her dismissively: 'The view from the fish shop window is of a neatly divided world. There are 'hard workers' like herself, and 'bludgers' – the welfare recipients and Aborigines she believes are ripping off the system.' This hard work/bludger opposition is the stock-in-trade of right wing tabloid media. It also shaped the view of society that *60 Minutes* had been promoting for years. Moreover, the choice of Curro to interview Hanson was a curious one. Then an unpopular figure in the *60 Minutes* stable (largely for having called a living legend of Australian women's journalism, Ita Buttrose, 'old'), Curro was rumoured at the time of the Hanson interview to be at risk of losing her job because the programme's audiences found her sarcastic and even 'a bitch'. So why send her up against Hanson?

How to create Hansonites

Not the least of Hanson's political successes was to mobilize against multiculturalism a new Australian *social* identity: 'the people out there'. Forged from the diverse elements attracted to her movement, and drawing on a historically deep tradition of mythology about the worth of 'ordinary Australians', this social identity unified everyone feeling excluded from the political, bureaucratic, financial and cultural centres of power in Australia – regardless (Hanson would often claim) of race, creed, or colour. Used as a referent, 'the people out there' designates a marginalized majority, even a mass. Used in the present tense of a TV interview, it interpellates an audience in an obliquely second person mode of address: in the here and now of the media moment, 'the people "out there"' effectively means '*you*'. In this way, Hanson spoke to the audience with a directness and immediacy common in day-time talk and variety television ('women's shows') but very rare in Australian TV political commentary – where 'men of power', including journalists and a few stray women in suits, publicly perform their intimacy for a peeping, eavesdropping viewer.

Hanson's capacity to break the rules of power TV and critique them to the audience was positively Brechtian, not least in her willingness to portray herself as learning. As we shall see, in her encounter with Curro she cut through to 'the people out there' in the first few seconds and demolished her opponent's game in four swift movements. However, in looking closely at those movements I want to emphasize Curro's moves rather than Hanson's. As a small-fry member myself of the cultural elite, I believe that critical academics have a duty to understand why our efforts at even small-scale media interventions can go very badly wrong. Moreover, the interview as broadcast by *60 Minutes* was, of course, edited: the elegance and punch of the segment I am discussing was as much a product of the programme-makers' art as of Hanson's rhetorical power. However, *60 Minutes* fully understood that power: 'The Hanson Phenomenon' opened with a Curro voice-over informing viewers that Hanson 'is a phenomenon not for who she is or what she says, but because so many are listening to her, and agreeing with her'. So while a face-off between Curro and Hanson organizes the text, it is by no means clear to me that Hanson and *60 Minutes* had fundamentally different aims. Both were in the game, I believe, of creating Hansonites, and, step by step, I want to see how Curro played it.

1. Create sympathy for the other by refusing to 'hear' her terms

Pauline Hanson [PH]: In World War Two we went and we fought the Japanese from actually taking over these shores ... this land of ours. And what's hurting the Australian people out there is that the government just can see them coming over now and virtually letting them take over. They don't have to be citizens here to own freehold land in this country.

Tracey Curro [TC]: And this gets to your idea then that we are in danger of being swamped by Asians. That's what you're talking about.

PH: No. What I would like to see is that there be a balance back to our immigration policy. And I have said that we have got forty per cent between 1984 to 1995, so far, forty per cent of migrants into this country are Asians. I would like to see more of a balance.

In this opening phase, Hanson immediately appeals to the audience and establishes herself as *sharing* with them her knowledge of past historical suffering ('we went and we fought the Japanese'), present economic injustice ('they don't have to be citizens here to hold freehold land'), and the follies of government policy (immigration statistics). Ignoring the past, Curro manoeuvres for moral high ground with respect to 'your idea' (a distancing, isolating 'you') of an Australia 'swamped by Asians' – a sensationalizing reference to Hanson's 1996 maiden speech in Parliament, in which she had scandalized the country by using that phrase. At this stage, Hanson is already claiming large-scale national and 'public interest' ground, while Curro goes personal and petty by trying to hold Hanson to an unfortunate term she had used a year before and which she simply swats away ('No.').

Now, Hanson has often been accused of inconsistency about racism. She did say, and clearly believes, that Australians ('we') are in danger of being 'swamped', an expression which – regarded from a critical and ethnicizing perspective – plainly predicates Australians as 'not-Asians'.[11] On the other hand, she has always refused association with the White Australia Policy. Hanson several times affirmed a belief that 'Asians' have always been part of Australian life and always will be; the issue, she would claim, is not the racial composition of the existing population but the balance of the immigration intake now and in future. Hers is a national-citizenship approach to defining Australian identity; from this perspective, an Australian citizen is Australian regardless of ethnicity or origin, and it follows that the 'we' who is now in danger of being 'swamped' by Asians in principle encompasses Australians of Asian background. However remote it may be from current academic ways of construing identity, ethnicity and race, and from the experience of many immigrants, this is a widespread, deeply entrenched understanding of nationality in Australia. Accordingly, One Nation in its early days was not short of a few Asian-Australian members to display for the TV cameras. So when intellectuals, politicians and lobby groups converged to decry Hanson as racist (as I, too, take her discourse to be), she could plausibly claim to be misrepresented – in the process, appealing across our heads to people who share her sense of nationality and who do not understand critiques of it, not least because they do not participate in developing those critiques.

Confronted with this appeal to the public, Curro performs a refusal of understanding ('not listening'). It helps here to ask why Hanson so emphatically says 'no' in response to Curro's invocation of the notorious 'swamping' remark. Curro wants to talk about one issue: racism. Hanson thinks she is discussing two distinct issues having nothing to do with race: one is foreign investment (owners in Australia should be citizens), and the other is the power to control immigration (we-who-identify-only-as-Australian should control 'the balance'). By saying 'no', Hanson denies that these issues may be the same, and that they involve matters of race. From my point of view, the link between them is both real and racialized in Hanson's own discourse; the function of her opening invocation of 'war with Japan' is precisely to conjure a figure of 'Asian invasion' that covers money and people, the past and the present, alike. However, that is an analytical observation. Dramatically, it seems to be *Curro* who is obsessed with the sensationalist theme of race ('this gets to your idea, then'). In this moment, Curro also takes up the intimidatory-journalist position, which against an 'ordinary woman' is potentially one of weakness. A zone of sympathy for Hanson – poor little Pauline, trying to make a serious point – is established.

2.   *Assert your own knowledge as power*

> **PH:**   … I would like to see more of a balance.
> **TC:**   Well, let's look at some *actual* numbers then. There are 866,224 Asian-born Australians out of a population of over 18 million. Now, is that in danger of being swamped?
> **PH:**   I don't believe those figures.
> **TC:**   Well, these are from the Department of Immigration …
> **PH:**   That's … they're … as far as I'm concerned, they're book figures [i.e., not the real numbers].
> **TC:**   [*lengthy pause, sneering for the camera*] Are you … xenophobic?
> **PH:**   Please explain?

The second phase of the duel involves a knowledge/status war, which Hanson wins hands down with an impressive display of courage. *60 Minutes* was a top-rating show, and Hanson's notoriety assured this segment a large audience indeed. In any circumstances, it takes considerable *sang-froid* to eyeball an interviewer unflinchingly and admit to a vocabulary failure after having been challenged at the level of fact. On an occasion when for once 'the whole nation' really is watching, it takes bravery. However, Hanson was standing on sure rhetorical ground. In refusing to believe 'authority' and counter-asserting her own mastery of facts, she was capably drawing on a tradition with deep historical roots in Australian popular culture – a tradition of contempt for big words and statistics, for knowledge based on books instead of a direct experience of life, and for the tricks that educated people play by intimidating others with words. Sardonically posed, Curro's question was aggressive merely at the level of tone and content. Softly delivered, Hanson's counter-question was violently effective at the level of the struggle for enunciative mastery and power. The latter is more important; in this moment, Curro rendered herself a puppet of the 'cultural elites', and Hanson the voice of the People.

A *60 Minutes* reporter might ordinarily know better than to appeal to 'actual figures' in the context of a show about social and political feeling; anti-intellectualism is grudge television's home terrain. However, Curro reacted as though being challenged in her professionalism by Hanson's imaginary immigration figures. It is quite possible that while Hanson was talking to 'the people out there', Curro was more narrowly bent on sending an image of *60 Minutes* as 'responsible' to other professionals – in other words, playing primarily to other journalists, to politicians and to opinion-makers. Whatever the reasons for her choice of style, the effect was to intensify the gendered class division of the scene of public debate: on the left hand side, Pauline Hanson, single mother, talking common sense with deeply rooted historical authority; on the right hand side, Tracey Curro, career girl with attitude, voicing the world view of the 'New Class' beneficiaries of globalization. With this division established, Curro went on to make a serious mistake.

3.   *Feminize your opponent*

   PH: Please explain?
   TC: Xenophobia means a fear of all things foreign.
   PH: No, I don't think I am. No, I'm not. Is there a problem? ... I find this very hard because ... I have to sort of clarify what all my ... what I think and feel about things ...
   TC: Precisely, because you are a Federal politician. You're not, we're not just sitting around in a pub talking about things. You're a Federal politician, you've been standing up in Federal Parliament making these statements, so of course you should be expected to be able to ... to qualify ...

PH: [*interrupting*] Which the majority of mainstream Australians are backing me on this issue because they believe in what I'm saying also. They can see it also. But it's all these minority lobby groups who don't like the fact of what I'm saying is, because it's going to upset their little world. They've got a problem with it, not I. All I know is what comes from here inside, and by talking to the people out there in mainstream Australia and their fears also.

TC: So it's from the heart not from the head.

Many commentators have noted that Hanson's femininity – at once strident and quavering, flirtatious and shrill – was a crucial condition of her success. Gradually pushed to the fringes of Australian politics after the Second World War, the raw anti-Asian, anti-migrant, anti-Aboriginal content of her positions had been peddled by various men associated with small extremist parties (such as Australians Against Further Immigration) with little effect except amusement in the mainstream media. Hanson's gender made all the difference. Portrayed by fascinated image professionals as a 'strine' Joan of Arc, she appealed not only to popular audiences as 'an ordinary attractive woman' – dressed 'nicely' but 'just like anybody' in clothes from your local mall – but also to a strand of ostentatiously perverse yuppie taste; from 1997, Hanson began to appear in glossy lists of the 'sexiest women in Australia'. Greeted as a welcome shock and a novelty after years of 'politically correct' government, her femininity in fact had a classical lineage: feisty, tough when she had to be, strong yet vulnerable and soft, the Hanson moulded by the 1990s media was a direct descendant of those 1970s film heroines who first emerged decades earlier in famous Australian short stories and novels – 'The Drover's Wife' (1892), *My Brilliant Career* (1901), *The Getting of Wisdom* (1910).[12]

To try to take advantage of Hanson's spasms of incoherence by implying, as Curro did, that they signify a feminized emotional condition ('from the heart not the head') was profoundly to mistake not only the sources of Hanson's attractiveness to her 'mainstream Australians', but also the degree to which men and woman alike could *identify* with that condition (whether or not they agreed with the content of her policy propositions). Curro here represents 'the suits' – the bosses, the economic 'facts and figures' people – whose heartlessness and indifference towards the plight of working people is the very point at issue. Hanson's virtue in this scene is to 'have' a heart; to feel for people, and care deeply enough to be able to face up to a bullying suit on national television. Above all, her much-touted status as a battling single mother of three secured her victory over Curro, the masculinized bosses' woman (or 'castrating bitch'). As a patriotic bearer of white children, Hanson is also a mother coming to the aid of the nation in its hour of need ('talking to the people out there in mainstream Australia and their fears also'). With Hanson in possession of the national heart, Curro is now given a lethally lucid blow.

4. Lose the argument

TC: So it's from the heart not from the head.
PH: I've been learning since I've been in this job. It's been a big learning
curve for me.

As a closing line, Hanson's final reply (at least, the last that the editors allow
us to hear and see at this point) deserves to be called a rabbit-killer punch. Splat!:
mother power seizes the intellectual terrain and redefines the heart–head relation, as the common sense voice of the People claims the capacity quickly to
master policy expertise (a 'big' learning curve is also a fast one). The only person
'feminized' here, in the negative sense of that term, is Tracey Curro.

After Hanson's reference to her 'big learning curve' (threatening even bigger achievements in future), the editors cut to student protest footage followed
by former Prime Minister Malcolm Fraser (Liberal) abruptly declaring
Hanson's views 'wrong' and her policies 'evil'. Hanson's opponents having
been given perfunctory space, the Curro–Hanson interview resumes. This editing in fact works to highlight Hanson's big rhetorical hit against Curro rather
than to subject what Hanson has said to scrutiny and criticism. Accordingly, in
the next phase of the interview Hanson rebukes Curro for 'overdramatizing'
(a hysterical feminine trait) when she accuses Hanson of wanting to cut Australia
off from the rest of world, and, in the last scene of the programme, Hanson
secures her claim to speak as a national mother. Asked by Curro if she could
not find room in her heart to care more about the disadvantaged of our society,
Hanson replies with the ultimate cliché of phallic maternal cool: 'I'm a very
caring person, but I tell you what – you've got to be hard, you've got to be cruel
to be kind'.

Learning from Tracey Curro

It is dangerous for critics of media to dwell on Hanson's performances. If one is
at all susceptible to their scary charm, the logic of fascination carries one quickly
into a vast network of camp jokes and self-consciously kitsch critique. While hers
is a powerfully aestheticized politics, and we need (in my view) to know more
about the practice of such politics than we do, an exclusively aesthetic focus on
Hanson's or any other kind of performative politics leaves too much out of the
picture. Hanson does not matter primarily as a made-for-TV demagogue; she
matters because of the ugly racism that her politics brought back into public life,
because of the anxiety and suffering that the rise of One Nation caused many
'ordinary', 'mainstream' Australians of Asian and Aboriginal descent, and

because of the damage her movement did to the international imagination in Australia, never mind the national image.

In conclusion, therefore, I want to frame this exercise in 'listening' to Hanson as an effort to understand better how to fight her kind of media politics or, more modestly, how not to aid and abet them. Cho argues powerfully that in cultural theory we need to understand the subjectivity formations we live with and inhabit instead of affirming universals, and I tend to think that 'universalizing' theoretical rhetorics of cultural difference – universalizing, that is, within the confines of a transnational academy of which 'theory' is the lingua franca – have failed to come to grips with the urgency of this need as it arises in relation to national and majoritarian subjective formations.[13] One reason for Hanson's success against Curro is that the former is a more attentive local 'historian' (or mythologist, if you prefer) than her cosmopolitan opponent. Hanson intimately knows the memory-laden turns of phrase that will emotively mobilize her constituency. Curro lacks this awareness and cannot see coming the traps that Hanson lays for her; she asserts the attitudes and the everyday buzzwords of a profession, not a people.

Let me illustrate this claim with one more example from 'The Hanson Phenomenon', this time an example of a trap that Hansonism lays for feminist academics and cultural studies professionals as well as for media workers. Coming back against Curro's charges of xenophobia and isolationism, Hanson has a furious burst of eloquence:

> Why are you making me out to look as if I'm a racist? Why don't you go and ask Japan their immigration policy? Or Korea, or Sri Lanka? Ask them how they feel about white people going into their own country! And you can respect their views, and they can be proud of their own homogeneity. Yet if I voice my opinion I'm made to look as if I'm a racist. I don't ... I won't cop that.

Cultural studies teaches us to deconstruct this kind of thinking with an angry fluency: there to be ticked off is the Orientalizing assimilation of all Asian countries to 'the same'; the breath-taking ignorance of the differing histories of Japan, Korea and, of all places, strife-torn Sri Lanka (presumably 'homogeneous' as 'not-white'); and the denial of the colonial past as it shapes the present, not only in other countries where a 'white invasion' was and still would be unwelcome, but of course in Australia itself. Yet to expose this thinking is not to counter it, still less to answer Hanson's fierce questioning of the authority of her critics. There is the trap. Hanson derives her own authority not from her knowledge or lack thereof, but from her *refusal to be bullied* by the powerful and more articulate: 'I won't cop that' is the essence of both her political position and her popular appeal.

Tracey Curro had no answer to Hanson's questions. I'm not sure that I would either if challenged to respond in twenty seconds on national television, not least because there is an important grain of truth in Hanson's accusation that Australian opinion-professionals came to practise a double standard of 'critique' in the Labor years (so one response might have been to say, 'okay, let's talk about problems in Japan, Korea and Sri Lanka as well as in Australia'). However, if we are to take seriously Kuan-Hsing Chen's formulation of cultural studies as a decolonizing project, we cannot afford to follow Curro's example when engaging in any mixed public or community debate, within or across national borders.[14] It is no good talking *about* the local, the specific, the different and the heterogeneous if we do not know how to speak to constituencies beyond our own academic and institutional milieux.

It is not only 'in' theory that the task posed to social movements by pressures toward globalization is one of finding, as Beng-Huat Chua reminds us, the 'appropriate words and levels' for intervention as well as precise analysis.[15] It is when we presume to speak publicly as critics and theorists of other people's fears and anxieties that we most need to be able to find the words and the levels that work.

NOTES

1 The Australian Labor Party (ALP) is the oldest and biggest party in the Australian political system; with roots in the nineteenth century union movement, it incorporates a range of views from socialist to right-of-centre social democrat. The once conservative Liberal Party is now dominated by right wing radicalism on the US model; rarely able to rule in its own right, it dominated government after the Second World War in coalition with the rurally based, protectionist National Party (formerly, 'Country Party'). These historic distinctions blurred in the 1980s, when the ALP in government (1983–96) embraced a mix of free trade, deregulatory and privatization policies while pushing a 'progressive' social agenda. Given the pain the economic policies caused working people, 'Pauline Hanson's One Nation Party' proved capable of attracting voters away from all major parties, while doing special damage to the National Party.

2 Michael Millett, 'Howard's Nightmare', *Sydney Morning Herald*, June 15, 1998.

3 Geoffrey Barker, 'Fish-'n-chips Fascism Takes a Battering', *Australian Financial Review* October 15, 1998; Nicholas Rothwell, Leisa Scott and Natasha Bita, 'One Nation Starts to Crack', *Australian* July 1, 1998.

4 See Ghassan Hage, '"Asia", Hansonism and the Discourse of White Decline', *Inter-Asia Cultural Studies* 1:1 (2000): 85–96.

5 See Tony Bennett, 'Elite', in *New Keywords: A Revised Vocabulary of Culture and Society,* ed. Tony Bennett, Lawrence Grossberg and Meaghan Morris (Oxford: Blackwell, 2005), pp. 99–102.

6 For example, John Frow, *Cultural Studies and Cultural Value* (Oxford: Oxford University Press, 1995); J.-K. Gibson-Graham, *The End of Capitalism (As We Knew It): A Feminist Critique of Political Economy* (Cambridge, MA and Oxford: Blackwell, 1996); and Bruce Robbins, *Secular Vocations: Intellectuals, Professionalism, Culture* (London: Verso, 1993).

7 Cho Hae-Joang, '"You Are Entrapped in an Imaginary Well": the Formation of Subjectivity within Compressed Development – a Feminist Critique of Modernity and Korean Culture', *Inter-Asia Cultural Studies* 1:1 (2000): 49–69.

8 Barry Hing, 'Pauline Hanson, the TV star', *Sydney Morning Herald* April 25, 2005, p. A13. In 2004, Hanson also won second place in a reality TV show, *Dancing with the Stars*.

9 See Meaghan Morris, *Too Soon Too Late: History in Popular Culture* (Bloomington and Indianapolis: Indiana University Press, 1998), pp. 219–234.

10 Melani Budianta, 'Cultural Identity Discourse in Indonesia during the 1997–1998 Monetary Crisis', *Inter-Asia Cultural Studies* 1:1 (2000): 109–128. I discuss these issues extensively in *Too Soon Too Late*, pp. 93–119.

11 On this issue see Ch. 3 of this volume.

12 See Brian Kiernan, ed., *The Portable Henry Lawson* (St Lucia: University of Queensland Press, 1976), pp. 96–103; Henry Handel Richardson, *The Getting of Wisdom* (Melbourne: William Heinemann, 1977): and Miles Franklin, *My Brilliant Career* (Sydney: Angus & Robertson, 1974).

13 See my 'Globalisation and Its Discontents', *Meridian* 17: 2 (2000): 17–29; and 'Humanities for Taxpayers: Some Problems', *New Literary History* 36: 1 (2005): 111–129.

14 Kuan-Hsing Chen, 'The Decolonization Question', in *Trajectories: Inter-Asia Cultural Studies*, ed. Kuan-Hsing Chen (London and New York: Routledge, 1998), pp. 1–53.

15 Beng-Huat Chua, 'Globalisation: Finding the Appropriate Words and Levels', *Communal Plural* 6:1 (1998): 117–124.

12

Uncle Billy, Tina Turner and Me

Like many other people, I first saw TV through the glass of a shop-front window. I don't remember it very well. It was near Martin Place in Sydney, but only a photograph tells me this; I do remember a sudden flash, and then the man with a camera demanding money from my mother in George Street. It must have been about 1958. In the Christmas holidays, we would take the twenty-hour train trip from Tenterfield in northern New South Wales to see my father's mother in Glebe ('don't tell anyone your Nanna lives in a slum', some of the family would whisper), and go to 'the city'. I loved riding the escalators up to heavenly tearooms with ice creams in urban flavours – peach, butterscotch, lime. I loved rolling down the slope towards the lake in Victoria Park, and dodging the cars in Glebe Point Road to get over to Peter's Milk Bar. TV was a flicker in a window, nothing special. I probably didn't know what it was. I certainly didn't know what it meant: no-one was telling me then that it could change the world I lived in.

Some histories of early television give me this same sense of a vaguely faulty memory. Based on white middle class American experience (give or take a back-yard with a Hills Hoist clothesline), they tell stories of the suburbs, the consumer society and the post-War nuclear family all growing round the TV set in the sacred place of the Home. These are now our dominant images of television's past, and the way 'we' were in the Australian 1950s. Slowly, I am beginning to feel that I should remember this too. Perhaps one day, I will: history as the public repetition of other people's stories can change our sense of a personal past, and soon we may all have been, once upon a time, the children of ancient Suburbans.

In fact, TV for me came gently into a way of life which (I now realize) had barely changed since the Depression. By the 1960s I was living with my other Nanna in East Maitland. She chopped wood to warm the bath, stoked coal to heat the stove, hauled washing through the wringer and fed the chooks before break-fast. Most of our neighbours did. At some stage my Great-Uncle Billy bought a TV, and Nanna and I would go over the road to watch it.

My main memory of this is not the set or a show but a *smell*. Like our own, Uncle Billy's house was old (my great-grand-father Ferry had owned it), dark (blinds were never opened), musty in parts (front rooms where people had died) and it still smelt faintly of the flood-mud caked into our ceilings by the 1955 Maitland Flood. Uncle Billy sometimes smelt too – of old age, and ancient singlets. Nanna perfumed her hankie in self-defence and wore flowery talcum powder. It all mixed in with the sweet scent of coal drifting in on the breeze every evening.

I loved these nights at Uncle Billy's, and they kept me hooked in to extended family living for longer than I might have been. We spread across four main family houses, and TV was another reason for constantly moving between them. Only in the 1970s did my generation split off into nuclear units living in distant 'homes' and a silence fall at last in our older family lounge rooms. TV at Uncle Billy's was a noisy and active experience. Nanna and I were into narrative: we hated missing the dialogue, and shared a passion for analysing character even on spectacle shows like *Bandstand*. Uncle Billy was a raging formalist. All he cared about was 'snow', and he would lumber up every five minutes to play with the reception. Our groans and sighs never stopped him. The rare perfect picture achieved, he'd begin to talk loudly or snore.

You have to grow out of television when you don't have one in your house. At 16 or 17 I graduated, like my cousins before me, to drive-ins and Town Hall dances. Yet TV made this easy. It socialized me, in a way: a bookish child, I'd had few friends except my cousins and talking to strangers was painful. But when I fell in love with Shintaro on *The Samurai* like every other girl in East Maitland, my alienation was over. I belonged to an intense and open community that spread out from school to the swimming pool and the pictures and the beach, and on to parties. Thanks to Uncle Billy and Shintaro, I grew out of both of them quite fast.

Then I had a premonition of something else that can happen if you fall in love with an image. August holidays with my parents in Maroochydore became (I thought) a nightmare. They wanted to walk and swim and go driving. Torn from my new friends in Maitland, I would curl up miserably, for hours on end, communing with the screen. I laughed with Jimmy Hannan and Bert Newton and picked boxes with Bob Dyer, but my heart went out to Michael Ansara as Cochise in *Broken Arrow*, and (with no sense of conflict) to whoever played the hero in *Tombstone Territory*. The theme songs of both made me sad, but I would run them over and over again in my head, until I'd feel a bit strange and unable to get up and start moving again.

Many years later, as a student in Sydney, I learned to call this feeling 'depression'. It swamped me for a while when I rented TV for company, and got so addicted to drinking Marsala all night with *The Golden Years of Hollywood* that I'd stay in bed all day. My TV didn't cause this, solitude and culture shock did. But in a few more years, I felt the same feeling rising in a tiny flat on the fringes of the city where one of my cousins was escaping three babies and the housework and the visitors by staring into the infinite depths of the midday soap opera world.

Both of these early experiences – learning sociability, losing it again for a while – still affect the way I see television. I am involved with it more as a process in time than an object in space, and I am sceptical of theories that treat it as intrinsically good or evil. For the first twenty years of its history, most critics who took TV seriously would denounce it for stupefying people: their average viewer was a passive, uncritical sponge. Today, the opposite view prevails. It is an item of dogma for many scholars that no-one is ever mesmerized, fooled or drugged by watching television: their ideal viewer is a happy little vegemite in total control of the image.

I don't believe either story. Watching TV is a volatile business, insignificant at some times and intensely emotional at others. I think of it as a set of events mediating relationships between people in particular situations. If time and change and history are left out of the picture when we talk about TV, 'the medium' is a myth and 'the viewer' is a phantom – both serving only to generalize the interests of specialized social groups. Australian TV can be very powerful, however, precisely when some such group manages to mediate the idiosyncrasies of so many others that new relationships can form in a resonant public event.

The 'What You Get Is What you See' 1989 Rugby League promotion with Tina Turner worked like that for me. I used to like going to the football. It was part of living somewhere, and some women took it very seriously: my boyfriend's Nanna in Maitland was capable of running down to whack the other side with her umbrella as they were coming off the field. But in the 1970s the game itself got sleazy, and TV football made it all seem just too ugly – an ocker in an armchair with a six-pack. I was no longer proud of once having knitted sixteen jumpers in a single season.

1989 was amazing: suddenly, the symbol of the League could be a black American woman singer taunting men falling flat on their faces in 'Walk of Life' sports blooper footage, while families from the many races of Australia milled cheerfully round the field as though gathering for a parody of *Beyond Thunderdome*. Any text layered with media memories is an open invitation to contribute your own: the ads made the League seem like *my* game again, and I felt as though I'd missed it (I don't think I had, before). Even the cynics could get involved: on the Big Day, when the Big Game of the Big League began, anyone casually glancing upwards would have seen an aeroplane delicately writing in the Sydney sky: 'Big Deal'.

This probably made it a classic postmodern event: an event with no 'outside', in the sense that criticism of it was included in the spectacle. For those critics who want to be outside the society with which they take issue (a position very different from having no choice about your exclusion), this extensive electronic familialism opens up a scary world where no sense of history survives. TV now has terrifying uses: the 1990 Gulf War, with its televised military briefings about the video replays of bombs falling on a land with no people, showed us that.

But something not altogether trivial was happening when, driving down Marrickville Road during the 1989 Grand Final (the VCR set up at home so I could catch the real thing later), nearly all of the cars had the Rampaging Roy Slaven and H.G. Nelson radio critique of the TV version blaring out of their windows. I'm not sure why passages of joy and humour between diverse strangers can't also be creative of history – like the desire for other people's stories that this moment made me feel. At any rate, a sense of history was certainly what seized me on that day, when a memory of Tina Turner dancing recalled the lumbering ghost of Uncle Billy, a man who only ever seemed capable of 'getting' exactly what he saw. I thought about my memory of watching this child of the nineteenth century watch TV in the 1960s and, for the first time in my life, I wondered what *he* saw.

Index